The
Executive
Money
Map

Library of Congress Cataloging in Publication Data

McLaughlin, David J, date.
The executive money map.

Bibliography: p.
Includes index.
1. Executives—Salaries, pensions, etc.—United States. I.   Title.
HD4965.5.U6M27   332'.024   74-30349
ISBN 0-07-045390-X

1234567890   KPKP   7321098765

The editors for this book were W. Hodson Mogan and Mary R. Grace, the
designer was Naomi Auerbach, and the production supervisor was Teresa
F. Leaden. It was set in Linotron 505 by Black Dot, Inc.

Printed and bound by The Kingsport Press.

For Lori and John Randall McLaughlin

Contents

Preface

In 1969, when I first had the idea of writing a book about pay from the individual's perspective, everything was different. Executive mobility was at an all-time high, and more and more people were having to decide which new job offer to accept. The stock market averages were at rarefied heights; stock options still seemed a surefire way of making a great deal of money. Taxes were in the news, of course; they always are. But the talk was about ways of vastly simplifying the tax structure in a "reform" bill wending its way through Congress. Thanks to rising affluence, many Americans began enjoying income levels that made taxes and active planning about how legally to minimize them a major consideration. Another feature of the landscape was the dizzying multiplication of ways in which individual executives were being compensated, though there was talk of simplification here, too.

With the rising preoccupation with personal values had come a new concern about how to manage one's career—and pay—to make life more satisfying, now and later. For individuals to accomplish this, it seemed clear to me that they were going to need much better maps than were available. For one thing, there were very few sources the individual could turn to for guidance about the hows and whens of pay. At least 80 percent of the literature is aimed at helping companies design or modify compensation plans—an interesting and occasionally helpful exercise but one in which very few individuals get a chance to participate. Although the body of literature was great and growing, much of it was also highly topical, hence subject to obsolescence with new tax rulings and other events. Finally, as at any country-club dance, certain glamorous girls like stock options get all the attention; plain Janes like insurance and profit sharing get only an occasional nod in an article, even though many more executive lives are touched by them. When I began the book, I wanted to redress this balance, at least to some degree. Given all the turbulence of the late 1960s, I also wanted to rethink certain basic assumptions on executive motivation and compensation design that I, at least, had used during my years of consulting work.

Quite obviously, a great many things have changed since I began to work on this book. Yet the need for it is even more evident now. The stock market gyrations—one is tempted to say tailspin—of the early 1970s dramatically demonstrated the personal risks that have always been inherent in the stock option as a compensation vehicle. The latest tax "reforms" have added rather than lessened complexity in this critical area; there is now even more confusion and more choice. Sustained high rates of inflation have seriously distorted many traditional pay relationships and created great uncertainty for the individual. At the same time, the changing values that became so evident in the late 1960s have started to find fuller (if quieter) expression in careers, money decisions, and attitudes toward work.

Personally, I think the trend to greater individualism in the employer-employee relationship is a positive development, even though it is certainly causing uneasiness in many executive suites. Most companies have tapped only a fraction of the energy and creativity of their personnel. That's true at the senior executive level as well as among the rank and file. Perhaps, as more individuals learn to manage their careers instead of being managed in them, companies will find new ways to motivate their employees. Inevitably, this will mean new approaches to compensation better tuned to changing times. I say inevitably because, whatever one's personal values, what we are paid influences our attitude toward life in all its dimensions, including productivity in our work and, therefore, the contribution of that work to the society.

This book, then, attempts to put the whole subject of pay plans in perspective. It should stimulate both executives and would-be executives to ponder and formulate personal goals and to make each key step in your career consonant with those goals. The book provides a framework against which you can measure where you now stand and, with the aid of specific guidelines, reference data, and exhibits, what direction you should take. It includes information on how to evaluate the impact of inflation on pay levels. And its four unique compensation planning work sheets (which appear as the Appendix and are also included as a separate pamphlet) should prove most helpful in practical, step-by-step planning.

David J. McLaughlin

Acknowledgments

Like many first books, this one was produced over several years. Throughout, I was encouraged by a number of good friends and colleagues who believed in me and what I was trying to do. I would like particularly to thank Lee Walton, former managing director of McKinsey & Company and now resident director of our Dallas office, and Jonathan Rinehart, an old friend.

Jonathan Rinehart took time to react to my first concept outline; he read early drafts, and when the book began to take final shape in 1973 he agreed to edit it. As a senior corporate executive with Eastern Air Lines, and later as an entrepreneur and president of The Jonathan Rinehart Group, he drew upon his own broad experience and contributed far more than editing help.

Lee Walton, along with a number of my associates, put up with my individualism and encouraged my efforts to bring a new perspective to the discussion of money and careers. A number of other colleagues read the manuscript and contributed helpful thoughts. I want to thank particularly George Foote, Donald Carlson, and David Kraus.

All consultants in the field of executive compensation, myself included, owe a great deal to Arch Patton, a pioneer in this area, whose book, *Men, Money and Motivation*, has become a classic. Arch Patton and, later, J. McLain Stewart of McKinsey put up with my early fumblings as a consultant, when I barely knew the difference between a stock option and an incentive bonus. Both taught me a great deal.

One simply can't complete a book of this nature without a lot of dedicated support in research, exhibit design, editing, and typing. Among those who have helped over the years are Bonnie Guillou, Beth Lehman, Jane Smith, Tom Simon, Sarina Thornton, and Bill Bolden. My special gratitude goes to Gene Zelazny, McKinsey's visual communications consultant, for his imaginative help on the jacket and all the exhibits; to Jane Pogeler, the editor in our Chicago office; and in particular to my secretary, Pat Mrozovich, who did most of the early typing from illegible pages and who coordinated things generally, including me from time to time.

To them all—and to the many client executives I have had the privilege of working with over the years—go my thanks for their very considerable contributions to *The Executive Money Map*.

CHAPTER ONE

Executive Compensation in a Changing World

In the fall of 1971, as the Nixon Administration was scrambling to set up the machinery for Phase II wage and price controls, a debate erupted over terminology. One economist proposed that a "compensation" board be established. John Connally, then riding high in Administration councils, added a blunt Texas perspective. "Who the hell knows what compensation is?" he snorted. "Call it pay." So christened, the Pay Board went on to prove that the former Secretary of the Treasury's approach was apt.[1]

For months the Pay Board, and later the Cost of Living Council, grappled with such niceties as the definition of a productivity incentive plan and how the government should fix the current pay value of stock option grants. It even created a new status symbol—being in "the executive control group." The honor was an uneasy one for some members, since they lost pay. During the succession of control phases few Americans may have learned what compensation was, but many began to realize it was pretty complicated.

All the preoccupation with compensation rules, and later debates on the definition of a recession and how to control inflation, have diverted attention from two long-range trends of fundamental importance: first, the level of affluence has been rising steadily and broadly; second, this rise has given birth to a whole new system of values and life styles. These are times when Miss America of 1973 can earn $75,000 in her year of glory, when the heads of at least three labor unions make over $100,000 a year, when a Carnegie Commission survey of 60,000 professors finds 15 percent of those in private universities doubling their salaries from outside work. Salaries in professional sports keep hitting new highs.[2] The $427,000 bonanza Joe Namath got for signing with the New York Jets in 1964 pales beside the reputed $3 million of Nate Archibold's basketball contract and the $600,000 annual salary for three years Wilt Chamberlain negotiated for as player-coach of the San Diego Conquistadors of the American Basketball Association. Tennis professional Stan Smith even made $150,000 a year while serving in the U.S. Army. A journeyman electrician in New York makes $76 a day, and New York City firemen get $18,000 a year. Suddenly the $938,000 paid the head of General Motors in 1973 to run a $35-billion corporation doesn't seem so out of line.

The double-digit inflation that ravaged the U.S. economy during 1974 cut into real income for many Americans for the first time since the great depression. But few economists expected the trend to last, and only a few extremists failed to leaven their warnings with a historical perspective. Hans Rosenhaup, president of the Woodrow Wilson National Fellowship Foundation, put it this way in a *New York Times* article on November 24, 1974: ". . . disposable 1973 income in real dollars was more than twice 1929 income and almost three times that of the early 1930s." Moreover, pay demands were moving rapidly to catch up with inflation. Union settlements rose from 5.8 percent in 1973 and 6.2 percent in the first quarter of 1974 to 11.3 percent by the third quarter. "Merit increase" budgets for management doubled over their historical levels in most companies.

By 1972, one out of four American families had an income over $15,000, and about one-third will be at this level by the time the nation reaches its 200th birthday in 1976.[3] In a longer-range forecast the chief of the Population Division of the Census Bureau estimated that the average constant-dollar income for families and single heads of households would increase from $9,779 in 1968 to $21,200 by the year 2000.[4] In spite of the wage controls of the early 1970s, new pay standards for financially successful executives are even more impressive. McKinsey & Company's 1974 survey of chief executive pay in the 581 largest publicly held U.S. corporations shows that the average cash compensation was $228,000. And graduate schools of business are now turning out some 25,000 men and women a year, many of whom command upwards of $20,000 for their first career jobs. In 1974, for example, the average offer made a Harvard Business School graduate was $17,600, double the level of ten years ago.

So at first the loudest cry of the 1970s sounds much like Sam Gompers' in the 1890s: "More!" For the immediate future, however, the fact will be not only more money, but more complexity: more complexity in the way it's earned, more complexity in the way it's protected from the tax collector by individuals, more complexity in the way it's employed by corporations as reward and incentive in the compensation arena. Our variegated society has already passed far beyond the simplicity of cash, or even John Connally's "pay." As any Pay Board member could attest, there has been an exponential increase in the nonsalary pay devices employed by corporations. More are inevitable. It is already very difficult for the average executive (or company, for that matter) to assess true compensation value with the maps available to date. And it is going to get harder.

Some historical perspective may help as a starter. To begin with, compensation was a highly secret business until the late 1940s, when innovators like my colleague Arch Patton[5] initiated the first executive compensation survey. At that time, most compensation was in simple cash or salary. In fact, a startling number of publicly held companies didn't even have pension or profit-sharing plans prior to World War II. In the twenty to thirty years since most of these plans were introduced, there has been a typical evolution. First the basic benefit levels were improved; then frills were added and employee contributions were progressively reduced and finally eliminated. The same years saw other new plans added to the pay package: employee thrift or savings plans, long-term disability insurance coverage, all-risk accident insurance running into the hundreds of thousands of dollars, comprehensive major medical plans, and, more recently, multimillion-dollar personal liability policies. All have added complexity.

To date the liveliest action has been in the executive stock arena. Here again things started slowly. The first really broad-based stock option plans did not start until 1950, and the original type of plan (the popular restricted stock option) remained the dominant stock incentive vehicle for more than twelve years. Starting in the mid-1960s, the pace began to pick up. The Revenue Act of 1964 introduced the qualified stock option. Shortly after that, companies began to experiment with restricted stock bonuses. By 1969, one large company out of six had some form of restricted stock bonus plan, usually in addition to a qualified stock option plan, and most companies had extended participation well down into the management ranks.

The Tax Reform Act of 1969 spurred further experimentation and change. In late 1970, when my associate David Kraus and I surveyed 165 large companies, we found that no less than two-thirds of them had entered the compensation complexity derby again in the first ten months of 1970.[6] The names of the new entries included nonqualified options, tandem options, and phantom stock options. Companies were beginning to finance the exercise of options directly, an unheard-of phenomenon in large publicly held companies a few years earlier.

As wage and price controls were imposed in 1971, the pace of stock plan evolution slowed somewhat. But this period also saw the development of a new substitute for options called the "performance share plan," essentially a stock bonus tied to long-term company performance. And the regulatory ground rules continued to change. Within three years of their birth, tandem options were effectively killed off by an Internal Revenue Service ruling on January 2, 1973.

The evolution of the tax structure has obviously had a strong impact on increasing the variety of executive compensation schemes, but it is by no means the sole explanation for the emerging crazy-quilt pattern. The increased diversification of American business has also played its part. In competing for executive talent, bank holding companies were forced to cope with the diverse compensation patterns of mortgage banking subsidiaries and data processing centers. Insurance firms plunged into the mutual fund business, and staid utilities launched real-estate development schemes. In such industries, highly leveraged incentives were and are the norm.

Other basic trends in the U.S. economy have also contributed to the growing complexity. As the new breed of professional manager replaced more traditional business leaders, the old compensation profiles of basic salaries, generous retirement plans, and a high level of security became increasingly dated. They yielded to plans pegged to corporate profit growth. The galloping transition to a service-dominated economy has been led by companies whose executives themselves represent major assets. Understandably, such companies tend to have a larger number of highly paid executives at the top than manufacturing concerns. And in a time of rapid expansion, highly visible venture-capital firms, which often take their cut from the stock gains of new high-technology companies, have had more influence on compensation patterns than their numbers or financial size would imply.

It is apparent, then, that the revolution in compensation has developed as a result of some pretty important trends in the U.S. economy. In the years ahead, however, even more pressure for change may come from social and psychological forces. As security and affluence have percolated through society, the vocational motivation of men and, increasingly, women has shifted markedly. This trend is likely to continue, and important changes in compensation will result. Call it the new life style, the quest for personal fulfillment, or whatever, the fact is more and more Americans are yearning for, and often actively seeking, a broader range of values in their work.

A brief, somewhat oversimplified look backward makes the point by contrast. At least through the nineteenth century, for all but the privileged or most venturesome few, simple hard work was man's lot. His options came down to a choice between toil on the one hand and poverty, even starvation, on the other. To be sure, there was available some choice of arena, and many Americans did choose to take their struggles westward. But the fundamental choice was inescapable. Inextricably intertwined with this essential fact, particularly in the United States, was the Protestant ethic, which made work a moral imperative as well as a practical necessity. As the society's elders are still wont to remind us, this value system not only enshrined growth and the pursuit of material gain—it built a great country.

But these values are now ignored by growing segments of the population and attacked by others. In a major survey comparing recent attitudes with those of five and ten years ago, Potomac Associates found that Americans' interest in economic status is dropping (as, interestingly, is our confidence in the country's future).[7] Few Americans are militant radicals, of course, but more and more of us are demanding work that is "meaningful," that can be performed in pleasant surroundings—in other words, work that has a variety of nonmaterial rewards.

Such demands, whether they exist as unarticulated, even unidentified, yearnings in suburban tract houses or as angry shouts in the streets, result from the fact that Western and particularly American society has reached a historic milestone: we as a society are capable of producing enough food, clothing, and shelter for all our citizens. Never before has man been able to do this. By definition, therefore, never before has he had to grapple with the consequences of this fact. Our system of distributing our entirely adequate production of life's physical necessities obviously lags behind the productive capacity. That serves to provoke the more idealistic into attacks on our system. But it does not alter the basic consequence that flows from the historic watershed. This is the assumption by most men and women, especially the young, that there will always be enough jobs and enough financial capacity to provide adequate compensation. This fundamental assumption underlies the expectation of rewards from work that transcend the material.

In the ranks of organized labor, such expectations can manifest themselves in fractiousness and rebellion among the rank and file, often, paradoxically, over demands for still more money. Yet even in union ranks the money demands are changing. The proposal that drew loudest applause at the 1973 convention of the United Auto Workers was not for increased insurance or higher pay. It was for overtime on a voluntary basis only. Among those with higher educations, the result is more likely to be an implicit belief in one's right to pursue, in time if not immediately, a broad variety of personal life objectives. Thus, within the context of relative affluence rather than the toil of the nineteenth century and earlier, one can legitimately aspire to raise horses on a ranch in New Mexico or corn and apples on a farm in the Hudson River Valley. It is easy to believe that one deserves, as a result of one's work, the time to write or to pursue a second career in public service, or perhaps even the capital to start one's own company. Today work is expected to feed the mind and soul, not just the stomach.[8]

One of the most vivid demonstrations of the new value system is the growing importance of the job's location. Stories abound of individuals with high corporate promise who have knowingly passed up major promotions rather than accept certain geographical transfers. "I'm sorry, I know it'll be a black mark for me, but Marge and I like it here in Phoenix. We just couldn't face coming to New York." Long the mecca for the talented and ambitious, New York City and the life style it connotes have repelled rather than attracted an increasing number of those moving up the corporate ladder. In part this reflects a steep marginal tax rate that climbed to 15 percent under Nelson Rockefeller, to which New York City has added up to 3½ percent since 1966. But it also is a sign that two- to three-hour daily commuting and an environment perceived as plagued with dirt, crime, and tension are increasingly incompatible with the newer values.

Again the implications translate into compensation action. Until very recently, pay patterns in the relevant industry were the dominant external influence on executive compensation levels. Today location is gaining as a major factor. While companies have long offered extra pay to lure a valued executive into hardship areas, they are going to have to broaden their definitions of hardship areas, and up the ante besides. A general deterioration in the quality of life can be partially offset by money, but it takes more than a normal "promotional increase." For example, Pitney Bowes, the postage meter manufacturer, found that a $30,000 manager would actually have 16 percent more spendable income working at its Stamford, Connecticut, headquarters than commuting to New York City.[9] And this does not reflect the cost of compensating the employee for the extra hours invested in a 2½-hour commuting grind. Location and the life style that it implies may well create the most immediate shock waves as the 1970s generation of executives make their own settlements with money. Some companies are reacting by moving to the suburbs. This is especially common in the New York area where a long list of corporate giants, led by such blue chips as IBM and PepsiCo, have moved out. Other companies are moving across the country to "more desirable" areas. Greyhound from Chicago to Phoenix and Johns-Manville from New York to Denver are examples. But most metropolitan companies won't move in the near future, and so "location" will be more and more explicitly factored into compensation thinking.

Similarly, heightened interest in second careers has major meaning for tomorrow's money. Less and less will prudent companies be able to assume their executives' careers will march inexorably to age sixty-five. To compete for the talent, therefore, there will be less emphasis on such traditional long-payout benefits as pensions and retirement programs, and more on capital-building vehicles and other avenues to greater personal net worth. In fact, the building of personal net worth is, I believe strongly, central to the new and broader definitions of compensation with which all of us will have to deal. As more people see work as an avenue to varied personal objectives, the traditional system of financial rewards will have to be profoundly affected.

Of course, money alone has never really been enough. Colonel Henry Crown, by that time a very rich man, said it well in an interview with the *New York Times* in 1960: "Money isn't the primary factor in what one does. A person does things for the sake of accomplishing something. Money generally follows." Most successful entrepreneurs have recognized this, and regardless of their field most leaders seem to march to an inner summons to achievement. Peoples' definition of achievement may be changing somewhat, but to date ours has been a highly competitive society and money has been one way of keeping score in the game. That's one reason why both compensation surveys and interoffice scuttlebutt on "who makes what" have such appeal. Money abounds in status implications; it's a yardstick of both performance and potential.

Several years ago I worked with a large Chicago manufacturing company that paid its three executive vice presidents the same salary, $70,000. All three were candidates for president. One year the company changed its payroll system. In the transition, two of the contenders wound up with calendar year earnings of $69,600 and the other with $70,673. The inferences drawn when these amounts were reported in the proxy statement eloquently confirmed the importance of money as a status factor. I've often been surprised to find new chief executives foregoing perquisities and stock awards to obtain a salary in six figures. As that humorist of the old school, Artemus Ward, put it many years ago, "When a fellow says it ain't the money but the principle of the thing . . . it's the money."

Contrary to some expectations, the new value systems are not going to change the essential truth of the axiom. Not long ago, at a conference that debated the changes in college student attitudes over the last five years, one astute observer put it this way: "Five years ago a lot of students were announcing plans to grow their own vegetables on a small farm in Vermont. No big corporations or Wall Street law firms for them. Now they're saying they want to make as much money as they can as soon as they can—so they can retire at fifty and grow their own vegetables on a small farm in Vermont." In 1971 the *Wall Street Journal* polled some leading law schools and found that at Columbia only four of 136 seniors were taking public service jobs and at Stanford only 6 percent were going into "pro bono" legal work.[10] Placement service officials pointed to a perceptible shift away from firms located in the large industrial cities like Chicago, Los Angeles, and New York, but they detected little acceptance of lower starting salaries. Even most communes levy a modest annual money contribution (I'm told the going rate is about $500), and the first two-year budget of Ralph Nader's Project for Corporate Responsibility provided for a 5 percent salary increase for second-year employees.

The millennium is not here yet, then. The principal effect of new values is still likely to be more complexity in compensation. Tomorrow's senior executives are likely to see their careers in a shorter time framework, and value trade-offs will be harder to quantify. It will take more money to overcome environmental negatives, unattractive job locations, or dull, slow-growth industry situations. Money will be used increasingly to buy leisure time and the independence to enjoy it. An economic landscape dotted with unprecedented shortages will mean a changing mix of economic rewards. In an energy-short environment such a traditional perquisite as a company car could seem almost immoral, for example. Persistent inflation is going to make cash an increasingly significant element in the mix. In sum, there will be changes, but the importance of money will not diminish.

If anything, I believe, money will be an even more important motivator, particularly in established companies where the excitement factor and growth potential are likely to be lower. As executive talent gets more sophisticated about compensation, the price of retaining the successful will increase. The most perceptive executives already recognize that it takes larger and larger sums of money to motivate. The difference between an average salary increase of 6 or 7 percent and the 10 to 12 percent doled out by many large corporations to their outstanding producers no longer turns on the fastest achievers. Levels of expectations have changed. We may be breeding a situation where in ten or fifteen years many successful managers will achieve financial independence in their late forties or early fifties and where no amount of additional money will prevent the early departure of experienced managerial talent for other careers. As always, the greatest rewards will go to the swiftest, and those who profit most will have a thorough understanding of their own money motivation.

"Know thyself" has been sound counsel ever since the Greeks

carved it on the temple at Delphi. But never has the advice been more relevant, for a basic understanding of personal values and goals is essential if one is to make one's way expeditiously through the range of career choices available today. In his books, *Self-Renewal* and *Excellence,* John Gardner provides a great insight into the value system and workings of the successful: "The man who wants to get back to the sources of his own vitality cuts through the false fronts of life and tries to understand the things that he really believes in and can put his heart into."[11, 12]

Some people are fortunate enough to fix early on a career that naturally fits their talents, and they may go like straight arrows to their goals. As Henry Crown said, "Money follows." But in an age of specialization and quickening change, most of us come upon one or more major career decision points, each of which offers Robert Frost's "road not taken." Men and women with will and ability come to such forks most often; they will always have the greatest number of options. Money, not just cash but the entire compensation package, will be an inevitable part of their decisions. It should also be one of their most useful judgment tools. It is to be hoped that they will employ it in the broad context of career compensation goals.

How much money does one really want? Over what time period? In what form? Most important, at what price? No one can answer these questions without thoroughly understanding both personal aims and the net income consequences of the compensation options that may arise. Is deferred compensation a good deal? Is a $40,000 salary and a shot at a $20,000 bonus better than a straight salary package of $50,000? In relation to personal values? How do you value a pension or insurance package? How relevant is a company's earnings-per-share and stock price history in appraising a 1,000-share option grant? What are the tax implications of exercising an option at any given time?

Much of this book is aimed at answering these kinds of questions. Specific compensation techniques can be analyzed in dollar terms, and this book is organized around chapters that deal with each of the major compensation vehicles. There is also an early chapter on taxes, since an understanding of the fundamental principles of taxation is indispensable to personal compensation planning.

Quite frankly, the individual has long been at a severe decision-making disadvantage vis-à-vis the employer in the extremely complex world of modern executive compensation. Although I hope this book will prove useful to companies and those who counsel on careers, it is written primarily for the individual executive, for those starting out on their career journey and those reaching forks in it. It is intended to make that journey less agonizing for the individual—and more likely to lead to the destination right for that individual.

Important as it is to understand the intricacies of compensation and taxes, the really important questions for the individual go deeper than the technical. My purpose is to stimulate some thinking about who you are and what you want to be, as much as to map the compensation road you may be going down.

CHAPTER TWO

Money and Careers: On Getting There from Here

When one's current position is a way station to greater things, we speak of having a career instead of a job. We focus on total compensation over time, not just salary. People with jobs are concerned about being paid fairly and making enough. Their focus typically is short term, on cash on the line; their only alternative is getting another job, until age and pension lock them in. The person with a career has a far subtler, longer-term relationship with money rewards; and the changing structure of career opportunities has complicated that relationship immensely.

For a long while, only a fraction of Americans had real careers, and even those were narrowly constricted. One selected an employer on graduation and made progress through some combination of talent and time. Career planning was internally focused. There are still bastions of this kind of career stability, of course, where promotion from within is the rule and management turnover is incredibly low. They include such prestigious firms as General Motors, Eastman Kodak, AT&T, the 3M Company, and E.I. du Pont. In the great depression, those working for such companies were credited with having had great career judgment.

In the decade after World War II, however, a whole new generation entered business. Their members were much better educated, and they were impatient. They were anxious to have a career and accelerate it, even at some risk. To the successive waves of young men and women who have followed them, the risks have seemed slight indeed. Today's college graduate defines serious unemployment as 6 or 7 percent and looks a little incredulous when reminded that over one-quarter of the working population had no jobs at all in the 1930s, to say nothing of careers. The 1975 master of business administration, after two decades of steadily rising offers to each successive class, has forgotten (or never knew) that starting salaries for Harvard Business School graduates declined some 25 percent from 1930 to 1935 and didn't get back to predepression levels until after the war.

The recent generation's attitude is brazenly summarized by several young M.B.A.'s recently interviewed by *Forbes* magazine after their first five years of work experience. Said one young man: "Security is not really something you have to worry about." And another: "All those who go to the Harvard Business School are guaranteed a life of financial self-sufficiency as long as they make even a reasonable effort at their jobs."[1] Ah, the arrogance of youth. The uncertainties and mini-recessions of the 1970s have already retarded starting salary growth and reduced the number of offers the graduate gets. Nevertheless, the whole system of careers has indeed been irreversibly altered. It would probably take another 1929 to overturn the pattern that has emerged.

The sea of changes in career thinking and acting can be summarized in three phrases: increased mobility, multiplying choices, and a narrowing time span. Collectively, they define a new environment for compensation options and decisions.

Increased mobility is perhaps the most conspicuous change in career patterns. The propensity of managers to move from one company to another has risen dramatically. When, in the mid-1960s, Dr. Eugene Jennings of Michigan State University updated an earlier survey of turnover patterns covering the 1948–1953 period, he found a fivefold increase in the twenty years. To describe this new breed of executive, Professor Jennings coined the phrase "mobile manager," typified by the new M.B.A.[2] A comprehensive study of about 5,000 M.B.A.'s from the classes of 1965 to 1968 showed that about one out of four changed jobs within two years, over a third by their third year, more than half by their fifth year.[3]

The mobile manager's motivations and personal planning

contrast dramatically with the one-company careerist. The heads of General Motors and the International Telephone and Telegraph Company illustrate the extremes. GM's Richard Gerstenberg had never worked for anyone other than the auto giant when he was made chairman after thirty-nine years' service. (His predecessor, James Roche, had forty years with GM.) On the other hand, Harold Geneen, archetype of the mobile manager, had worked for six companies prior to accepting the presidency of ITT. Not surprisingly, companies like ITT or Litton have a reptuation for revolving-door executives, and a startling number of their alumni now run other companies.

While Mr. Geneen and ITT perhaps represent an extreme, most surveys show that the typical executive will work for four to five companies before retiring. All indications are that this mobility will increase, a force loosed by decreased identification with the company and the fact that movement is a beguiling option in the quest for personal fulfillment.

The dizzying multiplication of career choices itself encourages still more rapid change. Whole new functions have emerged in the last several decades, such as corporate planning, electronic data processing, operations research, distribution management. There are even new choices within the same old departments, e.g., value analysis in purchasing, cash management in the treasury department, production planning in manufacturing. Moreover, rapid growth in the accounting, consulting, and legal professions has produced broadening intermediate steps or alternative career paths simply not available on the same scale only twenty years ago. The scope of the new job phenomenon became clear several years ago in a *Fortune*-sponsored survey of some 1,000 young managers. The study found that one out of three held jobs that simply had not existed before they filled them![4]

All of this has happened in an increasingly compressed time span. Individuals now get responsibility much earlier, even at the top. University of Michigan studies reveal the age of the average corporation president has dropped from fifty-seven to forty-nine since 1950. It's still going down. At the same time, job tenure is shortening. In 1962, 45 percent of the presidents of the nation's 500 largest industrials had been in office for more than five years. By 1967, the proportion had dropped to 35 percent and, by 1972, only one out of four had held the position over five years.[5] And the total career span itself is shortening. More executives are being fired, for one thing. Professor Jennings' studies show turnover among the heads of corporations doubling since the 1960s, with perhaps half of them having been forced out. Age sixty-five retirement is going to be out of date in the lifetime of most readers of this book. IBM has already shifted to mandatory retirement at sixty, and scores of companies have moved part of the way through liberalized early retirement schemes.

What does all this mean in compensation terms? To start with, executives had better prepare themselves to evaluate competitive pay packages more accurately and more frequently. Earlier responsibility, the higher pay that goes with that, and shorter career spans are already presenting managers with real opportunities for early financial independence. Those who relish such prospects should keep in mind that personal net worth can be built much more easily and rapidly in some occupations than others and that each opportunity is a product of the career choices that have gone before it.

Nor will all the choices be pleasant ones. The mobile manager will have to balance financial opportunity against such other symbols of independence as time for family, freedom to remain in a pleasant location, personal satisfaction with the company environment. Once again, a man or woman will need a clear understanding of personal values and priorities to make satisfying choices at the increasingly frequent decision points. Some sense of direction is necessary, for each decision tends to narrow the range of future options.

A long view can be most helpful in determining that direction. Priorities, even definitions, change over the span of one's career. And there is a fair measure of luck and trial and error in every one. But there are generally four discernible stages during which the career and money interrelationships become distinctly different. Broadly stated, these four phases are:

- *The basic preparatory period,* during which one attends college and perhaps graduate school and, with the advice of parents, professors, and friends, tries to decide on a career. In the process, one usually begins to limit one's horizons—and future income as well.

- *The formative period,* or the first ten to fifteen years when an individual is paid progressively less for education and perceived potential and more for experience and relative performance. This is a period of rapid compensation progress and greatest mobility, when rewards are largely in cash and success means rising above the pack as quickly as is decent. Money is often exchanged for experience, and compensation requirements do not limit options excessively; in each industry, there are scores of jobs in the $20,000 to $35,000 range.

■ *The turning point* comes sometime in one's mid-thirties or very early forties, when one is or becomes a partner in the law firm, vice president of the corporation, professor at the university. Cash income has progressed to the point where net worth is starting to build perceptibly. In business, there have usually been the first stock options and other special rewards, and the traveler now has the experience and track record to negotiate major increments in compensation.

Often this will mean the first grappling with fundamental philosophical questions since college. In compensation terms, all but the very cocky will be surprised to have progressed so much further than they expected a scant ten or fifteen years earlier; they now also have a lot more to lose.

■ *Finally, the brass ring* may beckon the very talented who have built wisely: a clear shot at the presidency, the hard offer to turn around a competitor, the unique package deal from the venture-capital company, an invitation to become general partner in the professional firm. Especially when a change in employer is involved, this is a time of negotiation in which one can often invent the rules, mixing and matching employment contracts, deferred income, founders' stock, or special limited partnerships.

At each of these four points the rules may seem to have changed, sometimes perversely. The profile of compensation develops, of course. If we are honest, our aspirations and our estimation of what we are worth both increase exponentially. There is the individual version of the small-company phenomenon, which finds it *has* to keep growing, and some will be reminded of the play, *Stop the World—I Want to Get Off*. For those who reach their level of competence early, the choice may be simple: to dig in, keep the nose clean, and concentrate on avoiding technical or managerial obsolescence. But for the person with the ability, energy, competence, and desire to progress further? The higher one's ambition (if it is backed with talent) the greater the range and importance of the choices. Actually, the process starts very early.

The Preparatory Period

The years prior to a young man or woman's entry into the full-time job market are dominated by educational decisions. And for some twenty-five years now the "experts" have been passing out incomplete, if not downright misleading, guidance. Their message has been: Go to college and get a degree, for that means success. Take subjects that interest you, but don't worry too much about a career. That decision can be postponed by going to graduate school; after all, if one degree is good, two degrees must be better.

The numbers of those who have followed this counsel are now legion. In 1939, the entire college population was only about 1.4 million. Within a decade, rising affluence and a series of GI bills sent that number soaring. From 1952 to 1969, total enrollment grew 289 percent to 7.4 million, while the college-age population increased by only 160 percent. For the first time, public colleges and universities began to turn out more graduates than private schools; by 1970 they accounted for nearly two-thirds of the total graduates. New colleges and universities popped up all over the landscape, an average of thirty-six of them a year from 1950 to 1970, and the number of college and university professors swelled from 246,000 to 600,000. By 1969, 27 percent of Americans eighteen to twenty-four were enjoying higher education.

But getting a college degree soon was not enough of a distinction. For that, one needed an LL.B., an M.B.A., or an M.Ed. In business, the M.B.A. began to come into its own. For years the number of masters' graduates in commerce and business had seesawed between 3,300 and 4,300. In the 1957–1958 school year, when Korean War veterans were graduating in some numbers, total new M.B.A.'s jumped 22 percent.[6] The numbers have climbed steadily ever since. By the mid-1960s the number of M.B.A. graduates passed 10,000 a year and it doubled again by the end of the decade. The number of institutions granting M.B.A.'s also doubled from 1950 levels. In 1975 alone there will be about as many M.B.A.'s as there were in all of the 1940s. By 1980, current projections are for 50,000 M.B.A.'s a year!

That's a lot of education, surely, but from the individual graduate's standpoint, what kind of career planning do all the numbers connote? Not much, I'm afraid. The only advanced education decision that carries its own fairly certain guarantee of higher income is to go to medical school. For most careers and certainly in business, education is not in itself a guarantee of higher pay but rather an admission ticket to the better jobs and more attractive companies. As the bachelor's degree became common, the price of the first-class ticket became a graduate degree. Even if it didn't necessarily guarantee more money, it did mean better access to the newer types of jobs with greater visibility and developmental potential—financial analysis instead of general accounting, production planning or inventory control instead of plant operations, product marketing instead of sales. Similarly, the graduate degree holder was more warmly welcomed by recruiters in the professional services and investment fields that preserve maximum career flexibility.

Unfortunately, the overemphasis on education also fooled many graduates into thinking that they were acquiring skills that could be immediately applied. The fact is, most graduates are paid more for their perceived potential than for a degree. At that, they are usually overpaid in relation to their near-term contribution to the company's fortunes. Although the new graduate may feel that a healthy starting salary is a just reward for educational investment, the employer is more interested in paying what is acceptable relative to other positions in the company and other companies' initial offering patterns. For this reason, it usually doesn't pay to exceed the minimum education "specs." Most businesses are uncomfortable with the Ph.D., for example, except in highly technical firms or very specialized job categories. Few positions in industry really require advanced education, and the young man or woman with a string of degrees is often suspected of being a last-minute convert from a career in university teaching.

Rather than going for a Ph.D., it is much more appropriate for the career planner to assess the supply and demand forces at work in the economy. In the 1960s, for example, our educational system churned out tens of thousands of scientists and engineers as the nation poured some $50 billion into the space program. Ph.D.'s in engineering disciplines increased fivefold. Predictably, aerospace employment peaked at the end of the decade and we soon had more than 100,000 unemployed scientists and engineers. We could well be repeating that pattern in the law schools, where enrollment is up sharply and the number of graduates has more than doubled since 1965. Unfortunately, our educational system has a poor prediction record on such trends. As former University of California Chancellor Clark Kerr testified on the new California Master Plan for Education: We need "much better manpower forecasts for the students who might be wasting years of their lives for nonexistent jobs."[7] Clearly, it is worth the effort to get the best possible feel of the job market long term—and that doesn't mean talking to the Lockheed recruiter about aerospace trends in 1969. Equally important, the advanced degree that begins to spell specialist should be approached with great care, particularly when one has limited experience on which to base long-term career interests.

Finally, the individual still in the educational process should realize that personality, character, and work habits will be the real controlling factors in both initial job offers and early career progress. Employers do give emphasis to class rank and grade performance in their recruiting. But that's *not* because brainpower or a particular degree is crucial, but because such measurements provide the only evidence available on such traits as maturity, competitiveness, and energy.

One wishes the students could experience the hiring process before going to school. Any perceptive veteran of the process can attest that personal characteristics, rather than education, are usually the controlling factors: the ability to express one's self, quickness of mind, evidence of imagination, good physical appearance. These are the elements that largely determine the number and value of job offers that a young graduate receives. The crucial ingredient of personality can mean a 200 percent difference in the starting offer, judging by statistics from prestigious business schools. Here, too, a good sense of career direction and an understanding (unfortunately rare) of the personality requirements of alternative career paths can be much more useful than top-of-the-class ranking. In other words, "know thyself—and early."

The Formative Period

The formative period, over which one builds the first stages of one's career, typically extends over ten to fifteen years and only rarely lasts past the age of forty. One's objective here should be to emerge from a mass of technical, sales, and administrative personnel to an upper-middle-management position, with the kind of experience and background that best preserves one's options. There is no milestone that marks the end of the formative period, no particular title or pay level. In industries that have generous title structures (banks and airlines, for example), it is probably a vice-presidency. In leaner, less-titled organizations, it may be a job at the director or even manager level. The position is typically four or five organizational levels below the chief executive.

What is a reasonable yardstick by which to measure financial progress during this formative period, when the emphasis is decidedly on cash? The most financially successful would say that initial pay should double in about five years and double again in the second five. Another useful rule of thumb is that to be in the upper quartile of a given peer group one should make about $1,000 per year of age by age thirty or thirty-five. Obviously, this depends partly on position, size of the organization, location, and the like, but these days it isn't at all exceptional to find the thirty-five-year-old making at least $35,000. Recent inflation, in fact, may well have increased the standard age-to-pay multiple to $1,500 per birthday, starting at age thirty-five.

Data on fast-track graduates of Wharton, Stanford, Harvard, and other prestigious schools help define the pay standards further during these formative years. A survey of several thousand M.B.A.'s from the top twelve graduate business schools showed this pay profile (Table 2–1).

Obviously, it takes more than average salary increases to get to these levels. In fact, when one relates starting salaries with pay levels five, ten, and fifteen years out, the average annual compound increase in cash income of "fast trackers" is almost triple the typical merit increase. A confidential alumni survey of 1,797 graduates of one Eastern university showed this clearly (Table 2–2). The in-

Table 2-1. Pay Progress of M.B.A.'s

Year M.B.A. received	1973 salary
1970	$19,330
1965	23,100
1960	28,390
1956	36,090

SOURCE: *The MBA Executive: A Survey of Accomplishment in Business.* MBA Resources, Inc., New York, 1973.

Table 2-2. Pay Progression of M.B.A.'s at One Leading University

Year degree received	Median salary		Annual compound rate of increase to 1970 (%)
	On graduation	In 1970	
1965	$10,000	$18,000	13.0
1960	7,500	26,500	13.8
1955	6,000	32,000	12.0

SOURCE: Confidential alumni survey of 1,797 graduates of a major Eastern university.

dividuals providing the data in the table progressed during a period when the average merit increase was 4 to 5 percent (inflation has now pushed that average to 7 to 8 percent). Similar data in the 1970s will probably show a 15 to 16 percent annual rate of increase for the most successful.

The key to such increases is promotions. During the formative period, the individual should be getting a meaningful promotion about every three or four years—every two years in the early stages. With the rate of promotion so important during this career phase, several fundamental career decisions begin to come into focus, and compensation provides an interesting perspective on them.

One of the early decisions concerns joining the large, stable "careerist" company. Except in certain specialties, companies like GM, Du Pont, Kodak, or 3M rarely recruit individuals above the classic entry levels. Whether to join this kind of company, therefore, is a decision that has to be made on graduation or, at the outside, within the next five years. Perhaps surprisingly, many prestige companies don't pay particularly well during the first ten to fifteen years of employment, although one can get excellent experience, of course. Moreover, while some large careerist companies like 3M have "stayed small" by breaking up divisions when they got too large and consciously maintaining a "new product" or entrepreneurial environment, other large companies have somewhat stultifying atmospheres. Only infrequently do they give independent responsibility early, a serious consideration for today's impatient graduates. The large blue chip nurtures its future top management carefully by continually testing and sifting talent. They profit from their managers' limited awareness of the outside job market. The cash compensation pattern in these companies is convex—an elongated ski-slope curve. Eventually the pay can escalate sharply, although it may take quite a while. Take the example of James McFarland, chairman and chief executive of the General Mills Company. McFarland joined the company in 1934 and at forty-three was still making only $18,900 a year after twenty-one years of service. Although a series of big moves boosted his pay dramatically a couple of years later, the *Wall Street Journal* quoted him as saying, shortly after he got the top job, "It's only in the last few years that I've made any real money, you know . . . . Salary has been important to me mainly as an indicator of how I was doing in the company."[8]

There are many considerations, of course, that go into choosing one's first employer, and many of them are as personal as a favored location or a perceived rapport. But in considering a company or industry one should pay attention to its growth prospects. That is generally what controls the promotional opportunities, the name of the game in the formative years.

A surprising number of stable blue chips have been able to sustain good growth, and above-average growth has been part of the appeal of the "academy" companies like IBM, Xerox, and Procter & Gamble. These organizations often deliberately hire more talent than they need and move personnel fast. As a result, their turnover is higher and they become a training school for others. Ex-IBMers, for example, have infiltrated virtually every company in the computer industry and a surprising cross section of industry at large. It is so sizable a talent pool that one enterprising former manager collects names and addresses and publishes them for money. His *IBM Alumni Directory* lists more than 1,500 executives, over 200 of whom are now board chairmen or presidents.

Most individuals, though, should not be selecting a company at this stage. Among the three main variables in this career-building period, the company is less important than the industry, and both of these pale before the importance of choosing a functional area in which to acquire skill and experience. The choice is critical because one's initial promotions are always within a functional area, in accounting or marketing or personnel. It isn't until individuals have emerged from the pack that most companies start transferring talent into other functions or selecting high-talent manpower for general management positions. Further, in-depth functional experience is the individual's insurance and passport: that is, what another company is going to buy should he decide to move. In a time of increased specialization, this career choice is all the more important.

Of course, one can deliberately choose the road of "the generalist" in a reach toward top management. This often means joining a consulting firm or other service business, since many companies simply do not have jobs for generalists or are leery of hiring the "well-rounded" M.B.A. type. As Robert Townsend of Avis said of the institution that grows some of our best generalists: "Don't hire Harvard Business School graduates. This worthy enterprise confesses it trains its students for only three posts—executive vice president, president, and board chairman."[9]

Industry specialization during the formative years can be a two-edged sword. Often a concentrated dose of five to eight years of significant jobs in one or more companies within the same industry is as valuable a career commodity as in-depth functional experience. However, it can be hard to break out of an industry even in one's mid-thirties, and often it is impossible after forty.

There is one other career-planning question fundamental to these formative years. Is it really wise to move from company to company? In one sense, this is like asking whether it is wise to gamble. The answer obviously depends on a person's objectives and fondness for risk. If a person selects a functional path, there probably should be several moves. The man or woman with an intense interest in finance—a function that pays well and has accounted for more chief executives in billion-dollar companies than marketing and sales in recent years[10]—must consider getting a certified public accountant's degree. This means at least three to five years with a public accounting firm and probably two or three moves to round out experience in specialties like cost or tax accounting.

In all circumstances, however, moves should be made for the right reasons. Too many young men and women jump from company to company during their first five years or so, out of frustration or just to make marginally more money. They may paint the development veneer over each change, but they rarely have longer-term goals or fully assess the career implications of their decisions. Some get overpriced in this early stage of their careers and wind up as well-paid but underexperienced managers, poorly positioned for more senior jobs. Others move frequently in search of their "thing," a very risky way to mature. The principal focus during these formative years should be on solid, marketable experience, preferably with one or more well-known companies or through clear promotions. One should opt for more experience, but only rarely for more money per se. In those cases when higher pay is in order, a person should negotiate it, however, not simply acquiesce to an offer after being already committed emotionally. There are two very common mistakes made during these formative years. First, individuals move for money—as little as a 15 or 20 percent increase—when no real promotion is involved. In a couple of years, momentum will take the average person close to that level without a job change. A useful rule of thumb is to project one's salary level for the next two years, then add 20 percent to that. Usually this technique will tell you to bargain for at least a 30 percent increase. The second common mistake is to succumb to the lure of the option or incentive bonus, which wily recruiters use to lure individuals after about their fifth year of experience, when they are still several years from such participation in their own companies. There is a lot of counterfeit money passed around that way and the wise will be careful to bite the coin.

One factor to be considered in job moves during this period is whether one has a powerful sponsor in the current organization. Many senior executives find a great deal of personal satisfaction in identifying "comers" in the crowd and helping advance their careers. And in most companies there are a few executives who enjoy envied reputations for developing young talent. Often the divisions or departments headed by such managers spawn an extraordinary number of promotions and populate the higher ranks across the whole company. In one large oil company I consulted with a few years ago, it was the supply and distribution group. Over a period of seven years it accounted for 18 percent of the people who were promoted into the company's $30,000 jobs, even though the group had less than 3 percent of the management work force. In another oil company, it was the exploration department; in a third, finance, which included corporate planning. This phenomenon is very hard to spot from outside, but many a sharp-sighted individual has ridden the coattails of the right sponsor up through the corporate hierarchy—or away to another organization. Six or seven key executives followed C. Lester Hogan to Fairchild Camera from Motorola, for example.

In the final analysis, although the choices en route are seemingly limitless, one has to be positioned properly at the end of this formative period. For this reason it is well worth setting an arbitrary time for moving on if one's basic compensation and position-level goals haven't been attained.

The Watershed Period

For most rising executives, the mid-thirties to early forties bring a time of intense and very basic soul-searching. Some of it is due to reaching the midpoint of life, to becoming conscious, probably for the first time, of all the things one will never be able to accomplish. For many, this can be a very trying time, and the psychologists are just beginning to explore it.

Work is almost certain to contribute to the whole mid-life conundrum. One suddenly comes to the end of the formative period. By this time, pay may have reached $50,000 to $70,000, and there are probably some stock options, although up to now they haven't been sizable enough to produce any real wealth. In fact, the executive's net worth is often under $100,000, and major expenses loom on the horizon, particularly college education for one's children.

It is a time for knowledgeable and pragmatic assessment of one's full potential and one's willingness to make the sacrifices that are now more clearly predictable as the price of further career progress. Often this time brings the best chances to do something radically different—to join a small growth company or found one's own company, to move from being a partner in the law firm to being general counsel in a large corporation. *More important, it is time to decide for sure whether to make a career commitment to a given company.*

Ironically, the choices that would have freshened the younger person like a summer sea breeze can, in mid-life, stir personal doubts, even depression. Studies at the California Institute of Technology's Industrial Relations Center have shown that some 85 percent of managers undergo a period of frustration and disappointment in their middle thirties from which one out of six *never* recovers. In his brilliant article "On Being a Middle-Aged Manager," Harry Levinson puts his finger on part of the problem: "Since only rarely can one have youth and achievement at the same time, there is something anticlimactic about middle-aged success."[11] Dick

Dougherty talked of it in his book, *Goodbye Mr. Christian.* Explaining why he left an excellent job at the *Los Angeles Times* to join McGovern's campaign, he said, "I was feeling menopausal and mutinous."[12]

For some, this is a period for a major course correction. I have three highly successful acquaintances who proved it: a forty-one-year-old dentist earning over $60,000 who moved his family to Australia and accepted a $12,000 public health position in Perth; an eminent professor at one of our leading business schools who accepted a vice-presidency at a large consumer goods company; a thirty-eight-year-old executive in the same firm who decided to go back to school for a Ph.D. and teach.

For most, though, the available career choices are likely to be a product of the experience accumulated during the formative period. Jess Unruh, the erstwhile "Big Daddy" of California politics, summed it up in an interview with the *Los Angeles Times* in July 1971, just after he had lost as the Democratic candidate for governor. Asked about his future plans, the forty-eight-year-old Unruh quipped, "I'm at a very awkward age. I'm too young to retire and I'm too old to learn a new trade."[13] As many men have done (and all should at such a point), Unruh had to go back to some pretty fundamental questions: Have I reached my full potential? Am I ahead of or behind the people I consider my peers? How far can I progress beyond this organizational level? And am I willing to move to ensure that next step? What do I want to do with my life?

Such questions demand answers. The temptation to defer them longer must not be yielded to. They are too important to what will follow.

One of America's most successful real-estate developers and entrepreneurs, Trammell Crow, observed about the many young people who succeeded in his unique partnership: "Everybody I hire thinks they want to make a lot of money, but you can't really tell until you see what they are willing to do. Often the most eloquent aren't willing to make sacrifices."[14]

In this time for searching career analysis, there are very important compensation considerations. First, one should make an objective appraisal of one's compensation in relation to one's real responsibilities. Often a reverse Peter Principle is at work, particularly in companies that weigh seniority too heavily in officer-level promotions. One who decided he was underpaid was an assistant treasurer of an East Coast utility who, after thirteen years' service, was literally running his department for $32,000 a year. This man, who had never changed jobs in his life, moved three times in the next four years, doubling his income in the process. Sometimes the opposite action suits an individual better. The forty-five-year-old vice president, finance, of an entrepreneurial food company on the West Coast recently searched his soul and concluded he was neither qualified for nor interested in competing in his current cutthroat atmosphere for the next ten years. He stepped back $5,000 in salary and accepted a controllership in a more mature and stable corporate environment.

One has to cast a hard eye on personal financial goals as well as requirements. Too many executives talk about wanting to "build their net worth" or "be in a position to retire at fifty-five" or "achieve financial independence" but don't get down to specifics. The head of one of the four largest personal financial planning firms in the country told me that eight out of ten of his new clients (mostly corporate executives) had not developed any long-term gross or net income forecasts, a fairly obvious first step in translating objectives into tangible plans. Even among the executives who have formulated specific goals ($500,000 net seems to be a common target for the thirty-five-to-forty-year-old vice president) there is a widespread lack of realism about how hard it is going to be to get there. Such net-worth goals are obviously not going to be reached through simple savings.

Goals even approaching these proportions cannot be achieved without stock option gains, deferred compensation, lump-sum settlement of retirement plans, tax shelter investments, or other noncash compensation rewards. While each of these pay vehicles is discussed in some depth in subsequent chapters, two facts should be emphasized in the context of careers.

First, there is wide variation from industry to industry in the incidence of special plans and payoff probabilities. Exhibit 1 shows the proportion of leading companies in twenty selected industries having the more common types of special pay vehicles. Any intelligent assessment of career alternatives at this watershed period should take such data into account.

An even more important consideration is the pay potential in specific companies, for there are sharp differences in compensation at an executive level. Exhibit 2 lists specific high-paying and

EXHIBIT 1

Profile of pay plans by industry.

INDUSTRIES

Special executive pay plans				Industrials	Other pay plans			
Stock option	Incentive bonus	Incentive stock*	Deferred comp.		Pension	Savings/ thrift	Profit sharing	Qualified stock purchase
70%	35%	5%	15%	Alcoholic beverages	95%	5%	10%	—
85	80	10	45	Apparel	90	25	25	15%
85	95	50	5	Chemicals	100	50	10	15
90	85	30	20	Diversified	90	45	20	15
90	80	30	25	Food products	90	35	20	10
70	65	—	10	Iron and steel	100	50	—	5
90	90	10	20	Motor vehicles/ equipment	100	50	10	5
100	60	40	15	Office machines	95	15	30	30
85	80	30	25	Paper/allied products	90	30	15	10
75	80	20	5	Petroleum	100	85	15	—
100	95	5	25	Pharmaceuticals	100	55	25	5
65	50	10	10	Tobacco	100	35	50	—
				Nonindustrials				
100	70	60	35	Airlines	100	15	—	30
55	40	5	5	Commercial banks	100	15	90	15
60	90	25	15	Investment banking	80	15	55	—
45	20	10	10	Life insurance	95	25	20	—
40	40	10	15	Railroads	95	5	—	10
85	55	5	25	Retail food chains	90	15	30	10
85	70	40	40	Retail trade	90	10	50	15
15	5	5	20	Utilities	100	40	—	20

*Includes restricted stock, performance shares and phantom stock plans.

SOURCES: McKinsey annual surveys, American Management Association, National Industrial Conference Board top executive compensation survey, Cole salary survey, various industry surveys and confidential studies.

EXHIBIT 2

Range of chief executive officer compensation by industry, 1973.

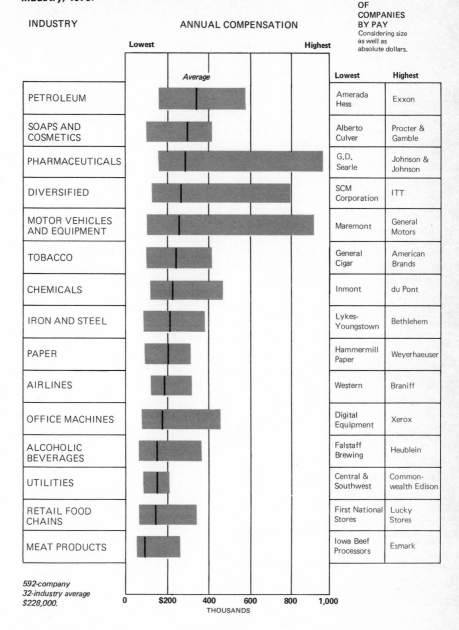

INDUSTRY	ANNUAL COMPENSATION	RANGE OF COMPANIES BY PAY Considering size as well as absolute dollars.	
	Lowest — Average — Highest	Lowest	Highest
PETROLEUM		Amerada Hess	Exxon
SOAPS AND COSMETICS		Alberto Culver	Procter & Gamble
PHARMACEUTICALS		G.D. Searle	Johnson & Johnson
DIVERSIFIED		SCM Corporation	ITT
MOTOR VEHICLES AND EQUIPMENT		Maremont	General Motors
TOBACCO		General Cigar	American Brands
CHEMICALS		Inmont	du Pont
IRON AND STEEL		Lykes-Youngstown	Bethlehem
PAPER		Hammermill Paper	Weyerhaeuser
AIRLINES		Western	Braniff
OFFICE MACHINES		Digital Equipment	Xerox
ALCOHOLIC BEVERAGES		Falstaff Brewing	Heublein
UTILITIES		Central & Southwest	Commonwealth Edison
RETAIL FOOD CHAINS		First National Stores	Lucky Stores
MEAT PRODUCTS		Iowa Beef Processors	Esmark

592-company
32-industry average
$228,000.

0   $200   400   600   800   1,000
THOUSANDS

SOURCE: 1974 McKinsey Top Executive Compensation Survey (1973 data).

low-paying companies in fifteen selected industries. In each case, there is a significant deviation from the indicated level of pay for the top three highest paid executives. Of course, this can be a function of many factors—tenure of these executives, bonus plan variations, and so on. More often than not, however, on the high side it is a deliberate policy to pay top dollar for above-average performance.

Before the final career commitment, the watershed evaluation should focus on the company's recent performance and prospects as well. Despite the proxy gadfly's complaints about overpaid top management, there usually is a distinct correlation between company growth performance and executive pay. This is clear from an analysis of the pay patterns of senior executives in the fifteen best and fifteen poorest performers among the fifty largest industrial companies in the country. During the last ten years, top-management cash compensation in the fifteen best performers increased, on average, 85 percent compared with 40 percent (less than the increase in cost of living) in the poorest fifteen companies. But this is only part of the difference. Option gains in marginal companies were practically zero (only three of the fifteen had any gains at all), while gains averaged 40 percent of cash compensation in the better-performing companies. The total difference in compensation: more than $1 million per company.[15] Needless to say, senior management pay affects pay for the next several organization levels down.

Even where performance and prospects are good, there may be real differences in attitude toward pay and net-worth building from company to company. Most publicly held companies face compensation constraints. Their boards of directors, regardless of their effectiveness in other areas, really do play an active role in compensation decisions, particularly in the adoption of new plans and in bonus and stock-plan administration. The board compensation committee (usually composed of at least three outside directors) is one of the few active standing committees in almost every company. The typical board is not receptive to frequent redesign of the top-management pay package. In my experience, most changes come only after a major external event, e.g., when there is a new tax law, when there has been a sudden exodus of top talent (a rare occasion, really), or when a strong-willed chief executive officer is in a position independent enough to force changes, i.e., has negotiated an individual package and can freely champion the cause of the remaining executive group. Moreover, it can take up to a year for most companies to complete major changes in special plans for top management—and as much as eighteen to twenty-four months if the plan is to be submitted to stockholders. Revising a pension plan is often a three-year proposition from start to finish. Such constraints should be guardedly weighed against the recruiter's promises.

Companies face other constraints as well. There are criteria and precedents for inclusion in special plans; there are merit increase budgets and guidelines that too often become rigid rules; there are salary ranges and job reevaluation checks and balances. Unfortunately, most companies worry most about "the average employee," unwise as this preoccupation is, and least about the unusual talent. When an employee nears the top of an organization, the compensation decisions are typically made by the president, who should have broader vision. But there is no such thing as instant equity in most companies, and the company's compensation time schedule is sure to be slower than the individual's.

What does all this mean to the executive who has reached the critical point of committing his future to one company? Basically, it means measuring personal goals against the company environment to assess the fit. It means self-examination and it means taking a hard, critical look at one's present or prospective employer. The most important thing is to focus on what I call the compensation environment within a company. How long did it take to adopt the last new plan or plan revision? If there are salary ranges, how many executives are paid above the grade maximum? If the company pays bonuses, how many of the eligible participants did not receive bonuses? How many got double the statistical average bonuses? How many of these were at the relevant organization level? Are all initial option awards the same size at the relevant entry level? When was the last time someone was jumped more than 30 percent in base salary in a year? At what dollar level does the president review all compensation decisions?

This sort of careful probing should produce an index of the company's flexibility and priorities. Equally, it will tell a lot about its overall management processes. One should look for the company that is concerned more with the outstanding individual than the standard performer, for the company that provides immediate supervisors with substantial latitude, for the company that can move swiftly to adjust its programs, for the company with a consistent and well-planned compensation philosophy, and for the management alert to the role of money at critical stages in a person's career—at the time of his first promotion, when financial responsibilities increase because of marriage and children, and after the settling-in period, when he develops a better understanding of the company environment.

One of the common characteristics of successful companies I have been exposed to is a willingness to break the rules, an ability to make radical distinctions in pay, to focus on replacement costs in valuing key executives, to make imaginative use of incentives that pay off for sustained above-average performance, and to grant extraordinary merit increases. Again, this sort of thing is hard for outsiders to evaluate. But it's very important.

Granted the company's compensation orientation will differ from the individual's. But the individual must have an underlying faith in the honesty and fairness of the company. Similarly, the individual executive must also be sure that there is a reasonable chance of realizing personal compensation goals in a given company. Whatever the formality with which one pursues this objective, imaginative compensation and career planning is essential if one is to avoid drifting into middle-aged frustration or obsolescence.

Negotiation at the Top

By their mid-forties, most people have made a twenty-year string of career decisions. They have passed through a personal watershed point and fixed on a course that represents their particular settlement with professional life. Many have already reached the level of their competence; but others will progress further toward the post of chief executive officer.

To some extent, the moving finger of fate writes the script. Mergers and acquisitions can play a part, and not only with small companies. Sometimes a key executive will change direction unexpectedly—as presidential contender John Zachary DeLorean did when he resigned his $550,000-a-year General Motors job at forty-eight—thereby opening the way for those in line behind him.[16]

Still, about 10 percent of *Fortune's* top 700 companies elect new chief executives each year, and about two-thirds of these come from within the organization. Most have more than ten years of service with their companies, which means that career planning for the majority over forty has become internally focused. For those who accede to the presidency from within, compensation is largely fixed by precedent and internal relationships. The number twos or heirs apparent in most companies make about 70 percent of the chief executive officer's pay. And very few internally picked CEOs will start at more than their predecessors. But when the opportunity does arise, the bargaining can be spectacular. Semon (Bunkie) Knudsen's negotiation for the position of chairman and chief executive of White Motors is a classic case in point. After missing out on the top job at General Motors, Knudsen left GM in 1968 to accept the presidency of the Ford Motor Company. That didn't work out either and he left Ford a scant twenty months later. The next time Mr. Knudsen was ready. He negotiated current pay of $200,000, plus $100,000 deferred compensation a year for ten years. But this was just spending money. As part of the deal, White agree to acquire a small company called Rectrons for 400,000 shares of White stock then valued at $8.7 million. Knudsen had formed Rectrons after leaving Ford; he and his family owned 60 percent of the stock.

As Bunkie Knudsen demonstrated, there are unusual opportunities for those who have learned the rules. The opportunity usually involves turning around an existing company, coming in as the professional manager in a family-held business or a new venture that has outgrown the founder. Very rarely, it can involve coming in as heir apparent in a large and profitable organization that for some reason hasn't developed a successor. All of these situations have high downside risks, even in the establishment company, where insiders can make it tough, as Knudsen himself found out in his short stint with Ford. But in such cases compensation is an open-ended question. One executive I know overcame the lack of stock by negotiating $375,000 a year *net* of taxes, a sum the company guaranteed for five years. Another swung a seven-figure loan. In the public company, particularly in the turnaround situation, huge blocks of stock, often fifteen or twenty times pay in options, are a favorite lure. For example, the package Robert C. Wilson recently got to turn around Memorex involved 250,000 option shares. This negotiation, incidentally, was a classic. In addition to options,

Wilson got a $200,000 base salary (guaranteed by Memorex's nervous lead bank, the Bank of America), a minimum bonus of $125,000 in 1975 and 1976, and a highly leveraged incentive that could boost his total cash pay to $600,000—with most of the figures adjustable for cost of living!

Whatever the specifics, three factors stand out in almost every situation. First, one has to negotiate a scale of payoff with major upside potential. Whatever seems like a lot should probably be doubled, at least to start the discussion, for in my experience executives in this kind of situation usually underestimate their worth. Second, there should be some protection, in writing please, against the *down*side risks—which is to say there should be an employment contract. Finally, if there is ever a time to harmonize personal objectives with career considerations, this is it. Few readers may ever get to this point—and of those even fewer need my advice—but fewer still will get a chance to play this high-stakes poker if they haven't planned well and known themselves when they came to successive forks in the road.

There is a fascinating element of luck in most careers. What we do with our lives is a highly personal thing. Our interests and aspirations change over time, even our self-confidence. While the careers of most business leaders can be analyzed in terms of the four major stages, there is a wonderful variety in the time span and relevance of each stage for any given individual, looked at with the benefit of hindsight. While there is a decided trend to a more intensive educational preparatory period, there will always be some who achieve the top ranks of business with a high school education or less. While a diversified and well-rounded formative period, followed by intensive functional experience when a person begins to emerge from the pack, is the logical way, some will stumble into the right job and the right company by chance. An amazing number of the really unusual situations seem to find us, instead of we them. The great difference between those who achieve their full potential and those who languish by the roadside seems to be that the former maintain their vitality and have the courage to move quickly when opportunities arise.

What seems clear is the imperative to know oneself. With such self-knowledge, one can, as the U.S. Navy teaches, "plot a broad course, but steer in small increments." As we've seen, the increments in terms of compensation can get pretty large in the event. Whether large or small, however, compensation increments do provide the most finite means of measuring whether we are keeping to the course we have set.

CHAPTER THREE

Money and Taxes: You and Your Shadow

I met a young man recently who is, as he puts it, "a victim of Wall Street and Wilbur Mills." Several years ago, Joe was a junior partner in a prestigious Chicago law firm, with an annual income of $48,000 and a clear shot at $100,000 within a few years. "It was a great job," he told me wistfully, "but the taxes were unbelievable. There I was: single, no house, no losses, no charity to speak of, no medical expenses. The best I could do was the minimum standard deduction. They say that taxes are the price of civilization. Personally, I'd rather have the money."

So in 1968 he left the law firm to accept a $60,000 general counsel slot in a budding West Coast conglomerate. The company's stock was selling at fifty times earnings and had climbed with inspiring regularity for the past three years. Joe was given a 10,000-share restricted stock grant that, according to his calculations, should have gained him $750,000 in 1975 and been taxable at the 25 percent maximum capital gains rate.

But conglomerates are not what they used to be, and Wall Street wasn't kind. Salting his wound, Congress in 1969 lowered the maximum rate on earned income and increased the capital gains rate to 35 percent on sums over $50,000, adding over $100,000 to his potential tax bill. That soon became a moot point as the stock plummeted. Today, this erstwhile conglomerateur is back in the law business with a small Chicago firm.

If nothing else, my friend's misfortune provides insight into the relationships between taxation and the individual's effort to build personal net worth. Taxes, and particularly the lure of tax-favored income, can distort sound career judgment. Tax rules and regulations make it much more difficult to judge the real value of a specific pay package or to compare job offers. The tax structure dictates the vogue of different forms of compensation. Perhaps most frustrating of all, taxes make it difficult to gauge the future consequences of a given career choice, since the rules affecting net income change with stubborn regularity.

Ever since the founding fathers sent up the cry of "No taxation without representation," we have been embroiled in one tax controversy after another. Initially, the debate centered around tariffs, duties, and excise taxes. But in the dark, early days of the Civil War when the Union resorted to practically everything but a national lottery, we introduced the first personal income tax. The Revenue Act of 1861 set a flat rate of 3 percent on income over $800. Needless to say, the tax was not particularly popular, and it was allowed to lapse in 1872. Congress flirted off and on with the income tax in the 1890s, debating both its desirability and its constitutionality, and finally laid the issue to rest with the Sixteenth Amendment to the Constitution in 1913.[1]

The real era of national income taxation traces back to that date, which was a cold February 25 incidentally. Almost immediately, Congress started to complicate the tax structure with deductions and a progressive rate schedule. Over the years, the rates themselves have risen or fallen with the tides of war and the state of the economy, but the trend has been steadily upward. No question about that.

By fiscal 1974, the federal government was collecting $117 billion in taxes from individuals, almost 150 times the *total* federal revenue raised from all sources during the five years of the War Between the States. The individual has become the prime source of revenue for the federal government, as Table 3–1 shows.

As the individual income tax has grown in importance, taxes have increasingly become an instrument of national policy.[2] They are a critical variable both in managing the economy and in setting national priorities. Tax stimulation and tax penalties are used to

Table 3-1. Sources of Federal Tax Revenue

	Percentage of total federal tax dollars			
Tax source	1942	1950	1960	1970
Individual income taxes	26.1	44.7	52.9	61.9
Corporate income taxes	38.6	29.8	27.9	22.5
Sales, gross receipts, and customs	27.9	22.3	16.4	12.5
Other taxes, including licenses	7.4	3.2	2.8	3.1

SOURCE: U.S. Department of Commerce, "Tax Revenue by Source and Level of Government," *Statistical Abstract of the United States,* 91st Annual Edition, 1970, Table 584, and 94th Annual Edition, 1973, Table 660.

redress the social order and to encourage certain investments and discourage others. As a result, our tax system has become increasingly subject to political as well as technical design influences. It also inspires certain emotions, the latest example of which is the public outrage at the fact that, on more than $800,000 income from 1970 through 1972, former President Nixon's lawyers and accountants calculated that he owed only $5,979.01 in taxes, equivalent to the bill of a man with an income of $17,000 a year.

At any point in time, the tax system is a creature of compromise and precedent. Most important to the executive, it is *subject to change.* And since the individual income tax accounts for close to two-thirds of the tax dollar, most change affects the individual taxpayer. Since the Sixteenth Amendment to the Constitution in 1913, there have been twenty-two separate changes of significance in the legislation governing the individual's tax levy—which works out to about one every 2½ years. The longest period between major legislative acts was ten years (from the Revenue Code of 1954 to the Revenue Act of 1964). So in assessing the impact of taxes on various forms and levels of compensation, we are talking about a variable that history suggests will keep changing during, say, the three- to five-year time span of a particular compensation award, or the critical years of a career decision.

In addition to changing rapidly, the tax system, like everything else, is getting progressively more complex. For example, it was not until 1921, when a separate capital gains rate was first adopted, that we began to distinguish between *types* of individual income. It was forty-three more years before the next tax calculation method, income averaging, was adopted in 1964. At that point, one had three sets of tax provisions to master. Five short years later, in 1969, Congress added three more provisions: a new rate and ground rules for taxing "earned" income; a new 10 percent tax on preference income; and a special method of averaging to determine the tax due on lump-sum distributions from certain qualified retirement plans. In the intervening years, a massive body of tax code regulations and precedents have accumulated to guide us on what we can and cannot deduct. We have created a bewildering array of methods for sheltering income and protecting investments from the steeply progressive ordinary income tax bite. By the end of 1973 the Internal Revenue Service had grown to a staff of over 70,000. The size of the book containing the basic revenue code has doubled in the last ten years alone; the interpretive manuals used by IRS agents run to 40,000 pages.

The twists and turns of our tax system have affected corporate compensation schemes immensely. The existence of a low capital gains rate, for example, made it clearly desirable to convert ordinary income into capital gains. This led to the restricted stock option plan of the 1950s, which enabled executives to buy shares in their companies at a favorable price and sell them six months later for a capital gain. The Revenue Act of 1964 changed the ground rules and led to the considerably less attractive qualified stock option. Restricted stock bonuses also had a brief run in the mid-1960s, when they received favorable tax treatment. They were virtually eliminated by the Tax Reform Act of 1969, a piece of legislation so complex that it was dubbed the "accountants' and lawyers' relief act." In the act's wake, we have seen the rise of a host of new executive stock plans, including the nonqualified option and the phantom stock plan. No doubt some subsequent law or ruling will diminish their appeal, and a mad scramble will ensue as corporations rush to adopt yet another scheme for converting one form of income to another more desirable.

Where does all of this leave the executive, buffeted by a rising tax bill and increasingly complex, rapidly changing rules and regulations? Should we allocate a major portion of our lives to studying the tax code? Or should we surrender and accept our sentence as inevitable? Neither alternative is acceptable. What the individual ought to do is plan ahead and develop a tax minimization strategy. For this type of planning, a general understanding of fundamental principles is much more useful than specific knowledge of the ever-changing rules and provisions of the tax code. Far more overpayments have stemmed from failure to grasp the underlying concepts of our tax system and to plan a personal tax minimization strategy than from lack of knowledge of a particular tax rule or provision.

For example, one basic principle here to stay is the concept that each successive level of income should be taxed at a higher rate. We are firmly committed to the graduated or progressive income tax by precedent, philosophy, and practical necessity. Recent legislation has reinforced this by imposing a higher rate on capital gains over $50,000. The progressive taxation concept carries over into state tax structures as well. There are only a few states (Illinois and Massachusetts are examples) that still employ a flat income tax rate. The progressive nature of both our federal and state tax systems weighs heaviest on the corporate executive, whose primary source of income is often a salary and bonus. As a man or woman succeeds financially, a larger and larger percentage of income must be turned over to one's silent partner, the tax collector. A study by Tax Analysts and Advocates, for example, shows that the executive earning $20,000 in 1972, whose income rose with inflation, would see the federal tax bite rise from 15 to 16.3 percent of income. A salary increase of 11.2 percent, to about $22,400, would involve a tax jump of 21.3 percent because of the progressive nature of our tax schedules. Moreover, the taxes would continue to outpace the individual's pay for some time to come. The $20,000 executive whose salary increases by 10 percent per year will experience tax increases of 19 to 20 percent a year until he or she reaches the 50 percent tax bracket—in about twelve years, when annual salary will total $57,061.[3]

Our tax structure favors builders, another important fact to keep in mind. Since we first adopted the separate capital gains provision in 1921 (the maximum rate was 12½ percent of the profits on assets held over two years), we have favored the creator of new values. From the entrepreneur to the real-estate developer, venture-minded taxpayers have enjoyed more favorable rates on their gains than have individuals who get most of their income from other sources. This reflects our society as much as our tax structure.

The low capital gains rate has also had greater impact on executive compensation in this country than any other tax provision. It is largely responsible for the myriad stock programs over the past several decades as corporations searched for compensation plans that would qualify at least part of an executive's income for capital gains treatment. Similarly, the financial appeal of founding or joining a new venture stems primarily from the potential for capital gains when the company goes public.

Like favorable tax rates, deductions are also used to stimulate certain kinds of behavior. Our tax structure encourages oil, mineral, and certain agricultural investments, and provides special depreciation breaks for real-estate investments. Tax-exempt bonds reward the supporters of municipal projects. The ability to deduct property taxes and interest on mortgage loans encourages home ownership. We encourage charitable contributions, which are deductible, and indirectly discourage political contributions, which, for all practical purposes, are not.

On a corporate level, the tax system encourages such employee benefits as profit-sharing and pension plans and life insurance, which are legitimate deductible business expenses to the company and, with few exceptions, are not taxed as current income to the individual. These same tax breaks extend to many "perquisites" such as country club memberships, chauffeured cars, and the like.

Like all tax provisions, these incentives and rewards are subject to change; and when the changes occur, the astute corporation will respond quickly by modifying its executive compensation programs accordingly. Virtually every new compensation scheme in recent years has enjoyed a few years of tax-favored status before the federal government recognized the full implications and stopped the leak through legislation or regulation. In today's complex environment, the value of the compensation package is thus affected by the company's speed and creativity in reacting to tax developments.

Corporate creativity is related to another fundamental aspect of our tax system as well. Neither Congress nor the Internal Revenue Service is a specialist on the relationship between executive compensation and tax law. The fact is few of the common executive pay plans are even mentioned in legislation. The tax consequences of executive compensation vehicles are often scattered through the law and depend upon the forms of taxation and deduction that apply. Understanding the full tax impact of qualified options, for example, requires a thorough knowledge of capital gains, earned income, and preference income provisions. While the IRS will usually rule on the tax treatment of specific plans when requested to do so, it is neither prepared nor staffed to provide templates for model plans or to spell out the tax implications of particular pay devices. It is companies that take the initiative in plan design.

Similarly, it must be the individual who takes the initiative in developing a personal tax strategy. No arm of the government is going to help an executive save on taxes. To paraphrase an old Chinese proverb, the man who waits for the government to show him the road to wealth will have a long, expensive wait. What is required is for the individual to develop a tax minimization strategy. There is nothing either dishonest or unpatriotic about managing one's own income and deduction sources with such a strategy. Mortimer Caplin, the former U.S. Commissioner of Internal Revenue, reaffirmed this basic point in a widely read article: ". . . It's perfectly legitimate and proper to plan your transactions in the most efficient way from the tax standpoint. Once Congress has adopted a policy, then every individual has the right to follow that policy and to take advantage, if you will, of every tax break the law allows. There's absolutely nothing wrong from a moral or citizenship standpoint for people to make their investment decisions on the basis of these stated tax advantages. Of course, *tax avoidance is to be carefully distinguished from tax evasion.*"[4]

I want to emphasize this point. The whole financial structure of an individual *should* be geared to (or reflect) a specific policy of tax avoidance. A fundamental compensation precept indeed.

Those who are willing to take the bull by the horns and plan a conscious tax strategy have basically three tax minimization tactics at their disposal. First, they can manipulate the form in which they receive their income in order to take advantage of the different rates associated with different types of income. Second, they can manipulate the timing of their income in order to defer receipt of a part of current earnings to a time when, presumably, total annual income will decline and they will consequently be in a lower tax bracket. And third, they can manipulate their expenditures and investments to take advantage of provisions that enable them to deduct certain types of expenses from their taxable income base.

Manipulating the Forms of Income

The first technique, manipulating the form of income, has given rise to almost all of the noncash benefits and rewards in the executive pay package. These include the whole spectrum of stock plans (see Chapter 8), many of which are intended to take advantage of the favorable capital gains rate, as well as such tax-free perquisites as executive physicals, company cars, club memberships, and so forth (see Chapter 10).

In turn, the development of these compensation vehicles reflects Congress's current recognition of four separate forms of income, each of which is taxed differently.

Ordinary income is only "ordinary" from the point of view of the government. From the standpoint of the individual, it is generally supplemental or windfall income from dividends, interest, deferred compensation programs, or gambling. The term "ordinary" reflects that this income is subject to the basic (or ordinary) progressive tax schedules and provisions and is not eligible for any special (or extraordinary) tax treatment. The maximum marginal tax rate on ordinary income is 70 percent.

Earned income includes salaries and cash or stock bonuses received as current compensation, and gains from nonqualified stock options. It differs in this respect from ordinary income, which does not have to be received as payment in connection with one's occupation. Like ordinary income, earned income is subject to progressive taxation, but it receives more favorable tax treatment in that the highest applicable marginal rate is only 50 percent.

Preference income includes eight specific types of income (linked to investments) that are taxed in a somewhat paradoxical fashion. On the one hand, these forms of income receive "preferential" treatment; on the other, they are subject to a penalty tax. The seeming paradox arises from Congress's desire to encourage such investments, but only up to a certain point. That point is reached when preference income exceeds $30,000 plus the amount of the taxes the individual would pay on other income. Beyond that point, any additional preference income is subject to a 10 percent penalty levy. For the average executive, the most common preference items are the paper gains on qualified stock options at the time of exercise and one-half of all capital gains.

Table 3-2. Changes in Federal Income Tax on Taxable Income of $50,000 and $100,000—1925–1971

Income year	Tax on $50,000		Tax on $100,000	
	Tax	Marginal rate (%)	Tax	Marginal rate (%)
1927	$ 2,980	13.0	$11,660	19
1935	7,700	27.0	28,000	50
1937	7,700	27.0	30,000	55
1940	11,780	40.0	36,780	56
1942	23,240	63.0	59,140	77
1944	26,820	72.0	67,320	87
1964	23,940	63.5	59,340	75
1968	22,590	60.0	55,490	69
1971	20,190	60.0	53,090	69

NOTE: Single taxpayer; income after exemptions and deductions.
SOURCE: U.S. Department of the Treasury, Internal Revenue Service, *Statistics of Income, Individual Tax Returns*, Treasury Publication #79, 1925–1971.

Capital gains are income from the sale of an asset that has appreciated in value since the time of its purchase. Capital gains on investments held over six months are taxed at a maximum rate of 25 percent on the first $50,000 and 35 percent on the excess over $50,000. One-half of capital gains is also subject to the minimum 10 percent tax on preference income.

The standard income tax schedules are the most basic ingredient in our tax system and, if history is any guide, the most subject to change. Starting with the Revenue Act of 1918, Congress began building our progressive tax structure by combining a flat normal rate with a progressive surtax schedule. Over the years, many a change has been made in the fixed and surtax rates and in the income level at which the highest marginal rate applies, as Table 3–2 illustrates.

The changes in tax rates have been accompanied by variations in the value of personal exemptions. In concept, the exemption is intended to protect a subsistence level of income against taxation, the theory being that no one should be forced to starve in order to pay taxes. In practice, however, the personal and dependent exemptions have generally been well below subsistence levels. At present, a husband and wife filing a joint return can claim $1,500 for themselves and $750 for each dependent. A taxpayer filing a separate return can claim a $750 personal exemption.

Beyond these basic schedules, there have been periodic special surcharges, most recently in connection with the Vietnam War.

From the standpoint of the corporation and the executive, the high marginal tax rates on ordinary income have provided a powerful incentive for the development of alternative forms of compensation that qualify for lower rates. Theoretically, the Tax Reform Act of 1969 reduced that incentive by providing relief for the taxpayer whose income consists primarily of salary and bonus. The 1964 law had already reduced the highest marginal tax rate from 91 to 70 percent. Instead of reducing this ordinary rate further, Congress elected to leave the basic rates intact and created a special maximum tax on *earned income.* On the surface, this new provision is disarmingly simple. The *earned income* provision of the 1969 act lowered the maximum rate on current compensation from 70 to 60 percent in 1971 and to 50 percent in 1972 and thereafter.

This should have made salary and bonuses more attractive relative to stock plans and deferred compensation, and to some extent it did. But only to some extent. The tax relief afforded by the earned income provision applies to relatively few people. The benefit does not begin to take effect until an individual passes the 50 percent tax bracket ($52,000 for a joint return, $38,000 for a separate return). And if that individual has other forms of income besides salary and bonus, the effects of the tax relief may be diluted or washed out altogether.

Under ideal conditions, however, the relief can be substantial. Consider the case of an executive earning $200,000 who has no source of income other than current salary and bonus. Say the person's deductions and exemptions total $40,000, leaving a taxable base of $160,000. Prior to the 1969 act, the executive would have been in the 68 percent tax bracket and would have paid $83,580 in federal income tax. Now, under the 50 percent maximum rate on *earned income,* federal taxes would total only $72,060, a saving of $11,520. This works out to about a 14 percent decrease in the effective tax rate.

In practice, however, this provision is rarely so beneficial. The highly paid executive frequently has such other income sources as dividends and interest, which are subject to the highest applicable *ordinary income* rates. For example, if $30,000 of an executive's $200,000 gross income came from dividends and interest, that $30,000 would be taxed by assuming that the other $170,000 is ordinary income and by calculating the tax due on the last $30,000 at the highest applicable marginal rate. In addition, deductions and exemptions ($40,000 in this case) are prorated between earned income and ordinary income. Thus, instead of realizing a saving of $11,520, this executive would pay $75,820 or a saving of only $7,760 from the pre-1969 tax bill. Of course, the executive may be able to moderate the effects of this ordinary income by controlling the timing of its receipt. But this requires rather complex forward planning at the time of the investment decision. To evaluate the tax consequences of alternative investments, it is necessary to forecast income by taxable category for several years in the future and run tax calculations for each investment case.

Yet another complication arises when the executive also has *preference income* in addition to earned income. There are two preference income items of particular interest to the salaried executive. One is the so-called "bargain element" in qualified options, or the difference between the option price and the fair market value when the option is exercised. For example, suppose an executive receives a 1,000-share option to purchase company stock at $50 per share under a qualified option plan, then exercises that right five years later when the stock is selling at $80 a share. The executive has not made any money yet; in fact, the stock must be held for three more years in order to qualify for capital gains rates. However, the executive creates preference income of $30,000 in the year when the option is exercised. If other preference income is also received that year, the total may be enough to activate the 10 percent minimum tax penalty on preference income.

The other source of tax preference income relevant to the executive is half of all capital gains (the excess of long-term gains over short-term losses). This includes gains from both private investments and the sale of stock acquired through option programs.

In practice, an executive is allowed a substantial amount of tax *preference income* on a tax-free basis. To repeat, the 10 percent levy does not apply until the preference items exceed $30,000 plus the amount of the taxpayer's other taxes paid that year.

Thereby hangs an interesting tale. A scant thirteen months after the 1969 Tax Reform Act, Congress further liberalized the preference income provision by providing that unused deductions (the tax element, not the $30,000 fixed deduction) can be carried forward seven years. At the same time, Congress eliminated the three-year carry-back provision that some taxpayers could have used to recoup some of the preference tax paid in previous years. The net effect of these new ground rules is that most executives should be able to avoid paying any preference tax at all if they are astute in timing their option exercise decisions and their capital gains income.

Even though an executive can avoid the 10 percent tax, preference income can still create a tax liability by reducing the amount of earned income that qualifies for the favorable 50 percent maximum rate. Preference income in excess of $30,000 offsets the amount of earned income that qualifies, so that the value of the 50 percent maximum rate is quickly eroded. Consider the case of a $200,000 executive whose tax bill comes to $72,060. Suppose that in addition to a salary of $200,000 he creates $150,000 in preference income through the exercise of an option or the sale of stock for a capital gain. Since the tax preference, even after the $30,000 deduction, is greater than the portion of the executive's earned income subject to rates higher than 50 percent (in this case, $108,000), the total tax jumps to $87,230. While the direct preference tax is quite modest, only $3,650, the preference income triggers an additional $11,520 tax on his salary.

Given the relationship between preference income and the taxation of earned income, qualified stock options and capital gains are far less attractive for highly paid executives than they were before the 1969 Tax Act.

Another provision of the 1969 act further diminished the appeal of capital gains opportunities by adding a progressive component to the capital gains rate. Prior to the 1969 law, most discussions of capital gains focused on the 25 percent alternative tax rate. If one held the capital asset six months or more, this was the maximum rate. The actual rate could be lower, of course, because the basic capital gains calculation (ignoring losses) was: (1) divide your total capital gains in half, and (2) calculate the tax on this reduced amount using your applicable ordinary income tax schedule. The rate could well be under 25 percent. The 1969 act retained this formula for the first $50,000 of gains, but beyond that point the maximum rate was increased, over a two-year period, from 25 to 35 percent.

The law also changed the ground rules for deducting net long-term capital losses, which used to be fully deductible from ordinary income, dollar for dollar up to a maximum of $1,000. The 1969 act cut the offset to 50 cents on the dollar and eliminated the opportunity to carry forward the undeductible portion to subsequent tax years.

The net result of these changes has been to reduce the relative attractiveness of compensation elements designed to qualify for capital gains treatment. Although the maximum capital gains rate is still fifteen percentage points below the maximum tax on earned income, there is far less incentive than there once was to provide capital gains opportunities.

Despite their decline from dominance, however, compensation schemes that are oriented toward capital gains continue to have some appeal, particularly in smaller companies where the direct cost impact of cash and other alternatives is more pronounced. Many of the compensation elements common to larger corporations continue to qualify for capital gains treatment. For example, any increase in the value of pension funds is taxed at the capital gains rate. Savings and thrift plans, qualified stock purchase plans, and restricted stock bonuses also qualify to some extent for capital gains treatment.

When all the dust from the Tax Reform Act of 1969 finally settled, corporations and their executives found themselves in this position: The tax rate on current cash compensation had declined from 70 percent to 50 percent, provided that the executive did not receive excessive amounts of preference income from exercising stock options or taking capital gains. At the same time, the maximum rate on capital gains had increased by ten percentage points on gains of $50,000 or more. That combination of circumstances meant that a great many executive compensation packages, especially those that used qualified options to provide capital gains opportunities, had suddenly declined in relative value.

Since 1969, innovative corporations have responded by devising new compensation vehicles. Two of the most popular current devices are nonqualified stock options and phantom stock (again, see Chapter 8), which are intended to provide capital accumulation opportunities rather than capital gains. These devices tend to focus executive attention on the ultimate goal of building personal net worth rather than on tax consequences of the vehicles used to achieve that objective.

To the extent that taxes reduce the individual's income, however, they impede the effort to gain financial independence. For that reason, it makes eminent sense to develop a conscious tax minimization strategy that takes advantage of the different tax rates associated with different forms of compensation. To some extent, of course, an executive is limited by the forms of compensation available in the corporation. Only the top few executives in most corporations are in a position to negotiate individual compensation packages. But all of us can and should be aware of the tax implications and interrelationships of the various components of our income. Exhibit 3 reviews the most common elements of executive compensation in terms of their tax treatment.

In general, fringe benefits are the biggest tax bargains in the executive pay package. Insurance coverage, expense accounts, company cars, club memberships, educational allowances, and many other noncash rewards are virtually tax free. For anyone in a fairly high tax bracket, the next best tax minimizer is still capital gains income, and the most common corporate vehicles for providing capital gains are still stock options or stock purchase plans. These must be handled with care, however, because of the complex interaction of tax provisions pertaining to capital gains, preference income, and earned income.

The lion's share of most executive income—salary and bonuses —is taxed at progressive rates up to a maximum of 50 percent. Pension and profit-sharing benefits receive special tax breaks, although legislation passed in 1969 and 1974 increased the tax on lump-sum distributions (see Chapters 5 and 6). The potentially highest tax rates apply to income such as dividends, interest, and most deferred compensation that is defined as ordinary income, all of which is subject to a maximum rate of 70 percent.

Manipulating the Timing of Income

Executives who hope to minimize their taxes by varying the timing of their income delivery can employ three techniques: One is to defer receipt of part of the income through a deferred compensation plan; the second is to spread one year's income over several years for tax purposes under the income-averaging provision of the tax code; and a third is to participate in some executive stock option or other plan where the individual controls the timing of the gain.

Deferred compensation programs come in a variety of forms (see Chapter 9), but all are based on the premise that the individual's income, and hence tax bracket, will decline following retirement. The idea is to postpone receipt of part of one's current earnings until they can be taxed at a lower rate. Although the concept is appealing, the practice is rarely as advantageous as one might

EXHIBIT 3

Checklist and summary explanation of tax treatment of various forms of compensation.

Legend:
- ■ Primary form of taxation
- ▨ Possible alternate or additional form

FORM OF COMPENSATION	ORDINARY INCOME TAX RATES (TO 70%)	EARNED INCOME MAXIMUM TAX (50%)	INCOME AVERAGING	CAPITAL GAINS (25-35%)	MINIMUM TAX ON PREFERENCE INCOME (10%)	TAX-FREE INCOME
Salary	▨	■	▨			
Incentive bonus	▨	■	▨			
Deferred compensation	■	▨	▨			
Other current income*	▨	■	▨			
Life insurance		■				■
Sick pay	■					▨
Long-term disability insurance						■
Medical insurance						■
Pension	■			▨		
Qualified stock purchase		▨		■		
Qualified profit sharing	■			▨	▨	
Company car		▨				■
Personal financial counseling		■				
Qualified stock option	▨	▨		■	▨	
Qualified savings plans	■			▨	▨	
Phantom (or simulated) stock option	▨	■				
Nonqualified stock option		■		▨	▨	
Company loans**	⊕	▨				■
Reimbursement of uncovered medical expenses						■
Club membership***		▨				■
Performance share plan		■		▨	▨	
Reimbursed business expenses						■
Tuition refund plans						■
Use of company airplane (personal)		■				▨
Restricted stock or property		■		▨	▨	

* Christmas bonuses, overtime, shift differentials, commissions, etc.
** For purchase of company stock.
***Luncheon club, country club, etc.

Salary: At higher income levels executive should do alternate calculations to see which provisions produce lowest tax.

Incentive bonus: Taxed like salary if paid within 1 year. Payouts stretching beyond 1 year (the "rollover" bonus) taxed as ordinary income unless subject to forfeiture.

Deferred compensation: Not eligible for earned income provision under the typical deferral arrangement, since funds are not paid out within 12 months after the year in which they are earned.

Life insurance: First $50,000 coverage not taxed. Larger amounts permitted in most states, but you are taxed on imputed premium, which varies by age under a special IRS schedule.

Sick pay: $100 a week tax-free under certain conditions.

Long-term disability insurance: No tax on value of coverage. Distributions under contributory plans can be tax-free.

Medical insurance: Coverage and payments tax-free.

Pension: No tax until payout. Under the normal form of payment (i.e., a monthly annuity), taxed as ordinary income. Any portion representing employee contribution is tax-free. Lump-sum distributions qualify for special 10-year averaging.

Qualified stock purchase: Under these broad employee plans, company stock is acquired without any immediate tax, typically on a payroll deduction basis. Gains at sale qualify for capital gains if sale occurs at least 2 years after grant and 6 months after purchase. Where stock is granted at a discount (rules permit up to 15 percent), the discount is taxed as earned income at sale.

Qualified profit sharing: No tax until payout. Under the normal lump-sum distribution the portion attributable to company contributions and investment gains is now taxed as ordinary income, using a special 10-year averaging rule. Tax can be delayed if distribution is in stock.

Company car: No tax if used for business purposes.

Personal financial counseling: Portion of the fee paid to counselor must now be reported as income. Any portion relating to tax or investment counseling can then be taken as deduction by employee.

Qualified stock option: No tax at time of award. At exercise, paper gains may be subject to pref-erence tax of 10 percent. Stock held for 3 years is taxed as capital gains income, but the "untaxed" half of the gain can increase tax rate on other income and can be subject to prefer-ence income tax. If stock is sold in less than 3 years, it is treated as a nonqualified option.

Qualified savings plans: Taxed like qualified profit sharing; company stock distributed under these plans is not taxed until sold.

Phantom (or simulated) stock option: Taxed when "paper" gains are distributed; treated as earned income if the plan includes a substantial risk of forfeiture.

Nonqualified stock options: Gains at exercise are subject to immediate tax (50 percent max-imum). If held for 6 months, subsequent gain over exercise price receives capital gains tax treatment.

Company loans: Tax treatment depends on rate of interest. Interest-free loans (or loans with less than 4 percent simple interest) may involve "imputed interest" income. Any interest paid is deductible.

Reimbursement of uncovered medical expenses: Often provided to top executive as an additional tax-free benefit.

Club membership: Tax-free if membership serves a legitimate business purpose. Company payment of country-club memberships and dues is scrutinized carefully and may involve imputed income.

Performance share plan: Under these plans because the stock bonus is not paid unless a certain performance is achieved (i.e., a particular EPS growth), ultimate payment is treated as earned income if paid within 12 months of the year in which "vesting" occurs. Any real stock distributed is valued at current market value.

Tuition refund plans: Reimbursement not taxed if education is directly related to the individual's *present* job. Otherwise it is income.

Use of company airplane: Typically employee will reimburse company and avoid any imputed income.

Restricted stock or property: Taxed as earned income, at fair market value, when there is no longer any substantial risk of forfeiture or the asset becomes transferable. Any income (i.e., dividends) during the restricted period is taxed as earned income. If recipient declares the restricted asset as income in year of receipt, subsequent appreciation is taxed as a capital gain (forfeited assets previously declared as income create a capital loss).

expect. Two critical assumptions are involved: that one's income will, in fact, decline; and that current tax rates will prevail at a future time. Both assumptions could easily prove to be wrong. Moreover, many deferred compensation programs fail to provide any return on the deferred sum, even though the individual could invest the money if it were received as current income. And finally, the tax rate on deferred compensation can be as high as 70 percent under present tax laws, while the maximum rate on current earned income is only 50 percent.

The second technique, *income averaging*, enables a taxpayer with a sizable jump in income in a given year to treat that income as though it were also earned over the preceding four years. It is said that Dwight D. Eisenhower's phenomenal success with his book, *Crusade in Europe*, helped focus attention on the need for some provision to cope with the extraordinary income rise. It doesn't take much royalty income to dramatically exceed the $21,000 average annual base pay that generals received during World War II.

Income averaging was first introduced in 1964 and later simplified and liberalized in the 1969 act to the point that it is often the best tax provision for the younger executive whose income is jumping 20 to 25 percent per year, as Table 3–3 shows.

Quite logically, the lower the base-period income, the greater the potential of this provision. The reverse is also true. In fact, when a married taxpayer's base-period income nears $40,000, the new 50 percent maximum tax on earned income is usually more advantageous, and one cannot use both.

Obviously, if all or a substantial portion of the current year's

Table 3-3. Analysis of Tax Impact of Income Averaging for Married Taxpayer with $18,000 Base-Period Income

Net taxable income in current year	Taxes to be paid		Saving
	Using ordinary tax schedule	Using income averaging	
$25,000	$ 6,020	$ 5,982	$ 38
30,000	7,880	7,582	298
40,000	12,140	11,037	1,103

SOURCE: Harris Trust and Savings Bank, "1973 Federal Tax Computation for Returns on 1972 Income," Commerce Clearing House, Inc., Clark, N.J., page 9.

income is from an inheritance, the Irish Sweepstakes, Las Vegas winnings, or other income that *does not qualify* as earned income, the averaging provision can still be attractive. For example, the executive with a $50,000 base-period income who receives a gift from "Uncle Charlie" that pushes total income in a given year to $500,000 can save $31,880 by using income averaging.

Unfortunately, income averaging and other provisions of recent laws have vastly complicated the executive's problem of timing stock option affairs advantageously.[5] The exercise of a qualified stock option can trigger preference income tax, as we have already discussed. But the ramifications affecting timing do not end there. The taxpayer fortunate enough to realize a significant capital gain can either pay a capital gains tax or count half of that gain as current income and use an averaging approach. But this means forgoing the use of both the capital gains rate and the earned income provision. Anyone with this kind of problem should consult a good adviser; in fact, providing counsel on stock option exercise has turned out to be one of the principal services of the new personal finance counseling industry that has emerged in recent years.

Minimizing Taxes through Tax Shelters

In an April 1973 episode of the popular television series "All in the Family," Archie Bunker's daughter Gloria discovered that Archie had failed to report $680 on his federal tax return. "How could you cheat on your taxes?" she asked angrily. To which Archie replied, "I'm just—what do you call it—exercisin' my loopholes, that's all. Like the big guys."

As we've been reminded recently, most of the "big guys" and a lot of little guys have done that legally over the years by claiming legitimate personal or business deductions, effectively "sheltering" their income. The most common approach is the so-called homeowner's deduction, which allows the 39 million Americans who own their own homes to deduct mortgage interest costs and property taxes from their federal taxes. According to two Brookings Institution economists, the various tax favors granted to homeowners cost the Treasury $9.6 billion a year in lost revenues. And the 50 percent or more of us who itemize our tax returns each year are costing the government another $20 billion with our deductions for charity, medical expenses, interest payments, state and local taxes, and so forth. These deductions frequently add up to far more than the standard deduction of 15 percent of adjusted gross income or $2,000, whichever is less.[6]

Under the tax laws, several of these deductible items, such as interest payments, are also deductible when the cost is incurred in connection with an investment. Moreover, Congress has created additional tax benefits to encourage certain types of activity, the drilling for oil, for instance. These provisions create a wealth of opportunities to shelter income. In fact, in 1971, the federal government effectively lost $77 billion in tax revenue from individuals and organizations that took advantage of legitimate tax breaks.[7] That same year, the total federal tax collected was only $191.6 billion.

There probably isn't any area of our tax code that stimulates more debate than these special rules and provisions, many of which benefit those who already have great wealth. The hue and cry reached a fever pitch when it was revealed that, under one of these special provisions (since repealed), Richard Nixon claimed a $482,018 deduction for a gift of his vice-presidential papers to the National Archives. All newspaper readers were promptly engulfed in the intricacies of the tax law. Issues such as the deduction of a portion of the cost of the former President's San Clemente home for "business purposes," the treatment of his $500,000 expense allowance, and the taxation of his Florida real-estate gains were analyzed and debated in the press, and television brought the whole controversy into our living rooms.

The former President's tax problems sparked another round in the continuing movement for tax reform, aimed particularly at taxpayers with high income who manage to avoid high taxes. Even before the detailed review of the President's form 1040, congressional leaders were sending up trial balloons. In the spring of 1972, Congressman Wilbur Mills tried a novel approach with HR 15230, which would have eliminated fifty-four special deductions unless Congress specifically reinstated them, item by item, after a programmed review over three years. A Nixon-Shultz proposal in April of 1973 involved a complex series of changes to put teeth into the minimum tax provision.

But while some reform is probably inevitable, it seems unlikely that we will move completely away from the basic concept of deductions. There is too strong a constituency for each of the vast number of personal and business deductions, and the whole history of tax legislation suggests that an effort to increase taxes on certain forms of income often winds up lowering it on others in the give-and-take of the political process. What starts out as an exercise in simplification winds up complicating, often creating new opportunities for "exercisin' your loopholes."

In short, the third alternative in a tax-minimization strategy is likely to be around for some time, and high-salaried executives willing to take the investment risks inherent in efforts to shelter income ought to consider what steps fit their own specific needs. In my judgment, potential tax savings, which begin to look attractive at about the 50 percent tax bracket, are merely the first item on a tax-shelter investment checklist.

The attractiveness of the shelters also varies depending on the risk and profit potential. Generally, the best investment opportunities are privately arranged, often by an investment counselor or an accountant, on behalf of a group of wealthy clients. The major brokerage houses also put together tax-shelter deals and offer them to the general public. According to one estimate, over a billion dollars annually is channeled into publicly reported tax-shelter investments, and perhaps twice that amount is privately placed.[8] There are even a few corporations moving into the business of creating tax shelters on behalf of their top managers, one of the really unusual compensation developments to surface in recent years.

The private investor in search of a shelter is generally well advised to seek good professional advice, since many of the deals being arranged today are quite simply poor investments and the list of those burned in bad deals grows longer all the time. One should also stay alert for the possibility that, in terms of both tax savings and profit potential, a single tax shelter will be less attractive than a combination of several.

Impact of State and Local Income Taxes

An individual's tax planning should start, and often will end, with an assessment of the implications and alternatives of our federal tax system. But most careers now involve several moves, and job change often implies location change. This brings the executive up against that most uneven of all tax realities, the state and local income tax picture.

For more than a decade now, state and local budget growth has far outstripped the growth in federal expenditures. To support the burden, 44 states and more than 170 cities have turned to some form of income taxation.[9] State and local taxes on personal income have increased steadily as a percentage of gross national product from a modest nationwide average of 4.4 percent in 1945 to 10 percent in 1972. Except for Texas with its oil revenue and Nevada with its gambling revenue, most of the six remaining states will almost certainly succumb to some form of income taxation. But while state taxes are almost inescapable, they are by no means equal. California's marginal tax rate is 11 percent on all income over $15,500, for example, while Illinois has a flat 2.5 percent rate. City taxes can widen the spread. Since 1939, when Philadelphia introduced one of the first municipal income taxes (it was canceled in 1973), an increasing number of major cities have lined up for the take. Some examples of city income taxes are shown in Table 3–4.

In summary, state and local taxes together can easily account for a 10 to 15 percent differential in the cost of living in, say, Dallas versus New York City. For years, the uneven state levies on income have affected residence decisions in New York City. Taxes in New York State are among the highest in the nation, while New Jersey has a commuter's tax but no state income tax, and Connecticut is a virtually tax-free haven. Discrepancies of this type seem destined to remain for the foreseeable future.

By way of guidance, Exhibit 4 shows total state income taxes payable in 1972 for a $50,000 adjusted gross income and summarizes the marginal rate above that level. Clearly, such taxes can amount to a tidy sum, even though, since they are a deductible item on federal returns, the net cost for an upper-income executive in these examples would be about half of the amount shown.

While local and state taxes will rarely be a controlling factor in a career decision, they do deserve analysis when a change in location is involved. Nor are the immediate tax consequences of the move the only factor to assess. The progressive slope of the tax structure should also be taken into account, particularly when an executive

Table 3-4. Large U.S. Cities with Municipal Income Tax

City	Date introduced	Present rate (%)
St. Louis	1948	1.0
Cincinnati	1954	2.0
Detroit	1962	2.0
Baltimore	1966	1.0–2.5*
New York	1966	0.7–3.5†
Cleveland	1967	1.0

*The Baltimore municipal tax is 50 percent of the Maryland tax, which is currently 2–5 percent.

†Rates shown for residents. Nonresidents pay a 0.45 percent wage tax.

SOURCE: Advisory Commission on Intergovernmental Relations, *Federal-State-Local Finances: Significant Features of Fiscal Federalism*, U.S. Government Printing Office, Washington, D.C., 1974.

anticipates a sharp income rise over the next three to five years. In Delaware, for example, the tax rates are steeply graduated. The dollar level at which state taxes hit the highest rate also varies considerably. The top marginal rate in Georgia and Louisiana is only 6 percent, for example, but the applicable earnings level is $10,000 for the Atlanta executive versus $50,000 for the executive in New Orleans.

Let me close this chapter with several general observations about taxes. Trade-offs, forward planning, and "what if" thinking are the key to an executive tax strategy. The executive must be willing to analyze the interaction of company compensation and personal income and deductions, since private transactions affect the tax rate on option gains, lump-sum pension distributions, current salary, and the like. At the same time, it is important to keep the issue of taxes in proper perspective. When tax minimization becomes a governing factor in a career or compensation decision, it is time to pause and reexamine priorities. A surprising number of executives get so preoccupied with taxes they overlook the asset value and risk characteristics of a compensation package. The important thing is to go beyond tax details to look at the basic principles as they apply in particular cases. It involves effort, but effort that is worth while. Benjamin Franklin wrote in *Poor Richard's Almanac* that "A penny saved is a penny earned." That's especially true when it's saved from the tax collector.

EXHIBIT 4

Summary comparison of personal state income tax levels.*

	1 Tax at $50,000 income	2 Marginal tax rate above $50,000	3 Maximum marginal tax rate		
	%	%	%		$
New York	8.5	10.5	15.0	over	25,000
Wisconsin	7.1	11.4	11.4	over	14,000
Minnesota	7.0	15.0	15.0	over	20,000
Delaware	6.8	12.0	18.0	over	100,000
District of Columbia	6.7	10.0	10.0	over	25,000
Vermont	6.7	Related to federal income tax liability			
Montana	6.5	11.0	11.0	over	35,000
Hawaii	6.4	11.0	11.0	over	35,000
North Carolina	5.2	7.0	7.0	over	10,000
Oregon	5.2	10.0	10.0	over	5,000
Idaho	5.0	7.5	7.5	over	5,000
South Carolina	5.0	7.0	7.0	over	10,000
Arkansas	4.7	7.0	7.0	at	25,000
North Dakota	4.7	10.0	10.0	over	8,000
California	4.6	11.0	11.0	over	15,500
Alaska	4.5	Related to federal income tax liability			
Massachusetts	4.5	5% on earned income; interest & dividends, capital gains on intangibles 9%			
Iowa	4.3	7.0	7.0	over	9,000
New Mexico	4.3	8.0	9.0	over	100,000
Georgia	4.2	6.0	6.0	over	10,000
Rhode Island	4.1	Related to federal income tax liability			
Colorado	3.9	8.0	8.0	over	10,000
Maryland	3.9	5.0	5.0	over	3,000
Virginia	3.9	5.75	5.75	over	12,000
Oklahoma	3.6	6.0	6.0	over	7,500

*The following states do not have a personal income tax: Florida, Nevada, South Dakota, Texas, Washington, Wyoming.

Notes: Column 1. 1971 effective tax rate at $50,000 adjusted gross income.
          2. Marginal tax rate at $50,000 net income after personal exemptions, 7/1/73.
          3. Maximum marginal tax rate, 7/1/73.

	1 Tax at $50,000 income	2 Marginal tax rate above $50,000	3 Maximum marginal tax rate		
	%	%	%		$
Utah	3.6	7.25	7.25	over	7,500
Arizona	3.5	8.0	8.0	over	6,000
Kentucky	3.3	6.0	6.0	over	8,000
West Virginia	3.2	7.5	9.6	over	200,000
Kansas	3.0	6.5	6.5	over	7,000
Missouri	3.0	6.0	6.0	over	9,000
Mississippi	2.9	4.0	4.0	over	5,000
Alabama	2.7	5.0	5.0	over	5,000
Louisiana	2.5	4.0	6.0	over	50,000
Maine	2.5	5.0	6.0	over	50,000
Illinois	2.3	2.5% on total net income			
Nebraska	2.3	Related to federal income tax liability			
Pennsylvania	2.3	2.3% on all taxable income			
Michigan	2.2	3.9% on all taxable income			
Indiana	1.8	2.0% on adjusted gross income			
Median rate	4.2%				
Connecticut		6.0% on capital gains			
New Hampshire		4.25% on interest and dividends: 4.0% commuter's income tax			
New Jersey		15% over $25,000 (N.Y. commuters only); 2.3% on all taxable income (Philadelphia commuters only)			
Ohio		3.5% over $40,000 (net income after personal exemptions)			
Tennessee		6.0% on interest and dividends			

SOURCE: Advisory Commission on Intergovernmental Relations, *Federal-State-Local Finances: Significant Features of Fiscal Federalism*, U.S. Government Printing Office, Washington, D.C., 1974, Tables 139, 141.

CHAPTER FOUR

Company Insurance: Anticipating Death, Disability, and Other Disasters

The changing patterns of careers and taxation establish the framework for the reward structure in the United States.

Both forces produce more and more complexity. No compensation device illustrates this more graphically than group insurance, which is also the first special form of pay an employee encounters.

When the newcomer joins a company, nobody explains the stock option plan, or the pension, or the incentive structure; the typical orientation session does not even cover how the salary system really works. But on the first day on the job at virtually every company across the land, nearly everyone gets a set of insurance enrollment forms and explanatory group insurance booklets. The new typist in the pool may not pay much more attention to the booklets than the new young professional, who probably feels invincible. If either is married, the medical plan will probably get careful scrutiny. For the rest, people are likely to settle for the impression that there are an awful lot of plans to protect employees against any conceivable disaster. The impression reflects the fact that for several decades American companies have been in a mad race with themselves to provide more and more forms and larger and larger amounts of group insurance. Together they add up to the so-called full circle of protection: life, accidental death, disability, group medical, dental, personal liability.

Since our tax laws exempt most insurance coverage from any imputed income to the individual, while allowing the company to deduct its cost as a standard business expense, major developments have often followed taxation trends. Particularly during World War II and the Korean conflict, when confiscatory tax rates were in effect, employee insurance got a vigorous forward shove. In addition, as individuals became more mobile in their jobs, particularly at the clerical levels and in blue-collar ranks, companies began to use insurance as a competitive personnel weapon. It is worth tracing this evolution a little more closely, because it foreshadows what we can expect in the years ahead.

Much of the initial attention focused on life insurance. Many companies funded their pension plans in the early years by purchasing individual pension contracts, much like those one can purchase privately today. While there are many variations, all such policies build up cash value over time; and absent a death benefit claim, all can be converted into annuities. As employee rolls grew, however, the individual pension approach became terribly expensive; companies were "funding" a pension for each of their employees. It was primarily to cut costs, therefore, that companies began switching to various forms of group funding. Under this approach, the company could rest on the actuarial assumption that only a fraction of the work force would ever actually collect a pension. Then, with retirement benefits and death benefits divorced, companies began to look at a cheaper form of "pure" insurance being developed by the industry, term insurance. It was inevitable that somebody would link the concepts of low-cost term coverage and the insurance needs of employee groups. What evolved was *group life insurance,* a form of term insurance purchased at discount prices. Typically, it was either paid for by the company or offered to the employee at some standard rate like 40 or 50 cents per month per $1,000 of coverage.

Montgomery Ward (now Marcor) pioneered one of the first group plans as early as 1912. But it was not until right after World War II that group life caught hold as an employee benefit. In 1930, the total group life insurance in force was only $9.8 billion, less than 10 percent of all life insurance values. By 1973, the total coverage had increased to $483.2 billion. Approximately one-third of the total face value of all life insurance now in force in this country is in company-sponsored coverage.

As a next step, companies began adding a form of double indemnity coverage to the basic life policies, providing additional payments under the so-called *accidental death and dismemberment* plans. The typical plan provided for twice the basic group life in the event of accidental death and partial amounts for such mishaps as loss of a limb or an eye. In the early 1940s, pacesetter companies began to provide *group medical* insurance benefits in the form of insured hospital and surgical coverage, usually group Blue Cross/ Blue Shield contracts. And starting in the 1950s, *major medical* coverage was added by an increasing number of companies. To illustrate how quickly a benefit can catch on, the Health Insurance Institute estimates only 4.7 million employees and dependents were covered by group major medical plans in 1955; by 1972 they found the number had increased to more than 80 million.[1]

The 1960s brought yet another new development: protection against loss of income because of a disability. The historical roots were in federal and state legislation passed over the preceding two decades. The 1956 amendment to the Social Security Act provided the first source of real long-term income to the disabled worker. Some state legislatures had already moved to require short-term income continuance. New York State's temporary disability law, for example, was passed in 1949; and other states were soon providing protection up to a maximum of twenty-six weeks. These legislated benefits provided a reasonably large benefit in relation to current earnings for lower-income workers, but the coverage was hardly adequate for most salaried employees. The private *long-term disability* plan, on the other hand, was designed to provide financial security to the permanently disabled by guaranteeing to continue 50 to 60 percent of pay. These LTD plans have now become common in larger companies, although their incidence generally is still low. In 1972 there were only 13 million individuals covered, about 70 percent of them under group plans.[2]

With the spread of disability insurance, unions, insurance planners, and company personnel departments began experimenting anew. Only about half of 1 percent of the population was insured against dental expenses in 1962, and most experts argued that dental work was not a good candidate for insurance. Dental problems rarely involve catastrophic expenses (typically covered under major medical plans anyway), and the cost of dental checkups and filling cavities can be predicted in the family budget.[3] The chance to offer an additional tax-free benefit and protection against rising dental bills proved irresistible, however. So by 1970 over 12 million persons had dental insurance. With only 6 percent of the population covered, there is a lot of room for further growth, and that growth is likely to come. Now serious attention is being given to group *automobile liability insurance* as well. District 15 of the Steelworkers Union provides its 65,000 members with free legal advice, and a number of unions have prepaid *legal insurance* plans. The possibilities seem endless: group credit insurance, group homeowners' insurance, perhaps even divorce insurance.

From the early life insurance contracts to group dental plans, it seems at first blush that most plans are aimed primarily at lower-level employees. Group insurance appears to be a form of protection and compensation provided by the benevolent company to truck drivers, secretaries, and trainees, a benefit not all that relevant or important to an executive. Nothing could be further from the truth. Insurance plans are designed to provide basic protection for all employees, it is true, but companies have been particularly ingenious in finding ways to use this tax-favored compensation to meet the needs of executives. They have tied the amount of insurance to pay level and even adopted special executive plans. Yet the average executive still fails to realize how important group insurance can be to him. For example, how would most executives score on the following quiz?

- Most large companies now provide
     two   four   six
  different types of insurance protection to their executives.
- The average mid-career married executive probably needs
     2–3 times   4–5 times   6–8 times
  his pay in life insurance.
- Group life insurance proceeds are
     always   never   sometimes
  included in a man's estate and subject to estate taxes.
- The maximum federal estate tax rate is
     27%   52%   77%.
- If your group life insurance is convertible when you terminate, you can buy
     one-year renewable term insurance   five-year renewable
     term   permanent insurance.

- The replacement cost of the above-average company insurance package for a forty-five-year-old $50,000 manager would be
  $900 $2,100 $4,700.
- Benefits under most contributory disability plans are
  taxed as earned income   taxed as ordinary income
  tax free.
- The amount of group life insurance that a company can provide is
  unlimited   limited to $50,000 by the federal government
  limited in certain states only.

The correct answer to each question is the last one, but few executives can more than guess their way to even four or five right choices. In part, this is because insurance, like taxes, impresses most people as a dull subject. It is also more than a little depressing. While few of us over thirty feel invincible any more, the prospect of a crippling disability or a $40,000 medical bill is a remote proposition that we would sooner not think about, thank you very much. So we tend to ignore or postpone any careful review of insurance. We even postpone, if the truth be known, reading the employee insurance booklets and certificates of coverage sent us by our friends in the personnel department. Nor have companies helped matters much. The fact is they contribute to general ignorance and lethargy by appearing to take over the insurance planning responsibility. The sin has been compounded by minimal or bad communication. It seems to employees that every few years some marvelous new coverage is added and existing plans are updated and revised. It is hard to confirm this surmise from the fine print, but most of us can be forgiven for assuming our coverage is pretty good and that "someone up there" is keeping fully abreast of the latest development.

The facts are not this comforting, of course. Many employee insurance plans are either poorly designed or obsolete. Few offer adequate total protection. Most programs have evolved piecemeal over a quarter-century or so, and there are often duplications, gaps in coverage, and hidden technical traps. Moreover, while many plans reflect a sincere effort to provide at least basic protection, it is naive to assume that altruism is the principal drive behind the phenomenal growth of employee insurance. On the contrary, most company packages are a tissue of compromises reflecting a rather broad range of pressures. Unions have played a major role in pushing for more and more protection; dental insurance is only one recent example. "Competitive considerations" have also played their part. When a company is reminded that its plan lags behind its rivals', it is likely to up its ante accordingly—even though any company package will lag somewhere when planners must contend with the couple of hundred provisions, limits, and rules in the typical company insurance package of six or more plans. Certainly there is pressure from the insurance industry itself with its $250 billion in assets, its very powerful lobby, its 450,000 salespeople, and its innovative line of products. There are negative pressures on progress as well: cost, considerations of equity between groups of employees, concern over precedents for future union negotiation. To protect private insurance sales, the insurance lobby in quite a number of states also has been successful in getting legal limits set on the amount of group insurance that can be offered by companies headquartered in those states.

While the general trend is clear—to add new coverage and liberalize what exists—specific programs are developed in fits and starts. It is thus easy to see why most companies have adopted a philosophy of gradualism in insurance planning: keep making improvements a bit at a time as competitors' programs improve, as the industry develops new concepts, or as the company can afford changes. This is not an unwise philosophy from the company viewpoint; however, it does mean that plans or specific provisions are likely to be at least a couple of years out of date.

A corollary of gradualism seems to be that companies rarely cancel what they have. Accidental death and dismemberment insurance provides a case in point. Many insurance carriers originally sold "AD&D" as part of a package with basic group life. Thus, the cost was often hidden. Now many companies have adopted broader, more comprehensive coverage through all-risk policies. Yet few have taken the trouble to redesign the basic group life package. It thus becomes possible for an individual to be overinsured against death in an automobile accident and underinsured against death from heart attack or cancer. Company planners also have a way of focusing more on technical provisions and plans than on categories or profiles of employee needs. Take group life insurance. Most companies provide the same protection for married and single employees, even though their needs are usually quite different. Too, under most group plans, the amount of coverage is a multiple of salary; dollar coverage, therefore, increases with age since most people's salary goes up with experience. But most people's insurance needs begin to decline as they reach their mid-fifties. Children become self-supporting, other assets have had time to grow, and, actuarially at least, one's survivors need to be protected for less time. All this reflects the fact that very few corporations can meet all our individual needs in any one standard program.

So insurance deserves a lot more of our attention than we give it. We should look at it in light of our individual situation and needs: family status, income profile, personal net worth goals, health, and the rest. Only in light of such criteria can one determine whether one's corporate insurance program is adequate. Having identified which of your needs are unmet, analyze whether they can be better met in a corporate context or on your own.

Life Insurance Protection

The questions of adequacy and comparative cost are surprisingly difficult to answer when it comes to life insurance. Yet this provides the most costly and, for the married executive at least, the most important form of insurance protection.

Any rational evaluation must begin with an estimate of the amount of protection required. There are many rules of thumb offered, a common one being that the married executive in his middle years requires six to eight times his pay in life insurance. Such guidelines are helpful only as a quick check, however; factors like the number and age of one's children, the spouse's earning ability, and other available assets significantly influence the total protection required. A much more precise approach is to project future family needs.[4] The projection should assume various times of death for the executive, for only these will give proper weight to the time before his children will be self-sufficient and the remaining life expectancy of his widow. The projections should include repayment of outstanding debts, educational expenses, monthly family income needs while the children are growing up, and then the widow's income needs during the balance of her lifetime.

For a typical $50,000-per-year executive, forty-five years old, married, the father of three children aged eight, twelve, and sixteen, the family's financial needs (adjusted for social security) might look something like those shown in Table 4-1.

As noted, the estimates in Table 4-1 are net of social security

Table 4-1. Family Income Needs

Family income fund	$310,000
Educational fund	60,000
Widow's retirement fund	130,000
Stock option financing loan	10,000
Uninsured debts (including home mortgage)	45,000
Total	$555,000

payments. These benefits currently range up to $500 per month for widow's pension and child support. Payments vary with the number and age of dependents, of course, and that means the benefits must be forecast on a year-to-year basis to calculate accurately the lump-sum benefit over the period of time in question. The lump sum should then be subtracted from the family's gross income needs to indicate how much protection should be provided by insurance, assets, and other income sources. For simplification, let us assume this social security calculation has been done in our example.

Once the coverage requirements are known—over half a million dollars in this case—the next step is to weigh the insured's death benefits against the required lump sum. Again, this can be harder than it sounds. Just itemizing the death benefits can be a problem. In many cases, the executive only vaguely recalls his individual insurance: the $1,000 policy given him at birth by his grandfather, the $5,000 whole life plan he bought from a fraternity brother's cousin at college. He may be even less familiar with the company coverage, which can come from several different sources. The most important sources of death benefits are basic group life insurance, supplemental group coverage, accidental death and dismemberment protection, company travel accident insurance, and all-risk accident insurance. Keep in mind that the value of some of these can vary according to the time and manner of death. There may also be profit-sharing payouts and a widow's benefit under the company pension.

The basic group life plan is designed to provide a certain amount of automatic coverage at no cost to the individual. In some companies, this is a low fixed sum, say $5,000 or $10,000. More often, coverage is expressed as a multiple of the individual's annual salary, say three times pay under a fairly liberal program. In addition to the basic program, most companies offer supplemental coverage on a voluntary basis to be paid for by the individual. The amount of supplemental coverage available has risen sharply in recent years. Some companies now offer as much as ten times pay. Others allow the executive to select any additional amount of coverage up to a stated sum, $400,000 for example. The permissible amount of group insurance will vary by location since twenty states still have some limit. Exhibit 5 shows the present dollar maximum applicable.

Under many group life insurance plans, the individual also receives additional death benefits through an accidental death and dismemberment, or AD&D, clause. Generally, this doubles the basic coverage in the event of accidental death. Most companies offer this protection at no additional cost to the individual and coverage is automatic. In contrast, all-risk accident insurance is generally voluntary and contributory. Like AD&D coverage, it only pays in the event of accidental death. All-risk coverage is generally offered in large amounts at low rates. A typical plan might provide up to $500,000 at a monthly cost of 6 cents per month per $1,000 of protection ($72 per year per $100,000 over coverage). Frequently there is also an option to cover one's spouse for up to one-half the employee's coverage at the same rates. This type of coverage is becoming increasingly common and is often found in conjunction with AD&D insurance.

As I said, the how of dying can be as important as the when, and AD&D is the most obvious case in point. Not long ago, an acquaintance of mine, a man with a chronic heart condition, died under debatable circumstances. He apparently suffered a massive coronary while at the wheel of his car, at which point he lost control and drove into a concrete bunker. The insurance company ruled that he died of natural causes. The ruling cost his family $500,000 in death benefits. But the when of death also deserves much more attention than it gets. In most cases, a man's insurance needs are greatest when he is relatively young. He probably has children to raise and educate and a wife who may outlive him by twenty-five years or more. Yet this is the time when his company death benefits are likely to be at their lowest. If basic coverage is a multiple of pay, the odds are it will be lower at thirty than at fifty-five. For the same reasons, the company's other death benefits are also apt to increase with the employee's age and tenure. Profit sharing and deferred compensation accounts build up over time. Stock obtained under option plans is more likely to be a significant source of capital for the

EXHIBIT 5

Group life insurance maximums by state.

$100,000

Arizona
Florida
Illinois
Maine
North Carolina

$80,000

New Hampshire

$75,000	**$60,000**	**$50,000**	**$40,000**	**$25,000**
Indiana	South Carolina	California*	Arkansas	Kentucky
Ohio		Colorado	Montana	Or 200% pay
Wisconsin		Hawaii	Puerto Rico	
		Kansas	District of	
		Louisiana	Columbia	
		Texas		
		West Virginia		

*For trusteed plans only.

SOURCE: *The Group Insurance Manual Volume 1, Life Insurance Association of America*, pages 6–7, 1973.

heirs of senior executives. Perhaps most important, widow's benefits under the corporate pension program typically do not apply if the covered employee dies before he is fifty-five. It takes a considerable amount of insurance to make up for this, since the widow normally receives two-thirds of her husband's pension.

In short, under most corporate insurance plans, adequacy is largely a matter of the circumstances surrounding the individual's death. If he dies accidentally at fifty-five, his coverage may be more than adequate. Under other circumstances, his heirs may find him woefully underinsured. Let us look again at our $50,000 executive. If he dies of natural causes at forty-five, there may be a significant gap between his family's income needs of $555,000 and his death benefits, particularly if he has subscribed to only the basic group life plan. See Table 4–2.

So the corporate insurance plan may not be enough to meet family needs. In this case, it falls short by $275,000, and the situation would be much worse if our typical executive did not have his personal life insurance policies and his other net worth items. Later chapters will explore ways in which personal net worth can be built most efficiently and wisely. For present purposes, however, some thought should be given to how our typical executive might start making up the deficit with more insurance. Would more company insurance, if available, offer the best vehicle from a cost-benefit standpoint? Or could the individual obtain equal or better coverage on his own? What are the relative costs?

At first blush, corporate insurance appears to be quite inexpensive. In most companies, basic group life and AD&D benefits are noncontributory, even if they are not necessarily "free." The individual incurs a federal income tax liability on "imputed income" from coverage in excess of $50,000. The company calculates (and reports) imputed income using an IRS schedule that shows the imputed income value increasing with age, as illustrated in Table 4-3. When the individual has contributed toward the plan, as in supplementary insurance, the imputed income figures are adjusted downward accordingly. But in most age brackets the imputed income is not great.

There is also the cost of the "contribution" for supplementary, and in some companies even basic, coverage. Under a typical plan, the employee obtains additional coverage by paying a flat rate of,

Table 4-2. Comparison of Family Needs and Family Assets in One Situation

Family needs		Family assets	
Family income fund	$310,000	Group life insurance	$150,000
Educational fund	60,000	Personal life insurance	50,000
Widow's retirement		Widow's pension	
fund	130,000	benefit (other than	
		social security)	. . .
Stock option financ-			
ing loan	10,000	Cash on hand	10,000
		Equity in real estate	24,000
		Company stock ac-	
Uninsured debts		quired on option	30,000
(including home			
mortgage)	45,000	Company savings plan	16,000
Total	$555,000	Total	$280,000
		Deficit = $275,000	

Table 4-3. Imputed Cost per $1,000 of Group Insurance

Age bracket	Assumed cost of protection*	
	Per month	Annual
Under 30	$0.08	$ 0.96
30 to 34	0.10	1.20
35 to 39	0.14	1.68
40 to 44	0.23	2.76
45 to 49	0.40	4.80
50 to 54	0.68	8.16
55 to 59	1.10	13.20

*To calculate the imputed income, you multiply the amount of group insurance in excess of $50,000 times the assumed cost and then subtract any personal contribution.

SOURCE: Commerce Clearing House, 1973.

say, 50 cents per month per $1,000 of insurance. For coverage of $200,000, this works out to $1,200 per year, or roughly 2 percent of our selected executive's annual income of $50,000. Under a representative plan, the total cost of $350,000 in company insurance, good for natural as well as accidental death, would be as shown in Table 4-4.

The key question, of course, is how the cost of the company coverage compares with an individually purchased policy. This leads us into the never-never land of life insurance pricing. It is hard to compare prices of any intangible product or service, but you practically have to be a chartered life underwriter to find your way through the life insurance price maze. There are many types of policies and an even greater range of special riders and provisions. Some policies pay dividends (participating policies); others do not. Further complicating comparison, all forms of "permanent" life insurance build up cash values and thus are really a combination of savings and insurance. In the last few years, however, there have been some widely publicized efforts to make some sense out of all the confusion. They have confirmed what experts have known all along: There is an almost incredibly wide range in the true cost of protection, even under identical policies.

Herbert S. Denenberg, former insurance commissioner of Pennsylvania, made one of the first well-publicized comparisons.[5] Among the fifty largest insurance companies licensed to sell in-

Table 4-4. Representative Cost of $350,000 Insurance for an Executive at 45

	Amount of coverage	(a) Executive's contribution	(b) Unadjusted imputed income	(c) Reported imputed income (b − a)	(d)* Tax on additional income	(e) Total cost (a + d)
Basic, non-contributory group insurance	First $50,000	0	0	0	0	0
	Remaining $100,000	0	$480	$480	$240	$ 240
Supplemental contributory group insurance	$200,000	$1,200	960	. . .	. . .	1,200
Total	$350,000	$1,200				$1,440

*At 50 percent marginal rate, and age 45.

surance in Pennsylvania, the range of the cost of permanent life insurance was 170 percent! Even wider variance was revealed in the comprehensive Consumers Union study of the "true" costs of one-year term, five-year term, and whole life insurance.[6] This study employed a sophisticated analytical technique called the "interest adjusted method" to compare prices and took into account such factors as earnings on the cash buildup of whole life policies and changes in term insurance premiums as the policyholder gets older. The study showed that to replace $350,000 in company coverage an executive might pay up to $12,000 in first-year premiums for a whole life policy. The standard annual cost of an equal amount of permanent insurance, on the other hand, could be as low as $3,200 taking cash buildup into account. Replacing the $350,000 coverage with term insurance would initially cost about $2,100 in annual premiums. Over twenty years, however, this coverage could cost about $5,000 more than the whole life alternative, depending on how much the executive earns on the amount "saved" through lower premiums in the initial years.

The Consumers Union study made it dramatically clear that

company group insurance is a bargain for the $50,000, forty-five-year-old executive. But unless the company coverage is free, younger executives can often pay more for group life insurance than for individually purchased term insurance, where the rate averages less than 30 cents per $1,000 per month over twenty years for a policy purchased at age twenty-five. To put these pricing problems in perspective, Table 4–5 compares the cost of company plans offering $100,000 protection versus individual term insurance at three different ages.

The analysis suggests that people should do more comparison shopping, particularly at younger ages. The insurance department of à company will argue that the costs equal out. That is true if one stays with a company and coverage is uniform throughout one's career. Where rates are relatively high, however, serious thought should be given to purchasing a private term insurance policy that is renewable (so as not to lose coverage if one becomes medically uninsurable), then switching to the contributory group plan at a later age when term premiums start going up sharply.

A couple of noneconomic questions are also worth considering. For example, should almost all of one's insurance be tied to the company? Most good insurance agents and financial planners think not. Group plans usually have a convertibility feature, making it possible to stay insured even when leaving the company. But the conversion options are almost always limited to certain types of whole life policies, and exercising them can involve a hefty cash outlay. Moreover, if in his mid-forties the individual happens to move to another company with lower, or totally different, death benefit protection, the cost of starting up private policies may be steep indeed. The fact is the individual executive should carry a substantial amount of insurance privately if he can manage it.

In summary, the life insurance issue is far more complex than it appears on the surface. The kinds of analyses I've been suggesting should not only be pursued with real discipline; they should also be updated periodically, at least every five years and more frequently during times of rapid change.

Long-term Disability Protection

The most valuable asset most of us possess is our ability to work. A thirty-year-old professional with senior-level ambitions can easily

Table 4-5. Estimated Annual Cost to the Individual for $100,000 Life Insurance

Corporate approaches	Age 25			Age 35			Age 45		
	Contribution	Tax on imputed income*	Total	Contribution	Tax on imputed income	Total	Contribution	Tax on imputed income	Total
Noncontributory	0	$14	$ 14	0	$34	$ 34	0	$120	$ 120
Contribution of $0.30 per month per $1,000 on second $50,000	$180	0	180	$180	0	180	$ 180	30	210
Contribution of $0.60 per month per $1,000 on full amount	720	0	720	720	0	720	720	0	720
Individually purchased† five-year renewable term	362	0	362	631	0	631	1,417	0	1,417

*Tax on imputed income is the average for 20 years.
†Data shown are the average costs over 20 years for a five-year renewable term policy, with provision for converting to permanent insurance, using price information for company ranked tenth in cost in *Consumers Union: A Guide to Life Insurance*, 3 parts, Consumers Union, Mount Vernon, N.Y., 1973.

earn $2 million or more over his next thirty-five years. Life insurance can protect his dependents if he dies, but a disabling injury or illness can eliminate or cripple his earning power and simultaneously burden him with staggering medical bills. The possibility of this happening is less remote than we'd like to think. Insurance experts estimate that close to half of the men now thirty-five will be disabled at least once for three months or more during their careers; two out of a hundred will be disabled for five years or more.

Early company-sponsored solutions to this problem varied widely and often depended on individual company philosophies. However, today's executive can look to several sources for income continuance in the event of a disability. In most companies, the executive will be paid under some sick-leave or short-term disability policy. At the professional and managerial levels, this is often full pay for three to six months, followed by half pay for an equal period. Length of service usually will determine how long full pay continues. The period of coverage, rarely less than three months, is usually coordinated with the waiting period under the contributory disability insurance plan. The long-term disability plan continues some 50 percent of one's salary for a stated number of years or to age sixty-five. The benefit here is dovetailed with social security and workmen's compensation, both of which also provide some disability income. The pension can provide yet another source of income for the permanently disabled. Under some plans, the individual receives his accrued pension, though at a reduced level, since he predictably will be drawing payments for more years than if he had retired normally at sixty-five. Short service with the company and a steep reduction of this sort can cut the disability income to a pittance. More and more companies, however, are now coordinating pension disability benefits with long-term disability insurance, which stops at sixty-five. Under this approach, pension benefits continue to accrue at the man's last earnings rate until he is sixty-five, thus building up a decent disability pension.

Because disability benefits can come from several sources—and coverage is only rarely designed as an integrated whole—the disability benefit also can vary sharply with age, current income level, and other circumstances. Almost certainly, however, the typical executive will be underinsured against disability. His principal protection is more than likely to be his company insurance, and most company disability plans not only limit the benefit as a percentage of pay but also have dollar maximums set as low as $1,000 a month. Furthermore, technical distinctions on covered disability may leave one unprotected against heart- or tuberculosis-related disability, for example. Benefits also may be adjusted downward for increases in other income, including social security, and there can be restrictions against obtaining other work.

In light of these sobering considerations, the executive needs to take three critical steps. First, he should thoroughly analyze his existing coverage and forecast his benefits. Second, he should subscribe to the maximum coverage available under his group plan; many insurance companies are reluctant to write group policies for more than $2,000 a month income, but some plans have optional coverage of $3,000 a month or more. Third, if his available company protection is low and his own salary is high, he should explore individual policies.

Individual plans should be examined with special care since they contain more hidden traps than most group policies. One particular snare is the term of benefit. Individual policies often limit benefits to five or ten years or cut them off at age fifty-five. Some individual policies are not automatically renewable; if they are renewable, the premiums may not be guaranteed.

By and large, individual coverage will be more expensive than group coverage, which involves employee contributions of up to 1 percent of "covered" pay. The $24,000 executive with a 50 percent benefit, for example, will pay between $120 and $240 annually for coverage of $1,000 a month. This is well below the individual rate, even for younger men, and particularly for women.[7] As in most other group plans, the rates do not increase with age, so company long-term disability insurance becomes more and more of a bargain as one gets older. In shopping individually, the executive should look for price guarantees, continuity of coverage, quality, and breadth of protection when it comes to disability coverage. This is not a type of insurance where saving $50 to $100 in premiums is necessarily worthwhile.

Medical Expense Protection

Most employee attitude surveys show that the company medical plan is the most popular and best understood of all employee

Table 4-6. Medical Insurance Protection

Area of medical expense	Numbered covered (all ages) (000)	Percentage of civilian population
Hospital care	162,989	80.3
Surgical services	157,670	77.7
X-ray and lab exams	142,441	70.2
Prescribed drugs	100,966	49.7
Private duty nursing	100,235	49.4
Office and home visits	91,581	45.1
Nursing home care	32,392	16.0
Dental care	12,210	6.0

SOURCE: Employee Benefit Plan Review Research Reports 301.9, Charles D. Spencer Associates, Chicago, Ill., April 1972.

insurance benefits. It is immediate and relevant. Some 80 to 90 percent of employees will be reimbursed at least once in a given year, and a really comprehensive program offers protection against one of the largest expenditures a family has to face. Moreover, most people realize that medical costs are rising rapidly. Medical care expenditures for individuals increased steadily from 4 percent of disposable income in 1948 to 7.7 percent in 1972. They now represent the third largest deduction item in tax returns of individuals who itemize their deductions. Most companies provide some form of medical expense protection, but not all offer a full range of protection, as Table 4–6 shows. And while eight out of ten people have basic hospital-surgical coverage, only about half have major medical insurance to protect against so-called catastrophes.

Where does all of this leave the average executive? He is probably covered in some sort of full-scale plan. While he may contribute some of the cost, the sum is likely to be modest; and half of his contribution, up to $150, is tax-deductible. Since most companies pay half to two-thirds of the total premium, the average executive is clearly getting a bargain under a group plan. His principal concern should be whether he does indeed have comprehensive protection. The major medical coverage is worth particular scrutiny since the maximums may be too low. Many plans still have a $25,000 top, for example, while the more progressive have increased to $100,000 or more. Moreover, certain types of medical expenses, e.g., psychiatric care, may be disallowed or only partially reimbursed.

The executive should also investigate whether his company has adopted one of the latest "perquisites," the direct reimbursement of medical bills. IRS rules permit the direct reimbursement of up to $5,000 a year in medical cost on a tax-free basis. An increasing number of large companies are setting up special plans (for higher levels of management only, to keep the numbers down) under which the company pays any medical expenses not covered or only partially covered under the group medical plan.

Other Executive Insurance Developments

Death benefits, disability income protection, and coverage for medical expenditures undoubtedly will continue to be the main areas of insurance coverage for most executives. Benefits in these areas will continue to improve. As unions push for new forms of group coverage, management will also benefit from new and broader protection at low group rates, and the economic worth of the company insurance package will be enhanced by a few hundred dollars annually. But other forces are also at work that open up whole new areas of possibility.

For the last dozen or so years, increasing attention has been focused on the needs of the higher-salaried worker. For one thing, there have been more and more of them: the white-collar percentage of the total work force has grown from less than 33 after World War II to 48 percent in 1974. Too, the disproportionate impact of income taxes on salaried workers impelled company benefit planners, consultants, and insurance men to seek new compensation means for attracting and holding these workers. The higher-salaried professional manager, especially, was considered to be not only more mobile but, in the planners' eyes, more sophisticated about insurance. So after decades of preoccupation with all-employee basic coverage, the focus shifted.

The turning point came with the introduction of long-term disability plans, the first plans designed primarily for the salaried and executive employee. Long-term disability for the $10,000-and-up salaried worker was the first new coverage. LTD was followed by various types of supplemental group life insurance to provide voluntary additional coverage at low rates. Then came the development and promotion of all-risk accident insurance. The future will bring more and more of these plans, not only because companies are trying to think of new ways to reward the salaried worker but also because of growing company concern about key personnel. A few short years ago, a trend developed toward *comprehensive personal liability coverage* of $1 million or more, often on a company-pay-all basis for key executives. These plans provide a form of extra protection for the executive who is sued, say, as a result of an automobile accident. His personal liability insurance may cover him to $300,000, but blanket company coverage takes over up to amounts of $1 million, $5 million, or, in one company, $25 million. The corporate desire to protect key executives from any financial disaster—and the times we live in—is exemplified by the growing prevalence of kidnap insurance, with annual premiums running $5,000 and more for a $500,000 policy.

More usefully, there is another trend toward making insurance more flexible in meeting the needs of the individual. As employees express their yearning for more choice in their relationships with their employers, companies have responded with the so-called cafeteria approach to compensation. The idea is to let the individual choose among many vehicles, including additional insurance of one type or another. Available are not only the existing group plans, but also new supplemental plans and even individually tailored insurance contracts. With more precise calculation of company costs, net of deductions and taxes, it is possible to offer the executive a range of options that cost the company approximately the same dollars to provide.

At the same time, there is growing emphasis on the net-worth-building aspects of the pay package, again including insurance. The most conspicuous new element is called split-dollar insurance, a concept originally developed for the owners of small, closely held companies but now adopted by the likes of General Electric and Chase Manhattan Bank.[8] Split-dollar is a hybrid use of permanent insurance under which the company and the individual "split" both the premium cost and ultimate payout. Typically, the company pays the portion of the premium equivalent to the annual increase in the policy's cash value, while the executive pays the balance (usually zero after the first few policy years). The death benefit is split the same way, with the company getting that portion equal to the cash value and the executive's beneficiary getting the balance.

Calculating Values of the Package

Whether split-dollar insurance or group personal liability, company insurance packages are proliferating. The future promises even

EXHIBIT 6

Value of insurance coverage for two $50,000 executives.

| | Executive A
Above-average program | | Executive B
"Standard" program | |
	Coverage	Approximate replacement cost	Coverage	Approximate replacement cost
Group life insurance	$200,000 noncontributory	$2,800	$100,000 contributory	$1,400
AD&D	$200,000	200	$100,000	100
All-risk accident	$500,000	600	. . .	. . .
Long-term disability	$30,000 per year benefit	1,400	$15,000 per year benefit	600
Medical insurance	Comprehensive	600	Hospital/surgical	300
Dental insurance	. . .	200	. . .	. . .
Personal liability	$1 million umbrella policy	100	. . .	. . .
GROSS COST Less individual contribution and after-tax impact		$5,900		$2,400
of imputed income		$1,200		$1,000
NET REPLACEMENT COST		$4,700		$1,400

Assumptions: Male executive earning $50,000, age 45, married, with two school-age children, located in California.

more. One consequence, of course, will be still greater difficulty in assessing the value of the company package, and relating that to insurance bought privately. One school of thought has long held that insurance isn't worth much anyway, especially if one considers the probabilities of collecting, particularly from life insurance. The virtually unprecedented recent inflation makes this school's arguments even more telling.

George W. Hettenhouse's pioneering study on the cost-effectiveness of different forms of compensation[9] (which also provides the theoretical foundation for the cafeteria concept[10]) assigned group life a low value, because about 725 out of 1,000 thirty-five-year-old men and even more women will live to sixty-five. This sort of analysis has always seemed a little academic to me, and I suspect it would sound the same to a new widow with two college-age children. You either believe in insurance or not. If you do, the fairest, most straightforward way to calculate value is either in terms of its cost to the company or in terms of "replacement cost." Exhibit 6 shows the cost profile of an average and a particularly generous program for a $50,000 executive.

Summing up, insurance is probably the least performance-oriented element in the executive pay package. Rarely if ever is it a controlling factor in career decisions. But insurance plans add up to a big slice of the compensation pie offered by the modern corporation. The variations between one company and another can run to several thousands of dollars in equivalent value.

It therefore behooves the prudent executive to apply the same hard-eyed analysis to the insurance package that he or she would to a major marketing or financial decision. Sorting out the values isn't easy, and one should keep in mind that individual needs can diverge rather sharply from those assumed in standard group plans designed for the mass of employees. But since risks as well as rewards are great in today's inflation-prone world, and since insurance is a substantial part of the reward companies offer the executives they want to attract and keep, the time spent on the insurance game is definitely worth it.

CHAPTER FIVE

The Company Pension: High-Stakes Poker

For most of this century, a third-generation Californian tended his vines in the Napa Valley and made his wine. He sent his two sons to West Coast engineering schools, saw them embarked on successful business careers, and then passed to his reward at the age of seventy-seven. The sons promptly fell into debate on whether to run the family business, one of the smaller vineyards in the valley, or to sell out. The major consideration was, of all things, the current pension status of the two sons. The younger, by then in his fifties, had achieved a fair degree of financial independence, largely through his fully vested company pension that guaranteed him $30,000 annually at age sixty-five. But the older son had worked for four separate companies instead of one; he was still seven years from having his pension vested. The latter's lack of retirement security swung the family decision, and the brothers sold the vineyard.

The disparity in retirement security is spread broadly through American industry. More than any other compensation element, the pension distinguishes the haves from the have-nots among those who work for corporations. In most billion-dollar companies the long-service employee can look forward to benefits of at least 60 percent of pay from a combination of company pension and social security. In two out of three cases a supplemental savings plan will boost total retirement income much higher, perhaps even to more than the employee made while working. At the senior executive level, pension incomes alone are often higher than the salaries three-quarters of the executive population earn at the peak of their careers. For example, the average projected pension for the chief executives of the five largest U.S. commercial banks is $107,000, according to recent proxies. My own guess is that there are over 150 companies that provide six-figure pensions to one or more retired executives.

But the have-nots are legion. To start with, 30 million Americans work for companies that don't have pensions. And the current average private pension in the United States is less than $2,000 a year.[1] While that level is increasing, it will be years before a significant proportion of the retired population receives adequate retirement income. My own maiden aunt is a good enough example. She retired, after forty-seven years with a large tool company, on a monthly pension (excluding social security) of $45—less than $1 for every year of her service. At that, she is better off than roughly half the full-time employed population; they work for organizations that have no pensions at all. Of the theoretically "covered" employees, moreover, many will actually leave their companies, or die, before their pensions are vested or guaranteed. The more extreme pension reform advocates have claimed that only one of ten workers ever collects his pension. The actual prospect isn't quite that dismal, but more definitive studies do tell us that probably no more than six out of ten collect anything.[2]

The odds have improved with the pension reform legislation finally enacted on Labor Day 1974, after more than ten years of study and debate.[3] For the first time there are vesting and funding standards and plan termination insurance. But the harsh fact remains that the pension picture for the average American is still a bagful of ifs: if the company has a plan, if you are eligible, if you meet the vesting schedule, if you live to retirement age, you collect . . . something.

One explanation for this situation is that pensions are a relatively recent phenomenon in the United States. The first U.S. pension plan was adopted by the American Express Company in 1875, years after the device had become quite common in Europe. The railroads were the first to embrace the concept as an industry but in general the private pension movement grew very, very slowly. By 1925 there were only 400 pension plans in the United States covering 4 million workers. One-third of these were in four plans: U.S. Steel, the Pennsylvania Railroad, the New York Central Railroad, and AT&T. During the depression pensions were still such a rare phenomenon that when Abraham Epstein wrote his classic 1933 polemic advocating what ultimately became social security, he classed the industrial pension along with public alms-houses, organized charities, and Benevolent Homes for the Aged.[4]

In the decade after World War II, however, most large companies finally adopted pension plans. Wage controls and the excess profits taxes of World War II and the Korean War were again probably responsible for the development. The pace of plan development quickened in 1948 when, in the Inland Steel case, the National Labor Relations Board ruled that company retirement plans were a mandatory bargaining issue. But the growth of pension coverage has now slowed to a trickle again, largely because many firms simply can't afford the pension price tag. Most of the 1.5 million U.S. corporations with under $20 million in sales are just too marginal economically to be able to afford a plan that adds costs of up to 10 percent of payroll. Thus the gap between the haves and have-nots is actually widening. Corporations that do have plans steadily improve benefit levels, add pension frills, eliminate employee contributions, and the like. The smaller fellows lag farther and farther behind.

For the individual executive, then, the presence of pension coverage is no casual consideration. Because the qualified pension plan is usually paid for by the company, with no tax payable by the individual until he or she retires, it would take a substantial private savings program indeed to fund a comparable asset. In a 1971 article, *Fortune* estimated that a twenty-five-year-old would have to invest 10 to 12 percent of his pay for forty years to produce a pension equal to half of his preretirement income.[5] But despite the very significant dollars involved, few executives are able to explain the benefits and provisions of their pensions. In part this is because most are covered by one of the more complex of the pension genera, the so-called *formula pension*. Under this type of plan the retirement benefit is calculated by applying a rate formula, say 1½ percent, to a specified individual earning base. The earnings base may be the average of the last five years of salary or, less frequently, an average of the last five years of salary plus bonus. In turn this figure is multiplied by the executive's years of service or his years of participation in the plan. As if this weren't complex enough, there are often alternative formulas to give weight to benefits under earlier plans or to guarantee a minimum pension. In contrast, the blue-collar *fixed benefit pension* is relatively straightforward. Normally a stated dollar figure, commonly $7.50, is multiplied by years of service to calculate the pension.

Finally, the formula pension seems much more remote than the *profit-sharing retirement plan,* under which each participant has a personal account that increases with every company contribution and changes with each year's investment results (see Chapter 6). In the early days most pensions worked in much the same way as profit-sharing plans. Insurance companies wrote individual annuity contracts for each employee; and the company duly bought a piece of the future pension each year, often according to a schedule varying with age. As with profit sharing, the participating employee knew each year how much of the future annuity (or pension) had already been purchased. But these relatively individualized pension schemes aren't very practical for the average company, and not just because of the substantial paper work involved. To control more directly the investment of the large sums flowing into their pension funds, most companies some years ago began setting up pension trust funds. Normally the fund is held by a bank and managed by the company, the bank, or an investment firm.

As this type of funding evolved, the pension plans for salaried workers became more and more complex. The initial formula was often straightforward enough, designed to produce a target level of pension by the end of a "normal" working career. But as the social security system developed, the pension rate formulas were gradually adjusted; lower rates were applied to the portion of earnings covered by social security (initially $3,000) and higher rates above that. Then formula "refinements" were added, with one formula applied for past service and another for future service. Soon other benefits were appended to provide for such contingencies as disability. By the 1960s the average executive pension was a maze of complex provisions, and most companies only compounded the confusion by the turgid, jargon-filled booklets in which they "explained" the plan to employees. No wonder few potential beneficiaries understand what might, some day, be coming to them.

If one thinks of the pension as a maze (see Exhibit 7) through

EXHIBIT 7

The pension maze.

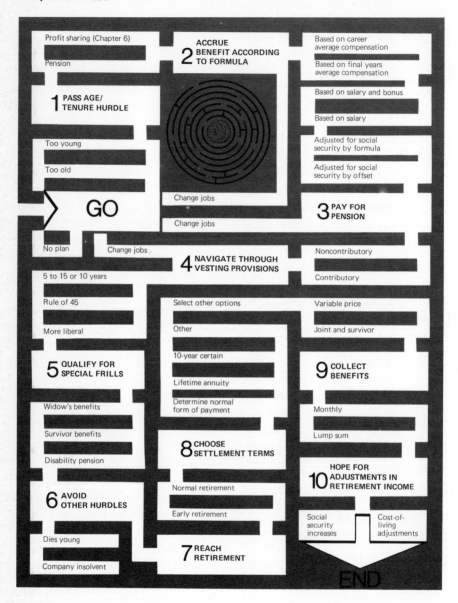

which the average manager must wander to earn and ultimately collect his pension check, there are seven main stages through which he must progress. They are: (1) getting into the plan (participation); (2) accruing normal benefits (the formula); (3) paying for the pension (contributions); (4) earning the pension (vesting); (5) reaching retirement age (normal and early retirement provisions); (6) gaining extra protection (pension frills); and (7) collecting the benefit (settlement rights and options). Each of these sets of provisions has to be understood to evaluate a plan properly, to compare different plans, and, perhaps most important, to do any realistic personal financial planning. So let's look briefly at each stage of the maze.

Stage 1: Participation

The simplest pension evaluation is also the most obvious: Is there a plan and, if not, is there any likelihood of one? This is clearly related to the size of the company one works for, as Table 5-1 shows.

Even where there is a plan, there may be barriers to participation, although the Labor Day law attempts to eliminate the most glaring abuses in this area. It used to be possible, for example, to define a fairly narrow eligibility period by applying criteria of length of service and minimum and maximum age rules. These combined to penalize both younger and older employees who joined their company recently. Starting January 1, 1976 (immediately for plans adopted after the date of enactment of the new law), the eligibility

Table 5-1. Correlation between Company Size and Prevalence of Retirement Benefits

Company sales	Pension (%)	Profit-sharing retirement plan (%)	Some retirement program (%)
Over $1 billion	96	3	99
$500–$999 million	92	6	98
$250–499 million	90	7	97
$100–249 million	84	11	95
$50–99 million	81	8	89
$25–49 million	60	19	79
Under $25 million	30	25	55

SOURCE: Special analyses of sample of 1,167 proxies.

requirements can be no longer than one year of service or age twenty-five, whichever is later. The only exception is that a plan which vests the pension fully immediately can have a three-year waiting period. Older workers benefit as well. Formerly, workers who joined a company in their fifties were often effectively barred from participating in the pension because of cost-motivated age barriers. Under the new law the company can exclude only those individuals who join within five years of their normal retirement date. Since most companies still have sixty-five as a retirement age, this means anyone joining before age sixty can be included.

Stage 2: Pension Formulas

Once in a pension plan, the individual encounters all manner of provisions governing the accrual of pension credit. What he or she can ultimately look forward to depends on the answers to a whole series of related questions on the plan formula.

For executives, the first and perhaps the most important of these is whether the pension calculation is based on annual earnings—the so-called career-average formula—or on some average of final pay. As a general rule, the executive is better off with a *final* average pay plan. A top executive's final five-year average earnings are likely to be 200 to 250 percent of his career average, so a "career-average plan" must have a formula *rate* at least twice as generous to produce as attractive a benefit. This is particularly important in times of sharp inflation. Some pension planners will argue that inflation can be offset by regularly "updating" the career plan formula, but a comprehensive McKinsey study of 490 major plans revealed that half of the career plans had *never* been updated.[6] And the benefits were on the whole clearly lower under career-average plans. In light of these facts, it isn't surprising that there is a trend to final average pay plans. When Bankers Trust Company surveyed retirement program trends in 1950, only 20 percent of the plans were of the final average type. By 1973 the number had grown to 83 percent, with most base earnings periods an average of the last five years of pay or the highest consecutive five years, or the highest five in the last ten.[7]

The second provision in question is the definition of "credited service," which is the multiplier in most formulas. Fine print can obscure this seemingly straightforward issue, too. For example, must the years of service be uninterrupted, or is there a clause that provides for leaves of absence? What happens in an acquisition or merger situation? Most plans carefully define service as "service to the parent, its stated subsidiaries or predecessor corporations." And past service credit isn't automatic. In addition, the technical wording of other provisions can affect the credited service. Some provisions limit the period quite subtly, by controlling when the participants can join and when they must retire. Others do so more directly. For example, if "credited service" is defined as years of participation in the pension plan (rather than years with the company), the waiting period ground rules become critical. A great many people have inadvertently lost critical benefits by not learning these ground rules. Under the 1974 law, companies can still count any waiting period as credited service—a provision that can be quite valuable to the future executive in a final pay plan. It is also worth checking any limits; some plans flatly limit credited service to, say, thirty years.

The third critical element in the formula is the definition of "covered earnings." With the growth of incentive bonus plans that at upper management levels can add 40 to 50 percent to base salary, whether or not the bonus is included is an important question indeed. For a variety of reasons, many companies do not include bonuses in the earnings base. For one thing, the IRS discourages too liberal a definition of covered earnings to prevent discrimination among employee groups. If the executive bonus is included, how about the laborer's overtime, or the foreman's shift differential, or the salesman's commission? Moreover, the IRS dislikes sharp year-to-year fluctuations in pension accruals, particularly as retirement age approaches. Nevertheless, in recent years a number of companies have managed to include at least part of the executive bonus in the earnings base, often on the grounds that the salary structure is "discounted" and the bonus is really part of total executive compensation. And some large companies include full bonuses, together with overtime and other such payments.

Fourth, there is the question of the pension maximum—an issue that has come full circle in the last thirty years. In the early days of most plans—in the 1930s and 1940s particularly—there was often a dollar limit on pensions in order to hold down cost and avoid the appearance of favoring top executives. Over the years these maximums have been raised substantially; the maximum at IBM is now

$100,000; at 3M, $125,000. In most cases maximums have been eliminated entirely; nearly three-quarters of the companies surveyed most recently by Bankers Trust had no maximum at all. However, the 1974 law reintroduces the maximum as an issue in plan design by stipulating that after January 1, 1976, the benefit under a qualified plan must be the lesser of $75,000 or 100 percent of the average of the highest three years of cash compensation. This is going to have all sorts of retirement program implications for upper management. Some companies may simply accept the limit; others may shift excess retirement funds to other vehicles, sweetening a savings or profit-sharing plan (see Chapter 6), for example. My own guess is that most companies will adopt supplemental nonqualified pensions to make up any lost pension opportunity, thus preserving the benefit "standard" as a percentage of pay. In any event, senior executives need to watch the maximum issue carefully over the next few years.

Fifth, one should consider the provision governing the relationship between the company pension and social security benefits. In the past, the "integration" of social security wasn't a real issue at the executive level. But with recent increases in both social security benefits and costs—as well as the growing popularity of the "offset" form of integration, under which part of the social security benefit is subtracted from the accrued pension—it assumes real importance for all of us. When social security was relatively new and annual company contributions were only $30 per employee, many companies ignored it in their pension calculations. With liberalization, the cost of company contributions has skyrocketed, however; a company's maximum per-employee cost reached $772.20 in 1974. Understandably, companies have sought to soften this rise by adjusting pension costs downward, explaining that individual benefits have climbed commensurately. And in fact the individual wage earner can now receive up to $320 a month from social security and a spouse can add 50 percent to that. Under the new funding approach adopted by Congress in 1972, which assumes a 2¼ percent increase in cost of living and 5 percent increase in wages, today's forty-year-old worker could collect $21,371 in social security benefits annually at age sixty-five.[8]

As the social security laws changed with increasing frequency, most companies shifted to the so-called "offset" approach, which chips away pretty effectively at company costs—and employee benefits as well. In this type of plan, a single rate (say $1\frac{1}{2}$ percent of average pay) is used to calculate the basic pension; then a portion (usually not more than half) of the individual's anticipated annual social security benefit is subtracted from the pension base. But some companies offset as much as 75 percent of the social security benefit, thereby directly reducing company pension benefits. In addition, under some plans the offset continues to increase as social security benefits rise, even after the employee's pension is vested. Under the new law, however, companies can no longer reduce the pensions of terminated employees or of retirees as social security payments increase. This has eliminated one abuse of the offset approach.

A final point worth noting regarding pension formulas: a given formula can produce a handsome pension for one executive and only a marginal benefit for a colleague with a different earnings history. Formula provisions interact and the interaction can produce some surprising results.

Stage 3: Contributions

The pension formula is only one of many variables in the pension maze. Employee contributions are another. In the smaller company especially, employee contributions of up to 6 percent of pay were often the only means by which decent plans could be set up. But the pressures of rising social security taxes, union negotiations, and the advent of thrift-savings plans have whittled away at employee contributions in different ways. A decade ago half the plans in existence required some level of employee contribution. Today 70 percent of the plans are paid for entirely by the corporation, and that trend is continuing.

There are some companies that fully fund a basic pension plan but permit employees to increase their benefits through voluntary contributions. Actually these supplemental plans warrant careful scrutiny. The "guaranteed" benefits often assume an unrealistically low alternative earnings rate on the money, while the interest rates paid on employee contributions vary widely indeed. I know of one manufacturing company, for example, whose plan pays 6 percent and one airline whose plan pays 2 percent, believe it or not. The only real advantage of contributing to such a plan is that the earnings compound on a tax-free basis. But an individually pur-

**Table 5-2. Life Annuity Beginning at Age 65
Purchasable with $1,000**

Age purchased	Approximate yearly benefit	
	Male	Female
35	$600	$500
45	300	280
55	170	160
65	95	90

SOURCE: Composite of five insurance companies' actual data.

chased annuity or whole life insurance policy has the same advantage and can yield a better return, depending on age and sex, as
Table 5–2 indicates.

It's obvious that while extra contributions or personal savings can
help supplement a pension, the average individual will be hard-
pressed to buy an adequate pension with after-tax dollars. Reform-
ers have always been bothered by the inequity of the present system,
which exempts the corporate pension from taxation until payout
but makes it difficult if not impossible to "buy your own pension."
There was a modest effort to redress this inequity in 1962, when
Congress adopted the so-called Keogh Plan to give individuals
without pension coverage a tax break. But the legislation limited the
plan to the self-employed and restricted the allowable contribution
to 10 percent of earnings or $2,500, whichever was less. The 1974
legislation raised the maximum allowable contribution to the lesser
of 15 percent of earned income or $7,500, with a $750 contribution
permissible even if your income is under $5,000. It also established a
way for employees who work for companies that do not have a
qualified retirement plan to begin to build their own personal
pension. The law permits such individuals to deduct up to $1,500
per year from their income (but no more than 15 percent of earned
income). They can put these monies in individual retirement
accounts. The earnings are not taxable until ultimate distribution.

While these new provisions begin to correct some inequities, the
individual with a corporate pension plan, particularly one that is
noncontributory, still has a decided advantage. As for those who
work for companies with plans that are still contributory, the
executive has little choice: if he wants a pension he pays the price.
At that he is usually much better off than those who have no plan

available. In a contributory company pension plan the company usually pays the lion's share of the cost. If the person leaves the company before the pension is vested the contribution is refunded.

Stage 4: Vesting Provisions

The ifs, ands, and buts surrounding an employee's right to his pension remind one of the old Army game. The Catch 22 for most participants is the so-called vesting provisions, the clauses that spell out how long or to what age you must work to "earn" your pension. Until the 1974 act there were still pension plans which had no vesting provisions at all. Only 2 percent or so of large-company plans were without such provisions, but 10 to 15 percent of small-company plans lacked them. In such companies, if you left to take another job or were fired in your twilight years, you often sacrificed your entire pension.

Being vested, of course, doesn't guarantee that the employee will get the pension. He or she still has to live to retirement age and the pension fund has to be solvent. So long as the enterprise remains in business and a plan is adequately funded over the years, there is limited risk that the money won't be there. But before this new law each year some corporations, usually small ones, "walked away" from their pension obligations. The most notorious large-company example, which provided a *cause célèbre* for reform advocates for ten years, occurred when Studebaker closed its South Bend, Indiana, plant in 1964, simultaneously distributing pension funds as far as they would go and terminating the plan. The distribution was sufficient to fund pensions for older employees, but some 4,000 employees between the ages of forty and sixty received only 15 percent of the vested pensions to which they were entitled. The obvious injustice of this type of incident understandably attracted public attention, and several related areas of reform were ultimately incorporated in the 1974 Act:[9] plan termination insurance, new funding ground rules, and new minimum vesting standards.

The new vesting provisions are perhaps the most important for the average executive or worker. All new plans and, after January 1, 1976, all existing plans have to choose among one of three vesting provisions or adopt a provision that is more liberal than any of the three choices. The three are: (1) 100 percent vesting after ten years of service; (2) 25 percent vesting after five years of service grading up to 100 percent after fifteen years; or (3) the so-called "rule of 45." Under this last provision, an employee must be 50 percent vested when his age and service total 45 (he still needs five years of service as a minimum, however). Vesting would then increase to 100 percent five years later. It is too early to tell which option most companies will elect but it is already obvious that the new law is no panacea. It is still possible to lose all of one's accrued pension if one leaves a company within five years, and to lose a portion of the credit under other circumstances. Vesting, then, remains a central issue in personal career planning and the evaluation of alternative pay packages. Moreover, while the new funding standards and termination insurance will help the mass of employees and prevent a Studebaker-type catastrophe, these provisions provide only limited security for executives. The benefit guaranteed under the new plan termination insurance is limited to $750 a month or $9,000 a year.

Stage 5: Retirement Age

Until social security was enacted in 1935, one retired only when one could no longer work. Some of the larger and more liberal companies provided for retirement at seventy, but most companies had no set age. With the enactment of social security, however, sixty-five became the norm and it still is the official retirement age under 97 percent of pension plans. The actual retirement age has begun to drop within the last decade, mainly through the curious institution of the early retirement clause. Three out of four pension plans now include a provision enabling the eligible participant to retire early with some benefits, usually as early as age fifty-five. Early retirement is a popular option with employees, but it does reduce the accrued value of a pension as companies compensate for the variable extra cost of a longer payment period. Most companies began by reducing the normal pension according to actuarial tables. In recent years, however, more and more firms—now about one out of three—have adopted schedules imposing lesser reductions. Even so, the reductions are significant, as Table 5-3 shows.

In fact the true cost of early retirement to the employee is even higher, because early retirement reduces the income base on which the pension is calculated. And this worker has accrued fewer years of credit. The loss is intensified in that the individual's salary

Table 5-3. Effects of Early Retirement on Normal Accrued Pension

Age	Actuarial discount (%)*	Typical liberalized provisions (%)	
		4% a year	3% a year
65	100.0	100	100
62	75.7	88	91
60	63.8	80	85
58	54.5	72	79
55	43.7	60	70

*Actuarial discounts will vary. Figures shown are from Joseph J. Melone and Everett T. Allen, *Pension Planning* (rev. ed.), Dow Jones-Irwin, Inc., Homewood, Ill., 1972.

predictably would increase each year that he remained with the company. Thus the "early retirement" pension is often only 25 to 30 percent of the projected pension taken at age sixty-five. In a case cited by my associate George Foote, the normal age-sixty-five pension was $31,500 while the pension starting at fifty-five was $7,500.[10] Be that as it may, most employees like to have the option of early retirement. Recent double-digit inflation has slowed the trend, but early retirement is still part of the growing American dream of independence. A few pacesetter firms now not only make it easier to retire early, they've lowered the *normal* retirement age from sixty-five to sixty-two (3M) or even sixty (IBM). Again, this seems to be the beginning of a real trend. The Aluminum Workers International Union won an age-sixty-two regular retirement in its 1974 negotiation with Alcoa, Reynolds, and Kaiser. These settlements will make earlier retirement a hot bargaining issue for other unions. The effect is certain to spread among unorganized workers as well.

Stage 6: Pension Frills

In the case of the pension, "extras" come in the form of provisions to pay the pension under circumstances other than retirement, particularly death (the so-called widow's and child's pension) or disability (the disability pension). These extras were a natural outgrowth of periodic liberalization, once basic pension benefits reached the level of adequacy. If a pension participant died at fifty-eight, there were moral and practical reasons why the surviving spouse should collect at least part of the pension the couple would have benefited from a few years later. Providing for the permanently disabled person was another obvious need.

The widow's and child's pension has never been as popular in this country as in Europe. The alternative approach in the United States has been to provide generous life insurance. As late as 1965, only about a third of pension plans had a spouse's benefit. However, the growth of liberal early retirement clauses has played a role in liberalizing plans generally; more than 50 percent now provide a death benefit, typically after age fifty-five. After all, if one can retire at fifty-five it is hard to explain why a pension built up over twenty or thirty years should disappear if one dies at fifty-five. The typical death benefit provision entitles the surviving spouse to a percentage of the pension accrued by the employee at the time of death. If the employee had accumulated an annual pension credit of $18,000, for example, the spouse might receive two-thirds of that amount, or $12,000.

The disability pension was designed to meet another real need. Up until the 1960s, the pension was often the sole means (aside from social security disability payments) of providing protection against loss of income. Two out of three companies had this coverage. But to control costs, the company often required a minimum period of service (generally ten years) before the participant was eligible to collect and, because the basic benefit buildup was often quite small when the disability occurred, the pension amounted to only a pittance. Long-term disability insurance provided an alternative company-sponsored means of offering income continuance for employees at relatively modest cost to the company. Since these insurance plans normally pay only until age sixty-five, they represent a new wrinkle in pension disability thinking. What do the disabled do on reaching sixty-five? A generous solution is to allow them to continue to accrue pension credits in cases of disability so that at retirement age income can continue. This is precisely what many well-designed plans now provide.

Stage 7: Settlement Options

Even after one has passed through the maze to retirement, pension variations and choices don't end. A pension, after all, is an annuity whose estimated cost reflects actuarial assumptions. Until the 1974 act most pension plans "guaranteed" the pension for the life of the recipient. Some liberalized the benefit by guaranteeing payment for a stated minimum period, usually ten years, although this often resulted in a distant relative or well-fixed beneficiary receiving an ongoing and perhaps unneeded sum. But because such "years certain" guarantees increased the annuity cost by about 8 percent for a ten-year guarantee, most plans put the settlement choice on the individual, making him or her choose among variations in the basic form of pension practiced by an actuarial reduction in the "normal" pension. Several of the more popular options and typical discounts are shown in Table 5–4.

Under the 1974 law, the ground rules have been changed, however, and again it isn't yet clear how companies will react. The law stipulates that after January 1, 1976, the normal form of the pension annuity must be a joint and survivor annuity that provides at least a 50 percent income continuation to a surviving spouse. This could prove costly indeed since the "J&S" pension is more expensive than the current life annuity. As a result, some companies may be forced to apply an actuarial reduction to the life annuity as a trade-off for paying the pension on a J&S basis. The unmarried retiree, of course, would have the choice of keeping the higher life annuity payment.

One other choice is worth noting. Some organizations offer participants the chance to hedge against inflation by taking all or part of their pension payments in such a way that the amount fluctuates with the pension fund's investment performance. Known as the *variable annuity,* this interesting option is still relatively rare. Given the stock market's performance in the early 1970s, it is likely to remain so for some time. Most companies reason that social

Table 5-4. Settlement Options

| Option | Retiree benefit | | Beneficiary pension | |
	Dollar pension	Pension as percentage of normal	Amount	Term
Normal pension	$10,000	100	0	. . .
10-year certain	9,200	92	$9,200	To 10th year
15-year certain	8,400	84	8,400	To 15th year
50% joint and survivor*	7,600	76	3,800	Life

*Assuming the beneficiary is a wife ten years younger.

security increases will provide some hedge against inflation; they consider their own obligation discharged once the employee has made his or her settlement choices. Even though most feel the cost of preserving the real income value of the pension is prohibitive, the inflation of recent years is forcing more and more large companies to reexamine their reluctance to increase retiree pensions. It looks as though automatic cost-of-living increases will become more common, particularly since federal government retirees already enjoy automatic protection under civil service laws. When the consumer price index increases 3 percent, for example, government pensions increase by 4 percent!

In some companies the executive has yet another unusual option, to take the entire pension in a lump-sum settlement. This is a costly provision indeed, and only companies with well-funded plans and substantial cash flows can afford it. The lump-sum settlement was quite popular in the 1950s and 1960s, when deferred compensation schemes were in their heyday. Executives with deferred accounts scheduled to pay $50,000 a year clearly had no interest in adding a monthly pension check to their income; it could do little more than increase their tax burden. Lump-sum settlement offered an attractive alternative, especially since the government offered a special capital gains tax break on lump-sum pension settlements distributed within one year of retirement. One of the barn doors was closed in 1969, however, when the new tax law declared the employer's post-1969 contribution taxable as ordinary income with a seven-year averaging provision. No one was very happy with this provision; it proved both complex and inequitable. The pension reform legislation of 1974 attempts to simplify the situation thus: the portion of the pension accrued prior to 1974 qualifies for capital gains treatment; post-1974 pension credits are taxed as ordinary income, averaged over ten years. In effect this means that small distributions are taxed at a somewhat lower rate than under the 1969 law, while large distributions are taxed at substantially higher rates.

Personal Pension Planning

Pension planning is tough plodding, but the amount of money involved makes it very nearly essential. The multiplicity of technical provisions can trip up the unwary. I know one woman who planned to leave her company thinking she was fully vested in her pension,

Table 5-5. Proportion of Retirement Income Provided by Social Security*

Final average pay	Social security benefit as percentage of final average pay
$ 20,000	28.8
30,000	19.2
50,000	11.5
100,000	5.8
200,000	2.9

*Assumes maximum primary benefit plus one-half primary benefit for spouse.

SOURCE: Social Security Benefits, 1974, A. S. Hansen, Inc., Commerce Clearing House, Inc., Chicago, Ill.

only to learn that she didn't have the required ten years' uninterrupted participation because of a three-month leave of absence taken several years previously. Another friend, who had been religiously making personal contributions to his company's plan for thirteen years, was shocked to learn the company was paying him only 2 percent interest on those contributions.

At a minimum, then, individuals should carefully study the plan on which so much of their future financial security rests. This means studying the text of the plan, not merely the summary in the employee booklet. The scrutiny should begin long before retirement is imminent; distant vesting horizons make this a must. And any supplementary actions will need considerable time to take effect. The overall analysis should begin with a determination of how much retirement income will be needed. This is a highly individual matter but most experts agree it should be considered in terms of a percentage of preretirement income. For years a common standard, from all sources, was a benefit of 50 to 60 percent of one's final average pay. Social security levels have increased steadily and a man and his wife retiring at sixty-five in 1974 could be getting as much as $5,488. While that meets part of the need, the proportion is obviously increasingly small as one's income increases. Table 5–5 makes this clear.

Since social security will provide only about 18 percent of the needed retirement income for the $30,000 executive—and only 12 percent if he or she is single—the company pension must be 40 percent or more of final average pay to yield an "adequate" benefit. This standard is easily met in most large company plans, but on the average the U.S. private pension system doesn't even begin to produce this level of benefit. In fact, it has been estimated that it would cost $60 billion to raise the pension income of those now retired to 50 percent.[11]

Ironically, even though the national average falls far short of the standard, the "haves" have recently begun to redefine retirement income targets at 75 to 80 percent of final average pay. A Representative can retire at 80 percent of his final five-year average salary after sixteen terms in the House—which translates into a $34,000 pension under current congressional pay schedules. Recent union contracts reach toward the same standard. The 1974 settlement with the Aluminum Workers, in fact, contained such liberal benefit increases that a cost-control provision was written into the contract to limit the combined pension and social security payments to 85 percent.

For an executive pension to come up to this level a final pay plan would have to have a formula rate of 2 to 3 percent per year of service. Very few do. However, companies with supplemental profit-sharing or thrift plans can produce a total benefit of 80 percent or more. So staying put in the large stable company is one way to become a "have." The large company, large union, and large government retirement patterns offer a kind of ultimate standard, but most executives will have to settle for substantially less in theirs unless they accumulate major assets through investments or such other corporate compensation devices as stock options. For every company that begins to approach the standard there are a score or more that fall far short. Whatever the industry, variations among competing companies in cash pay rarely exceed 30 percent for like jobs; but there are variations of up to 300 percent at almost any managerial level in pension benefits. Some of the variations among plans have been reduced with the reform legislation. Differences will narrow in eligibility requirements, vesting rules, and pension funding. But even here the thrust is to safeguard the employee's benefits, not to standardize them. Nor does the new law extend coverage to the millions of Americans who presently have no plans.

It is clear, then, that the good pension has considerable value. A rough rule of thumb is that a pension at age sixty-five is "worth" about ten times the yearly benefit. In other words, a $50,000 pension is worth about $500,000. This is a substantial asset, even at face value. In actual fact, it is worth more than $500,000 in replacement value. Under existing tax laws, the individual would have to pay close to twice as much as the corporation for a pension worth $500,000. The qualified pension plan is funded in pretax dollars and the contributions compound tax-free. Personal savings do not enjoy either advantage, and while a privately purchased annuity compounds tax-free, it must be purchased with after-tax dollars. Even with the new law's provision for financing one's own pension through an individual retirement account, it's still hard to accumulate much of a sum under current limits. At a maximum of $1,500 a year, or $45,000 over thirty years, it would take extraordinary investment results indeed to accumulate a very sizable sum.

Certainly things have improved in the pension area in the last forty years. We have come a long way in our attitude toward pensions since Abraham Epstein wrote in 1933: "Company welfare plans have been instituted primarily for the purpose of increasing the worker's loyalty, reducing labor turnover, frustrating unionization and strikes, and making possible the retirement of inefficient executives who could not otherwise be easily discharged."[12]

The pension is no longer a simple reward for faithful service but an earned right, a major element of compensation. If enough individuals begin to understand that, and can find their ways through the pension maze, we may even see the beginnings of a climate for still more fundamental change. But for some time to come, a great many executives will have to settle for far less than they need for retirement security unless they can supplement the pension through other means. The next three chapters deal with three forms of compensation designed to do just that—by building one's personal net worth. The first vehicle is the profit-sharing plan.

CHAPTER SIX

Profit Sharing: Incentives for the Masses

The father of modern profit sharing is reputed to be a nineteenth-century Parisian house painter named Edmé Jean LeClaire. Profit-sharing enthusiasts like to tell the story of the first year's awards. It seems that the forty-four painters and helpers to whom LeClaire announced this bold new plan on February 15, 1842, were more than a little skeptical about whether he would deliver on his promise. So a year later to the day, LeClaire assembled them and proceeded to dump 12,266 francs in gold on a table in front of them.[1] Other companies soon heard of the new scheme. While few matched LeClaire's showmanship, profit sharing became quite popular in Europe during the latter half of the nineteenth century, and ultimately it migrated to the new world. Procter & Gamble, for example, instituted a profit-sharing plan in 1887.

As with most compensation devices, the basic concept of profit sharing is simple. Management adopts a formal plan to give employees a percentage of the profits, typically distributed in proportion to base pay. Over the years, however, three types of plans evolved. The first is *cash profit sharing*; like LeClaire's gold franc caper, it involves an immediate payout from each year's earnings. Such plans have never been very popular in this country, except in banking. The second is the *profit-sharing retirement* plan, under which payout of funds is deferred to provide the source of retirement income. Usually, this plan is used in lieu of a pension. Finally, there is *supplemental profit sharing,* another deferred payment plan the most popular version of which is the so-called *thrift* or *savings* plan. The supplemental plan is similar to the profit-sharing retirement plan, but it normally supplements a pension. Usually it involves lower contributions and more liberal vesting and withdrawal privileges. The supplemental plan may also have objectives beyond boosting retirement income: it can encourage investment in company stock, for example, or provide a source of emergency funds for participants. Under the typical savings plan, the company matches employee contributions rather than allocating a percentage of profits.

When Procter & Gamble, Sears, Roebuck, J.C. Penny, and other profit-sharing pioneers instituted retirement plans around the turn of the century, they had two main objectives: to motivate their employees and to provide a vehicle for accumulating retirement funds in a period when pensions were still rare. The plans were often announced and promoted among employees with an odd mixture of old-fashioned morality and Midwestern populism, best articulated by the legendary Robert E. Wood of Sears, Roebuck: "We think in the long run it is not only good ethics but good business. If the company has a prosperous year or a series of prosperous years, we believe in the policy of sharing them . . . I think the only way you can run a business successfully is to have the employee with you."[2] Initially, most small companies starting out on profit sharing have an evangelical gleam in their eye and high hopes for motivating the participants. Unfortunately, this attitude often gets diluted as the corporation increases in size. With the advent of income taxes the retirement-savings and capital-accumulation aspects of profit sharing began to dominate profit-sharing planning.

Throughout the evolution of the tax structure, profit-sharing advocates have made sure that deferred profit sharing stayed protected under the changing tax code. They have done well. As the rules now stand, an employer can contribute up to 15 percent of an individual's pay to a qualified deferred profit-sharing plan (up to a maximum of $25,000), which is to say one that does not discriminate between classes of employees and conforms to other provisions of

Section 401(d) of the Internal Revenue Code. The company gets to deduct its contribution, the employee avoids any immediate tax on the contribution, and the amount can compound on a tax-free basis. In addition, the individual employee can contribute up to 10 percent of his or her earnings to such a plan; any investment gains are also sheltered from taxation. For decades the qualified profit-sharing plan enjoyed another generous tax advantage: any lump-sum distributions were taxed on a capital gains basis. Congress reduced the tax advantage in the 1969 Tax Reform Act and eliminated capital gains treatment on post-1973 amounts in the 1974 Employee Retirement Income Security Act, substituting a ten-year averaging rule. Even under these rules, though, the tax advantages can be significant.

At Sears, Roebuck, even clerks' retirement benefits are substantial. The Sears employees who retired in 1973 received lump-sum payments averaging $82,304. Sears is easily the most famous profit-sharing company. Through 1973, the fifty-seventh year of its plan, Sears distributed more than $3.9 billion to its retirees.[3] But the kudos for executive net-worth building go to another profit-sharing pioneer, Procter & Gamble. Its 1972 profit-sharing contribution for officers alone was $559,548. That award boosted the accounts of top officers to six and seven figures; the chairman's account reached $6.1 million.[4]

Profit sharing has a lot of appeal for the small company adopting its first retirement plan. It does not require the same fixed commitment as the pension, under which the company promises to provide defined future benefits and must fund the costs regardless of profitability. Moreover, the profit-sharing plan usually seems more meaningful to a management group likely to be still in their thirties and forties. One can figure out one's share of the company contribution each year, and most plans issue detailed status reports on the value of each individual account. The very essence of these plans is that the individual receives a contribution—as opposed to the pension's promise of future benefits—and shares directly in the investment results. Because of these attractions, the few large companies that can afford the cost have continued their profit-sharing plans. Xerox, Eastman Kodak, Procter & Gamble, Carter Hawley Hale (formerly Broadway-Hale), and Polaroid are examples. Not surprisingly, such companies tend to be very profitable, high-margin businesses, largely if not totally nonunionized. But for the most part profit sharing is a feature of smaller, newer companies. Of the 18,000 new plans approved by the IRS in 1971, for example, the average covered only seventeen employees. And the device rarely endures beyond the early decades of a corporation's life. Less than 5 percent of the nation's companies with sales over $500 million still have profit-sharing retirement plans. Most have long since shifted over to the pension.

Unlike profit sharing, the pension guarantees a fixed retirement benefit to employees who are within hailing distance of sixty-five. And as a company matures, the roster of such employees is likely to grow. The pension provides much greater security since the ultimate benefit is determined by the plan formula, instead of by annual contributions and unguaranteed investment gains. Although it's cited less often, another reason companies move away from profit sharing is that the price tag of any meaningful plan is very large when the work force becomes sizable. Thus, the pension offers the opportunity to cut costs, as well as to develop a larger benefit for those who stay with the company until retirement. Capitol Industries, a Los Angeles-based record and tape company, provides a reasonably typical example of what happens to employees when a company switches from profit sharing to pension. After successfully operating a profit-sharing retirement plan for some sixteen years, Capitol substituted a pension supplemented by a contributory stock purchase plan. Under the new arrangement the company's contribution is limited to $2^{1}/_{2}$ percent of the executive's salary, compared to the 15 percent payable under profit sharing. The executives who collect the pension will probably do as well as or better than under the profit-sharing plan, but the abrupt reduction in the company contribution must have been something of a shock to the younger participants. Fortunately, accrued funds aren't taken away when a shift like this is made.

The supplemental plans like that instituted by Capitol Industries are usually called *thrift* or *savings* plans. Technically and functionally, however, they are a form of qualified profit sharing without the "profit" trigger. This kind of savings plan started out in a handful of highly profitable industries, drugs and oil particularly, where there already were lush pensions in effect for the employees, who were relatively few compared to the company's size. The underlying concept again was simple. The employee would be invited to make contributions to a qualified deferred trust. Typically, the amount ranged from 1 to 6 percent of salary. The company would then "match" this contribution at the rate of 25 to 50 cents on the dollar. The money was often used to buy company stock. These savings or thrift plans started to appear in significant numbers in the 1950s, about the time when companies were coming under great pressure to set up pensions requiring no employee contribution. By adopting a savings plan and shifting employee contributions to that vehicle, companies could begin to apply the brakes to further liberalization of the increasingly costly pension benefit, while touting a new two-part retirement program still financed in part by employee dollars.

Some companies were also attracted by the opportunity to improve and diversify an employee stock-purchase plan. Stock-purchase plans were already provided for in the law, and companies like AT&T, IBM, and Honeywell had adopted them to offer modest stock options to all employees. Stock-purchase plans must conform to very rigid rules, however, and normally they involve purchase through payroll deduction of a small number of shares over a two-year period. Because the stock price can be discounted up to 15 percent from market value, the device proved to be an attractive, relatively inexpensive form of compensation, particularly in the 1950s and 1960s when stock prices were generally moving upward. The plans rarely involve a company "contribution" of more than 1 percent of pay (considering the discount on stock price as the contribution).

But members of management soon noted that the stock-purchase plan excluded officers—who are eligible for qualified stock options instead. The thrift or supplemental profit-sharing plan, on the other hand, offered an additional scheme for building net worth, one that could produce sizable sums. And so, popularized by obliging personnel departments, the shift to savings plans was on. Few participants complained and it is easy to see why. When W. W. Keeler retired as chairman of Phillips Petroleum in 1973, his savings account totaled $199,185.[5] In another company that adopted such a scheme to bolster an already generous pension plan, the new savings element alone produces accounts averaging slightly over $100,000 for the current officers upon retirement.

The result of all of this is that while there are few old-fashioned profit-sharing retirement plans in the top 1,000 companies in the country, there are now hundreds of supplemental plans. Generally

Table 6-1. Correlation of Supplemental Profit-Sharing and Thrift/ Savings Plans with Company Size

Company revenue ($ millions)	Percentage of companies with		
	Thrift/ savings	Supplemental profit sharing	Some supplemental plan
Over $1 billion	38	21	59
$500–$999	32	19	51
$250–499	16	19	35
$100–249	8	17	25
$50–99	7	22	29
Under $50	3	14	17

SOURCE: Special analysis of sample of 1,167 proxies.

speaking, the prevalence of such plans increases with company size, as Table 6–1 shows.

A great many executives, therefore, are beginning to encounter profit-sharing programs and to ask some pretty basic questions about their value and implications. What is a profit-sharing or savings plan worth? Should a top executive contribute as much as possible? What provisions should one be particularly alert to in the combined pension/thrift program? Is a profit-sharing retirement plan better than a pension, on average? What factors influence its real value? The answers to these from the individual's viewpoint emerge from an analysis of five aspects of any profit-sharing plan, whether retirement or supplementary savings: (1) the basis and level of company contribution; (2) investment policies and results; (3) employee contribution arrangements and withdrawal rights; (4) vesting provisions; and (5) available settlement options and special tax questions.

Company Contribution

There is an almost incredible range in the level of sustained contributions that companies make to their profit-sharing plans, but the standard is fairly clear. In a profit-sharing retirement plan where there is no pension, a contribution averaging much less than 10 percent of pay will not produce an adequate benefit unless there are extraordinary investment results or a very long period of service. Yet many profit-sharing retirement plans do not approach this level of contribution. The Profit Sharing Research Foundation surveys

**Table 6-2. Range of Company Contributions to Retire-
ment Profit-Sharing Plans**

Average company contribution as a percentage of participant's compensation	Proportion of profit-sharing plans (%)	
0–1	1.4	
2–3	5.6	
4–5	18.0	45.8% under 10%
5–7	6.9	
8–9	13.9	
10–11	12.5	
12–13	5.6	
14–15	36.1	

SOURCE: B. L. Metzger, *Profit Sharing in Perspective*
(2d ed.), Profit Sharing Research Foundation, Evanston,
Ill., 1966, page 125.

indicate that about one out of every four companies with plans
contributes less than 5 percent of pay and 46 percent of the
companies do not meet the 10 percent contribution level, as
illustrated in Table 6–2.

As one might expect, the contribution standard in the savings or
thrift plan is almost always lower than in the pure profit-sharing
retirement plan. The median contribution is about 3 percent, still
up sharply from the 1 to 1½ percent level of ten years ago.[6] But as
supplemental plans have evolved, a wide range in contributions has
developed, although oil companies continue to lead the parade (see
Table 6–3).

A number of profit-sharing and thrift plans boost their regular
contributions by allocating forfeitures—the invested funds of terminating employees—to the remaining participants, rather than
using them to reduce company contributions. About one out of five
thrift plans follows this practice. The typical approach is to allocate
forfeitures the same way the regular contribution is distributed—
i.e., in proportion to pay—but some companies allocate them in
relation to account balances. Obviously the latter course benefits
the long-service and highly paid participants. Again, the amounts
can be significant. In a company with generous contributions of 15
percent and high personnel turnover, forfeitures can add 1 or 2
percent of pay to each participant's account.

Beyond the contribution level itself, there are several related provisions an executive participant should focus on. For example, is the contribution based on salary alone, or on total cash compensation? Most plans still use just base salary, but a few (General Mills, for example) have recently moved to include bonuses. Is there a dollar limit on the contribution, or on earnings covered? The most recent Bankers Trust study found that 13 percent of savings plans imposed an effective limit on company contributions. The median dollar limit was $1,200. There may even be a dollar limit in a profit-sharing retirement-type plan. Sears, Roebuck, for example, limits the covered salary in its profit-sharing plan to $15,000, effectively holding company contributions for executives to a modest amount, or about $1,800 in recent years. But because of this limit Sears has a supplemental pension, something of a reverse twist.

Other facets of the contribution picture to examine include the stability of contributions year in and year out, any special approach to the allocation of the company contribution (some companies

Table 6-3. Range of Company Contributions to Supplemental Profit-Sharing Plans

Range of effective company contribution as percentage of participant's compensation	Illustrative formulas
0.5–2.0	Company matches 25 percent of employee contribution, which is limited to $450 (Du Pont). Company matches 50 percent of employee contributions of 1–6 percent; company contribution limited to $350 per employee (Colgate Palmolive).
2.0–5.0	Company matches 50 percent of employee contributions of 2–5 percent; additional contributions at company discretion (Coca-Cola).
6.0–10.0	Company matches 100 percent of employee contributions, which vary from 2½ percent for under seven years' service to 10 percent with ten years' service (Shell). Company matches 60 percent of employee contributions of 2, 4, 6, 8, or 10 percent (Exxon).

SOURCE: *Bankers Trust 1972 Study of Employee Savings and Thrift Plans,* Bankers Trust Company, New York, 1972, pages 81, 82, 106, 206, 217.

factor in length of service as well as age), and the form of contribution. Normally the contribution is in cash, of course, but I know one successful real estate developer who contributes land and other properties to his company's profit-sharing fund. This has helped the company's cash flow and, to date, the investment results have averaged a spectacular 30 percent a year since the mid-1960s. A plan making noncash contributions may well be challenged by the IRS though, thus jeopardizing the tax status.

Fortunately, in a profit-sharing plan there's no complex formula to master. In contrast with the basic pension benefit, profit-sharing retirement, or savings plan, contributions are normally not complicated by adjustments for social security. One reason is that they are very difficult to integrate. One can lower the company contribution on the portion of earnings that are covered by social security, but this is both complicated and extremely annoying to employees. Most companies don't even try it.

Investment Results

The investment results on profit-sharing funds are as important as the company contribution rate in determining the value of the individual's account. In the typical plan, 60 to 70 percent of the ultimate payout comes from investment gains. Because the plan is sheltered from taxes and makes its payout after a long period of time, the investment results are buoyed by a compounding effect. This is truly a situation where money makes money, as Exhibit 8 illustrates.

Too many people overlook the obvious: profit sharing is a big compounded earnings game. The trick is to get as much money as possible into the tax-sheltered trust in your early years. Several companies have sustained returns of over 20 percent per year; one of the largest West Coast retailers achieved an average annual return of 22 percent for thirteen years through 1969. Several factors make these 10 to 20 percent returns possible. Most profit-sharing trusts are professionally managed. While I know of no definitive studies, the comparative performance of the so-called diversified profit-sharing funds seems to be better than that of mutual funds or pension trusts. The major reason for the unusually high returns is that many plans are invested heavily in their own company's common stock. Although such a policy obviously carries serious risk

EXHIBIT 8
Profit-sharing projection factors.

| | | Rate of investment growth | | | | |
		1%	5%	10%	15%	20%
6%	5 years	5.74	6.19	6.81	7.48	8.21
pay	10 years	13.72	16.20	20.07	25.05	31.43
progression	20 years	39.74	55.38	88.01	146.22	250.93
8%	5 years	5.96	6.43	7.06	7.74	8.49
pay	10 years	15.06	17.67	21.74	26.95	33.61
progression	20 years	49.15	66.92	103.33	167.22	280.64
10%	5 years	6.22	6.68	7.32	8.02	8.78
pay	10 years	16.55	19.30	23.58	29.04	35.98
progression	20 years	61.19	81.48	122.32	192.78	316.10
12%	5 years	6.47	6.94	7.59	8.30	9.07
pay	10 years	18.19	21.10	25.61	31.32	38.57
progression	20 years	76.60	99.90	145.94	224.01	358.64

as well, about half of the assets of the fifty largest profit-sharing plans are invested in company stock, compared with less than 10 percent for corporate pension funds.[7] Throughout most of the 1960s, at least, there was a close correlation between superior results and the degree of concentration of assets in company stock.[8] And finally, of course, no taxes are paid during the buildup of the funds.

What goes up often comes down, however, and overinvestment in a particular stock can be risky, especially during a bear market. Even Sears, Roebuck (whose profit sharing was totally invested in company stock until 1939) has seen its stock go down in about one year out of four since 1916, most recently when it plummeted from around $105 to $55 from mid-1973 to mid-1974. For this reason, most companies diversify their holdings to at least some degree. Profit-sharing retirement plans generally do this by diversifying a single fund, while supplemental plans offer the participant a choice of two or more funds. A typical savings plan might provide that company contributions must be used to purchase company stock, while employee money can be invested in one of several funds, say a diversified common stock fund, a fixed-income account, or company stock. Obviously, a senior executive and an unmarried clerk have different objectives and attitudes toward risk; a range of investment options therefore has much to recommend it. I must admit, though, that some companies get carried away by a good thing. One I know offers nine different selections, including four mutual funds and a government bond fund. Most companies with savings plans make investment in company stock mandatory for company contributions and offer one or two additional funds. That would seem to offer adequate choice.

Faced with such investment choices, the individual again has several critical decisions to make. Only rarely, however, does he or she enjoy the professional counsel that the dollars involved justify. Should one "play the market" by switching one's account back and forth between a common stock and a fixed-income fund? About 48 percent of savings plans permit this type of switching one or more times a year. Other companies limit the privilege to older, longer-service participants, who may particularly need this flexibility. Another decision involves balancing faith in the company against the risk of a narrowly based portfolio. Executives are frequently overcommitted to company stock in option plans anyway, yet many profit-sharing and savings plans put even more eggs in that same basket.

Employee Contributions

It has always seemed somewhat irrational to *force* employees to contribute substantial after-tax dollars to a retirement plan. Forcing them to contribute to a profit-sharing plan is even less rational. Our tax structure clearly favors direct company contributions, simply because funneling a portion of them through the employee's salary check assures that Uncle Sam will take a slice. Yet many companies believe that employees will appreciate a plan more if they con-tribute—and anyway, doesn't sound morality dictate that they should help provide for their own security? About 15 percent of profit-sharing retirement plans therefore *require* employee contribu-tions as a condition of participation, and 3 percent even distribute company funds based on the rate of employee contribution. In situations like these, the individual has a simple choice—contribute to the plan or forgo retirement security.

Voluntary contributions to a supplemental savings plan obviously represent a more discretionary decision. In this case, the issue is not retirement security but investment return and liquidity. Generally speaking, it makes sense to contribute, since virtually all companies match at least a portion of the employee's contribution. The question is how much to contribute. The IRS limits the maximum voluntary contribution to 10 percent of pay, but few corporations will match that much, and the median matching rate is 6 percent, as illustrated in Table 6-4.

Typically, you can contribute less than the matched amount; you can almost always suspend contributions; and you do have a range of investment choice. However, it is wise to look closely at the provisions governing suspension and withdrawal, which determine how much real control you will have over the funds you do contribute.

Virtually all plans permit the individual to stop contributing without withdrawing from the program, but there are often restrictions on how frequently this can be done. In fact, 37 percent of plans permit it only once a year. Once the employee stops contributing, he or she often has to stay out of the plan for a specified period ranging from six months to two years. During such a hiatus, the company may not contribute either. Occasionally there is also a limit on how long a person can leave his funds in the plan without contributing again; this period can be as short as a year.

The withdrawal privileges are even more important in assessing the wisdom of contributing. All but a handful of savings plans permit participants to withdraw their own money. About two-thirds permit withdrawal of at least a portion of company contributions. However, the approach and conditions under which these withdrawals can be made vary sharply from plan to plan. There are two basic types of provision here. Early savings plans usually provided

Table 6-4. Corporate Matching Rates in Voluntary Savings Plans

Maximum matching rate (%)	Percentage of plans
Under 4	13.2
5	24.4
6	39.4
7–10	3.3

SOURCE: *Bankers Trust 1972 Study of Employee Savings and Thrift Plans, op. cit.*, page 16.

for *periodic distribution* of a portion of an individual's account, usually at the employee's election, on a so-called "class" basis. This meant treating each year as a separate account partially paying out three to five years down the road. Under this type of provision, one could arrange to have both company and individual funds paid out for a number of successive classes to obtain an annual income. Only 28 percent of savings plans still have this kind of feature, however. The more common approach now is simply to permit voluntary withdrawal subject to limitations on frequency, say once a year, and amount, usually expressed as a percentage of accrued vested funds. In addition, companies often impose a penalty for withdrawal, such as suspension from the plan or forfeiture of some of the accrued company contributions.

Profit-sharing retirement plans tend to be much more strict about withdrawal of contributions, as one might expect, since the principal objective of these plans is to build up an adequate fund for retirement purposes. Three-quarters of noncontributory plans and over one-third of contributory profit-sharing retirement schemes do not permit any withdrawals at all.

There are several aspects of the contribution issue that are particularly important for executives, many of whom have attractive alternative investment opportunities. First, the individual should evaluate the relationship between the profit-sharing/thrift plan and stock options. Ideally, the supplemental plan should provide a means of investment diversification. But if the company contribution is totally invested in company stock, the executive needs to have a lot of faith or a very attractive "discount" from the company's matching practices.

Second, in evaluating the supplemental plan as an investment, an executive should focus on the after-tax return of the profit-sharing plan versus that of other investments. Table 6–5 shows the kind of taxable return one would need to match a range of results.

Obviously the tax-free provision can be a particularly important advantage to the executive in the higher brackets. The higher the return the greater the risk, on the other hand, so some executives are understandably nervous about investing in profit-sharing plans even where there is a clear tax advantage. An increasing number of profit-sharing and thrift plans meet this concern by providing a fixed investment bond fund that guarantees a stated return for three to five years. Interest rates have gone up recently, of course, and yields have been between $7^1/_2$ and $8^1/_2$ percent.

Table 6-5. Compound Pretax Rate of Return on Investment Needed to Match a Profit-sharing Fund at Various Rates of Return (assumes 10-year period)

Marginal tax bracket	Profit-sharing yield (%) of				
	5%	6%	8%	10%	15%
40	10.5	11.6	13.7	15.8	21.0
50	12.5	13.6	15.8	17.9	23.3
60	15.1	16.2	18.4	20.6	26.0

The higher-paid participant also has to be sure he or she doesn't run afoul of a technical provision in the 1974 pension reform law that introduces a new limit on employee contributions, which for years have been permissible up to 10 percent of pay. That limit still applies, but the section of the law written to limit executive pensions (see Chapter 5) contains new profit-sharing limits as well. Unfortunately the ground rules also consider a portion of employee contributions in determining the new maximum alternative standards of $25,000 or 25 percent of pay. You must add together the contribution the company makes for you that year and your share of any forfeitures *and* the lesser of (*a*) voluntary contributions in excess of 6 percent or (*b*) one-half of your actual contributions. After January 1, 1976, these three annual additions to your account can't exceed $25,000 or 25 percent of your pay. Moreover, the limits are lower if you participate in both a pension and a profit-sharing or thrift plan. You can't enjoy both the maximum pension and the maximum profit sharing, only 140 percent of the combined limits. For example, if the company elects to split the limit evenly, the profit-sharing maximum would be reduced to 70 percent of the limit that applies to free-standing plans: $17,500. If the company elects to make the pension the core plan (which I believe is more likely to be the case) the profit-sharing annual addition would be limited to 40 percent—that is, $10,000 or 10 percent. Finally, the profit-sharing plan's contribution rules may include a number of special wrinkles. For example, the plan may permit the individual to make retroactive contributions to "make up" years when he or she did not contribute. This has to be individually negotiated with the IRS, but it can be a valuable benefit for the executive whose income jumps sharply after a period of years when he made no personal contribution to the savings plan. Some participants will even borrow to make a large lump-sum contribution. Since the loan interest is itself tax-deductible and the profit sharing accrues tax-free, it is possible to obtain a 3 or 4 percent return with virtually no risk. The individual executive may also use his or her profit-sharing asset to secure a loan made for tax-shelter investments, thus building net worth on a leveraged basis.

Vesting Provisions

Generous company contribution plans and a superior investment track record are worth a lot less if one stands to lose the funds in one's account on leaving the company. Virtually all plans vest fully on death or permanent disability, and participants can usually withdraw their own contributions. But most plans penalize participants who leave the company, particularly people with short tenure. Fewer than 4 percent of retirement plans and 6.5 percent of savings/thrift plans provide immediate and full vesting. In all other plans the short-service employee who leaves forfeits all or a portion of the company contribution and the investment gains thereon. Those funds that are vested, on the other hand, can be withdrawn upon termination or, in most plans, left in the trust fund to continue appreciating until retirement. In a profit-sharing retirement plan, one's account is vested gradually, in relation to duration of service or participation, as Table 6–6 demonstrates. The requirements tend to be demanding, but they are more liberal than those governing the average pension.

The supplemental plans tend to be more liberal in their vesting provisions. Over half of these plans relate vesting to years of participation, often on a graduated schedule, but full vesting occurs

Table 6-6. Vesting Requirements of Profit-Sharing Retirement Plans

Years required for full vesting	Years of service (%)		Years of plan participation (%)	
	This period	Cumulative	This period	Cumulative
5 or less	0	0	14	14
6 to 9	4.3	4.3	6	20
10	34.9	39.2	66	86
11 to 14	12.9	52.1	4	90
15	8.7	60.8	6	96
20 or more	39.2	100.0	4	100
Number of plans	23		50	

SOURCE: Metzger, *op. cit.*, pages 67, 68.

Table 6-7. Vesting Requirements of Supplemental Savings Plans

Years of participation required for full vesting	Percentage of savings plans	
		Cumulative
Under 5	10.4	10.4
5	49.1	59.8
6 to 9	9.7	69.5
10	21.1	90.6
Over 10	9.7	100.0

SOURCE: *Bankers Trust 1972 Study of Employee Savings and Thrift Plans, op. cit.*, page 25.

within five years in most supplemental plans, as Table 6–7 shows.

Another approach to savings plan vesting, used by about 40 percent of companies, is "class-system vesting." Under this provision, company contributions vest three years after the date the contribution is made. The time period varies, but three years is average.

Settlement Options

The well-designed profit-sharing plan can serve several objectives: provide a source of primary or supplemental retirement income, offer a vehicle for building net worth, or encourage investment in company stock. Each of these diverse purposes forces decisions on payout options that normally do not arise with the ordinary pension. Because of the tax consequences, these decisions deserve particular care, since large sums can be involved.

The profit-sharing retirement and thrift plans by their very nature build up an account value. Most plans make the final settlement in lump-sum form, therefore, regardless of whether the employee dies, becomes disabled, retires, resigns, or is fired. In more than half of the profit-sharing retirement plans and nearly half of the thrift plans, lump-sum distribution is the only available form of payout. Prior to the 1969 Tax Reform Act, such lump-sum distributions were taxed on a capital gains basis (except for employee contributions, which were not taxed at all since they were made with after-tax dollars). Since 1969, however, company contributions have been taxed under the ordinary income tax tables, although special averaging provisions in the 1969 and 1974 laws softened the sting somewhat. Under the Employee Retirement Income Security Act of 1974 you calculate the tax as if the lump-sum distribution were your only income and spread this over ten years. But with large amounts the total tax bite on lump-sum profit-sharing settlements can now theoretically rise to a 70 percent rate compared to the old maximum of 25 percent.

While it will be a number of years before the full impact of these changes is felt, companies are already moving to add other payout options that are also taxed as ordinary income. The most common choices offered involve installment payments, the right to purchase an annuity, or, in a few thrift plans, additional benefits under the company pension plan.

There is a need for careful tax planning here too. For example, there are ways to cut the income taxes on a lump-sum distribution—most dramatically by arranging to have the distribution made in company stock if that is feasible under the plan. The IRS does not consider this a "direct transaction" and one is not taxed until the sale or exchange of the stock. This same benefit may be available when distribution is in other companies' stock, not just the employer's stock.[9]

Estate taxes, as well as income taxes, must be weighed in analyzing the relative advantages of lump-sum distribution and, say, an installment payout over ten or fifteen years. The death benefits under a qualified profit-sharing plan (excluding any portion attributable to employee contribution) are not subject to estate taxes if receivable by any beneficiary except the deceased employee's estate. An individual who takes an installment payout can thus avoid estate taxes on the remainder of the funds, while an individual taking a lump-sum settlement is likely to have these funds taxed as part of his or her estate. State and local taxes, which are dramatically uneven throughout the country, can sometimes also be minimized (see Chapter 3) by moving to a state where the tax climate is more favorable.

Net Worth Potential

The profit-sharing plan that works—one in which sizable contributions are made and the investment results are good—can be an excellent retirement vehicle, often better than the average pension.

It is certainly more tangible and personal. But the intriguing development in recent years has been the emergence of the supplemental plan, which has become an important source of capital accumulation at the executive level. As we have seen, the potential for building net worth depends largely on three plan factors: the rate of contribution, the investment results and length of the period involved, and the executive's rate of compensation progress.

By weighing these factors in each case, it is both possible and extremely important to estimate what the size of the profit-sharing account will be at retirement, another way of calculating its contribution to total net worth. The individual needs this projection in buying insurance (see Chapter 4), in investment planning, and in making job comparisons. Some financial advisors use computer models to project ranges, but a close approximation can be made using the tables shown in Exhibit 8 and the following formula:

$$\begin{array}{l}\text{Profit-sharing} \\ \text{multiplier} \\ \text{factor}\end{array} \times \begin{array}{l}\text{Assumed} \\ \text{contribution} \\ \text{rate}\end{array} \times \begin{array}{l}\text{Current} \\ \text{salary}\end{array} = \begin{array}{l}\text{Ending} \\ \text{value of} \\ \text{account}\end{array}$$

Exhibit 8 is organized so that one can simply pick out one of four assumptions on how fast pay will grow (6, 8, 10, or 12 percent a year) and then find the factor that reflects a reasonable time period and rate of investment growth. For example: An executive at the $20,000 level who assumes his salary will advance at 8 percent a year should turn to the "8% pay progression" section and make specific contribution and investment gain assumptions. If the funds are likely to grow at 10 percent a year for twenty years, the factor is 103; 103 times the contribution rate (15 percent) equals 1,545; multiplying this by current salary ($20,000) gives you the projected end value of $309,000. If, on the other hand, the contribution was only going to average 5 percent, and investment results 6 percent, profit sharing would build up to only $73,000 over twenty years. Differences of this magnitude are *not* uncommon, incidentally.

In the years ahead, this new profit-sharing species will help provide real independence to the generation of management in its thirties when the plans were first adopted. It will write another honored chapter in an already honorable tradition. The qualified profit-sharing plan is a distinctly American institution, with strong and vocal advocates. In fact, it is the only pay plan with its own lobby, and its own association, the Council of Profit-Sharing Industries. The plan's cousin, the savings plan, doesn't yet evoke the same evangelical fervor but it may in time because it has made possible significantly greater financial security for more than 20 million working Americans.

CHAPTER SEVEN

Executive Bonuses: Incentive and Otherwise

In a *Wall Street Journal* cartoon one portly tycoon confides to another, "I'm holding on to my cash. I think money is going to come back." Money was indeed coming back as U.S. business moved into the 1970s. Annual McKinsey compensation surveys showed the nation's leading chief executives gaining as much in pay between 1968 and 1970 as they had in the preceding seven years. Poking beneath the surface, however, it wasn't so much holding on to cash that was responsible, but a resurgence of bonus plan use that had begun in the mid-1960s.

In some ways history was repeating itself. At the turn of the century fewer than 5 percent of U.S. corporations used incentive bonuses as part of their compensation plans. The bonus's popularity picked up in 1918, when that granddaddy of U.S. corporations, General Motors, adopted one of the first plans. In his book *My Years with General Motors*, Alfred P. Sloan, Jr., attributed much of GM's success to its incentive system: "When the plan was first started," he said, "it made a tremendous contribution in encouraging executives to relate their own individual effort to the welfare of the whole corporation. Indeed, the bonus plan played almost as big a role as our system of coordination in making decentralization work effectively."[1]

Inspired by the GM example, many companies not blessed with an Alfred P. Sloan rushed to adopt bonus plans, sometimes with unfortunate results. By 1928 some two-thirds of the major U.S. companies were using bonuses, and awards had grown to ridiculous proportions. Eugene Grace, then head of Bethlehem Steel, got a $1.6 million bonus in 1929, which seems a particularly hefty emolument compared to his base salary of $12,000.

The Great Depression cured such excesses the hard way. By 1932 only about one executive in ten was receiving a bonus, and the awards were not even within hailing distance of the million-dollar range. After World War II awards became significant again. By the 1950s the proportion of manufacturing companies with incentive plans had climbed again to about the level of the late 1920s. By the 1960s bonus schemes were proliferating in new business sectors. The oil industry offers a case in point. As late as 1963 only three of the country's largest petroleum companies had bonus plans: Texaco, Gulf, and Sun Oil. But when Standard of New Jersey moved in 1964, the others quickly followed. By 1971 only Getty was a holdout among the twelve largest oil companies in the country. (Getty's performance compared quite well despite its lack of incentives, incidentally.) Airlines, banks, and property and casualty insurance companies soon joined the parade. The trend was dramatic. McKinsey surveys of thirty-one industries found companies with bonus plans jumping from 50 percent in 1967 to 63 percent by 1969 and 76 percent by 1973.[2]

From the company's point of view, an incentive bonus has much to recommend it. Like the best of executive stock plans, it motivates the executive to focus on both company profitability and individual achievement. From the stockholder's point of view it puts a percentage of executive overhead costs in the variable as opposed to fixed cost category. At the same time, incentives are generally welcomed by company executives, since existing base salaries are rarely if ever cut when an incentive system is installed. In most cases, the first and second award years are heady days of added compensation and general incentive euphoria. As time passes, however, previous awards inevitably establish a level of expectation. If company performance falters or inept administration creates inequities, an incentive plan can also sow the seeds of executive discontent. It is also subject to abuse. The Watergate investigation uncovered a number of corporations that fudged bonus plans to provide funds for political contributions, including one billion-dollar company that provided double bonuses to executives who had contributed to political campaigns. Such problems have rarely slowed the adoption of new plans, however. Indeed the wage controls of the 1970s created still more pressure for the bonus, a weapon to be wielded against two-digit inflation without boosting fixed costs.

Given their many advantages, even greater use of incentive bonuses is in prospect for the 1970s. This entails still more questions for executives, for even cash isn't a straightforward commodity in today's environment. The bonus dollar is not necessarily worth 100 cents. That point was driven home forcefully to me not long ago during a call from a friend who was negotiating for the top job at a Midwest manufacturing company. He had been offered his choice between a $120,000 salary and a $100,000 salary plus a bonus that could reach $40,000 or $50,000. Anyone who has worked for a company with an incentive bonus system will immediately recognize my friend's dilemma. In practice, a bonus is about as predictable as a floating monetary exchange rate. Faced with such a choice, how should an executive weigh an incentive plan? What are the key design elements that affect the individual most directly?

Four bonus program elements deserve special scrutiny: (1) the incentive formula itself; (2) the structure of the bonus; (3) the administrative process and philosophy that condition it; and (4) the payout options that are offered.

The Incentive Bonus Formula

When they enter the bonus race for the first time, a great many companies are determined to find the perfect vehicle—the plan that will anticipate every contingency, spell out every detail. They remind me of the two University of Cincinnati professors who recently unveiled a model incentive plan for baseball players.[3] Ingenious though their result was, their plan illustrates the absurdities involved in trying to substitute rules for judgment. Under their system, one had to calculate for each player both defensive and offensive performance indexes. The latter alone had nine variables; the formula itself would baffle a Ph.D. in operations research.

The overriding fact is that an incentive bonus is largely a judgmental proposition—and, therefore, most efforts to mathematize the process have failed. However, the publicly held company usually does formalize at least one element of the system—the method used in setting the size of the bonus pool. Even though a bonus scheme does not legally require stockholder approval unless payments involve company stock, most companies submit their plans to stockholders. And wisely, I believe. Not surprisingly, therefore, most managements feel stockholders will be more comfortable if the company profit results required before bonuses can be paid are set forth quite specifically. So most plans do publish formulas defining those requirements, as well as the percentage of profits that can be spent for bonus purposes.

But although the formulas are on record, few executives take the trouble to study how the bonus pot is actually set, or other relevant rules, for that matter. There are nearly as many specific formulas as there are companies, of course, but Exhibit 9 defines the most common approaches.

Reviewing a formula should tell one something about a corporation's goals and standards, since the formula usually establishes a minimum performance level. Keep in mind, however, that technical definitions can have a major influence on the size of the fund. For example, is the plan based on before- or after-tax corporate earnings? Usually it's the former, on the theory that participants can't really affect the corporation's tax rates. Is the bonus accrual based on total profits, or just net operating income? One conglomerate's chief executive insisted on including capital gains and losses from securities transactions in the minimum profit calculation, reflecting both his company's emphasis on EPS growth and the fact that profits from securities transactions had been accounting for about 12 percent of recent total profits. The stock market decline of the 1970s cut the bonus pool of that company by two-thirds. How does the plan treat extraordinary items? When the International Textbooks Company's bonus pool was wiped out in 1970 because of "unusual and nonrecurring charges," management obtained stockholder approval of a retroactive change in the formula to "exclude from net income nonrecurring or unusual gains or losses." This move restored the bonus pot to $122,000 (although, quite properly, the senior officers could not participate retroactively).[4]

The individual executive looking at a bonus plan should obviously give thought to the realities of the profit hurdle. The popular fixed-formula incentive came into favor ten and more years ago, when the cost of capital was considerably lower and the number of

EXHIBIT 9
Executive bonus plans.

Types of incentive bonus plans	Percentage of plans	Illustrative formulas*
1. FORMULA	85	
a. Percentage of profits after investment hurdle involving return on stockholders' equity, invested capital, assets, sales	50	10% of after-tax profits in excess of 6% of capital investment (General Electric)
b. Straight percentage of profits	20	5% of pretax profits (construction company)
c. Percentage of profits after dollar hurdle involving dividend coverage, fixed profit figure	10	8% earnings after net income exceeds $3 million (chemical company)
d. Combination formula	5	5% of after-tax profits if return on stockholders' equity equals 12% (manufacturing)
2. GOAL-BASED—Bonus fund based on relationship between actual and planned results using corporate profits, competitive measure, divisional/subsidiary goals	10	Actual bonus pool will vary from 0 to 150% of the sum of target bonuses based on division results compared with profit plan (aerospace company)
3. DISCRETIONARY	5	Board of directors approves a sum based on previous award patterns and a judgmental assessment of current year's results (paper company)

OTHER DESIGN PROVISIONS	Carry-forward of unused funds	Bonus restrictions	Award form	Timing (payout option)
	Unrestricted	Stipulated dollar maximum	Cash	Immediate
	Limited	Cap on percentage of salary	Stock	Installment
	Not permitted	Unrestricted	Other	Deferred

* Any type of plan can be based on pretax or after-tax earnings. Some formulas include only operating income; others include all income and adjust for capital gains or losses.

participants far fewer. The changes brought by intervening years have conspired effectively to raise the hurdle for many companies. Chrysler executives, for example, went without awards for several years because smaller cars and inflation effectively raised their hurdle. In 1972 Chrysler finally faced that fact and dropped the minimum earnings barrier from $115.8 million to $50.2 million. General Motors, which in 1970 skipped its first bonus in twenty-four years, revised its formula to decrease the leverage.

Whether he or she participates in the corporate or divisional bonus plan is a question of great importance to the division-level executive. More and more, diversified companies are turning to separate division plans to ensure that the executive's payoff will relate more closely to his own unit's performance vis-à-vis its profit plan.[5] Other companies now relate a given portion of the bonus, say 75 percent, to division performance and the remainder to overall corporate performance. This design theory is not universally accepted, as Hank Nave, former president of White Motor, discovered. When Bunkie Knudsen was brought in from GM over Nave's head, the two men found they disagreed on many things. But the last straw, as Mr. Nave recalls it, went like this: "Knudsen and I completely disagreed about payment of incentive compensation to division heads. I mean, just because corporate management makes mistakes . . . doesn't mean that men who do outstanding jobs shouldn't be rewarded."[6] Knudsen's GM philosophy prevailed, and Nave left to join Mack Trucks. From the individual's standpoint, a divisional plan is usually preferable. For one thing, the division plan normally is not submitted to stockholders and hence can be modified more easily.

One should also look closely at the provision regarding carry-forward of unused bonus monies. Such a provision adds considerable flexibility, obviously, and even more if unused funds carry forward indefinitely rather than just to the next year. Consider the experience, starting in 1969, of three of the country's largest aerospace firms. Company A's bonus formula prohibited any fund before net profits exceeded 10 percent of stockholders' equity. Unhappily, that milestone was not reached in 1970, or 1971, or 1972. Company B's plan permitted the board of directors to carry forward to future periods any portion of the pool not used. This feature enabled Company B to build up substantial reserve, and the company paid bonuses selectively in two of the three years when

Company A did not. Company C took yet another approach when it drew up its plan in the mid-1960s. The plan instituted divisional bonus plans that applied to all but a handful of senior executives and corporate staff officers. When the three years of hard times came, Company C was able to provide incentive monies in three of its six divisions, even though the corporate plan itself did not generate any funds.

Most companies develop their bonus formulas pragmatically, gearing them both to the number of participants and to the "ideal" size of the bonus pool at various levels of company performance. Some formulas are rather rigidly designed to produce just this mystical amount of money. But most provide room for maneuvering to accommodate new participants or to permit the board of directors to exercise judgment on the amount of payout. In one large company, the board has not used more than 60 percent of the available fund in the last five years.

When the formula is too closely tuned to the funds actually needed, companies may be forced to redefine the eligibility criteria—sometimes surprising would-be participants in the process. For years General Motors has used salary levels to determine eligibility. In 1961 the entry level was defined as a salary of $9,600. Over the next ten years that level was raised in five steps to $15,000. Then, in 1971, it was jumped 60 percent to $24,000. Some 10,000 executives suddenly found themselves dropped from bonus eligibility.

Adding up all this experience, there are some important lessons here for both the individual executive and the company that hires him. First, anyone joining a company where a major portion of pay will come from an incentive bonus should study the details of the formula plan. That study should address *all* the formula provisions. By the same token, the company should make a real effort to explain its formula mechanics to all plan participants. After all, an incentive plan is intended to motivate people. If those people are unaware of the ground rules, or are led to finagling to beat what they perceive as "the system," neither the people nor the purposes of the bonus are served.

The Structure of the Bonus

There are two schools of thought on how to fit bonus plans with salaries to provide competitive cash compensation. One point of view, an appealing one conceptually, is that bonuses should be an extra awarded only to outstanding performers. Under this theory, the base salary structure should be competitive in itself. Then the bonuses paid to the deserving few will truly represent extra compensation for superior performance. The more widespread theory holds this approach to be impractical, pointing out that most plan participants will wind up receiving awards anyway. In companies acting on the latter philosophy, base salary structures are often discounted, therefore, so that only when bonuses are paid is total compensation really competitive.

While the two philosophies are quite different, actual results may not differ all that much. I have only encountered one company that has been able to make a highly selective award system work. Few companies can live with a plan that singles out only the stars year after year. After all, even the most dynamic organizations need a substantial number of average managers to keep the corporate machine running day to day. The company staffed entirely with strategic geniuses is about as effective as a football team made up of quarterbacks.

On the other hand, the theory of discounting a salary structure is difficult to translate into practice, at least over time. Even within a closely knit industry there may be as much as a 30 percent differential in the compensation paid top executives. There can also be significant variations among job groups and their competitive rankings. Many factors contribute to all the variations. Historic pay levels may really change only when top management does. The degree of unionization at the level where the rank and file meets management can have a significant effect. Industry compensation trends almost certainly will. When a bonus element is added to all this, "competitive" statistics become even more confusing. And while they can be related to an "average," a lot of the comparison is really little more than technical legerdemain.

Most companies espouse a philosophy under which base salaries plus bonuses equal competitive total compensation. But the bare fact is that companies with incentive plans pay more. The American Management Association's annual surveys have consistently confirmed this. In 1973, the premium averaged about 22 percent. Moreover, at upper management levels the pay advantage in bonus companies is likely to be even more substantial: at least 25 percent and upwards of 40 percent, according to some surveys. If most participants in most plans receive awards, and most bonus companies pay some compensation premium, what distinguishes one bonus company from another? The answer lies in the manner in which the individual awards are varied.

Even if most participants wind up with some award, most companies with incentive plans do make distinctions in the size of individual awards. Thus the bonus structure used to distinguish among participants goes to the very heart of an incentive plan. A few bonus plans still function essentially on a profit-sharing basis, with all the participants receiving the same percent-of-salary award, typically from 10 to 20 percent. The only "incentive" is that the percentage increases when corporate profitability rises. Another plan that minimizes the variations is the old Christmas bonus of from two to four weeks' salary, paid at year-end to a large number of employees. A variation of this was very popular among securities firms when they were in their heyday. Finally, some companies vary the awards only by organizational level, with no recognition of performance differences among individuals.

Most corporations, however, favor a more judgmental process, one that varies the award in response to differences in individual performance. The most common approach incorporates three main design elements: a target bonus, usually expressed as a percentage of pay, that increases by organization level; some device for adjusting the target bonus according to the size of the incentive pool; and a further adjustment for individual performance.

The target bonus is an important administrative standard and perhaps the most accurate indicator of what one is likely to receive. Most companies set the target at somewhere between 10 and 15 percent of salary at the entry levels, increasing it in even increments up to 40 or 50 percent of salary for senior management. The theory behind the graduations runs this way: At the higher levels, more of a person's total pay should be subject to risk, and the award should increase with a position's impact on profit results. To some extent, the practice also reflects the common view that pay schedules should be adjusted for tax rates. Crawford Greenewalt, the former chief executive of Du Pont, made a strong argument that "If compensation is to provide incentive, the scale must be calibrated . . . with a sufficient difference between one level and the next to make promotion attractive."[7] He went on to say that for the progression to be meaningful it must be on an after-tax basis.

In fact most companies bonus setups serve Greenewalt's principles rather well. In the first place, almost every company maintains an orderly salary pyramid within the bonus group, with the differential averaging 12 to 15 percent. Moreover, there is usually a two-grade separation between a superior and a subordinate. Finally, the compensation differential at successive levels is further accentuated by a structure that uses an increasing target bonus percentage. The plant manager, for example, has a 15 percent target bonus, the director of plant operations 25 percent, and vice president of manufacturing 35 percent. Thus even the plant manager, who receives twice the "normal" bonus, still winds up with both a smaller percentage and fewer absolute dollars than the manufacturing vice president. Because most bonus systems accentuate the hierarchical nature of corporate compensation, therefore, they do in fact increase the premium for promotions or higher grade assignments.

The scale of target or normal bonus percentages varies from industry to industry. In the insurance industry, for example, the bonus structure will typically range from 10 to 35 percent of salary while bonuses of up to 100 percent are not uncommon in the retail industry.

The weight of the bonus element in some companies can produce dramatic effects on total compensation. When General Motors failed to pay bonuses in 1970, for example, James Roche's pay dropped $400,000. In the investment industry, where awards may reach 200 to 300 percent of pay, the *average* partner compensation in one troubled securities firm dropped from $124,000 in 1968 to $25,000 in 1969.

Individual Award Administration

The first key question from the individual's standpoint, then, is what's my target bonus? Right behind it comes how can the amount be adjusted to reflect superior performance? Most companies do not write a limit into the formal plan these days; even when they do, the limit is set fairly high, e.g., 50 percent of pay. But the award can be and in practice is limited in actual administration, through other guidelines or the philosophy of administration.

The administrative apparatus represents a real constraint for most participants. Back in the chairman's office there is undoubtedly a set of guidelines that provides a framework for adjusting target bonuses

Table 7-1. Weight Given to Individual Performance in Adjusting Normal Bonuses

Performance judgment	Plan moderately leveraged for individual performance (%)	Plan highly leveraged for individual performance (%)
Unacceptable	0	0
Below standard	75	50
Standard	100	100
Above standard	125	150
Outstanding	150	200

based on individual performance. After the size of the bonus pool itself is determined, the normal individual bonuses are adjusted according to performance. Table 7–1 shows the performance weighting used in two large companies.

In most companies, the actual distribution of performance—and, therefore, the deviations above and below normal bonuses—tends to follow a bell-shaped curve that is skewed slightly upward. The majority of the participants receive the standard award or better. High performance ratings are especially common at upper management levels where an individual's efforts are surely more evident, presumably more valuable, and where it is more likely that personal interests will come into play. Few chief executive officers have the philosophy Bob Townsend expressed and apparently followed at Avis. He had an agreement with the board whereby they could cut but not increase the rating he gave himself. (According to Townsend, his self-administered ratings were "satisfactory" each year but one, when he gave himself an unsatisfactory mark.)[8] Fewer still have the discipline of Alfred P. Sloan, who in his later years reportedly called key executives down to his Boca Raton retreat for detailed explanations of the performance of subordinates and the rationale for bonus recommendations. Sloan halved one division head's own award for recommending identical bonuses for his managers from one year to the next.

How objective are the performance judgments that underlie the bonus decisions? Most companies have developed elaborate appraisal processes to provide an objective performance measure. In the 1960s, the favorite technique was the goal-setting or management-by-objective process, under which each participant agreed to several quantitative or qualitative objectives at the beginning of the plan year. Many of these goal-setting systems have now collapsed under the weight of paper work they generated or from lack of commitment by top management to the formal, planning-oriented style these systems require.

The goal-setting, or management-by-objective, plan can be a beautiful thing when it works. That happens in about one out of four companies that try it, in my judgment. It establishes a reasonably objective record of executive accomplishment and emphasizes the need for forward planning. Because of these advantages, most personnel departments hold up the goal-setting or other task-oriented appraisal process as the standard, strongly preferring it to the loose and informal appraisal approaches of earlier years. Much of the debate about the "best" appraisal system, though, ignores the practical realities of any bonus plan. The final decisions in 95 companies out of 100 will be made on a judgmental basis, regardless of the formal administrative system. Furthermore, in most companies the ultimate judgment is a relative judgment: the person relative to his or her peers, the individual compared to the incentive group as a whole, the man today measured against the same man a year ago.

An executive weighing an offer from a bonus company—particularly an offer whose total compensation depends heavily on the prospective bonus—has the right to ask the company for more than its philosophy. He or she ought to know how the plan really *works*. Did the company pay bonuses in each of the last five years? What percentage of eligible participants actually received awards? For the bonus group as a whole, how did the average bonus, expressed as a percentage of pay, vary from the expected norm? What were the three highest bonuses, again in percentage of pay terms, and what level of executive received them? What percentage of the bonus fund was actually paid out?

The administrative process also deserves attention. In many companies, management starts the review process with data from a number of sources, including a written or verbal critique from the department head. Typically, this beginning is followed by a good deal of top-management discussion during which other aspects of a person's performance and potential emerge. The end result under such a system, when conscientiously practiced, can be far more objective than under a much more elaborate and formal system. Some companies go too far toward informality, of course. One large chemical company has an elaborate appraisal process that generates highly detailed bonus recommendations. It also has a very strong-minded president who ignores the process. He takes a work sheet to his country home and develops his own recommendations over a long weekend. It's important, then, to know how much influence one's immediate supervisor really has in the hierarchy. As one very competent young manager told me, "Give me a strong, well-positioned boss as an advocate, and I don't worry too much about the administrative system." In more formal processes, one should assess the extent to which the company's budgeting, information, and control reports spell out the results of one's individual activity. These many reports provide the data that top management scrutinizes month in and month out; they create impressions that are favorable, unfavorable, or neutral. But the formal information systems are not always the source of top management's day-to-day personnel judgments, and it would be naive to think they are in the average corporation. Subtle, imaginative, and honest self-merchandising is a hard necessity in most instances. Total humility regarding one's accomplishments may be admirable in a monastery, but the modern corporation is not nearly so pure an institution.

Among management purists who decry anything but a formal, well-documented process, the major concern is that subjective judgments about an individual's personal life, managerial style, or even potential are likely to be given undue weight. My own feeling is that it's simply unrealistic to expect top management's biases to be wholly eliminated from any process as important as bonus awards. And after all, this is only one in a long list of decision-making areas that critically affect our careers and incomes. Subjective judgments are certainly involved in salary actions, promotions, committee assignments, participation in special plans, and the like. In essence, it comes down to this: If one has a basic, persistent doubt about the fairness or wisdom of management decisions in such areas, then it is time to move to a new environment.

The Bonus Payout Options

Once the executive has explored the intricacies of the bonus formula and evaluated the bonus structure and award system, it is time to ask the next critical question: In what form and over what time period will the incentive award be paid?

It used to be fashionable for corporations to use incentive plans to hold key executives. This was accomplished by either deferring a part of each year's award until retirement or stretching payment over a period of years, with any unpaid portion subject to forfeiture. Using money to hold people is a debatable proposition at best, in my opinion, and as a practical matter it takes sizable sums to do the job. Even the entire amount of the average bonus is not enough to offset a well-designed competitive offer. There is also something inherently illogical about the mandatory deferral of a bonus intended to reward performance for a given calendar year. Fortunately, most corporations have moved away from the "golden handcuffs" theory of incentive payout toward a philosophy of individual choice. This shift is particularly advisable in organizations with many younger executives. For example, it was the acquisition of Hertz that forced RCA to modify its bonus payout methods; the car-rental company's younger executive group rebelled at a five-year payout of awards.

Where the individual does have a payout option, important considerations come into play. All too many highly paid executives use a bonus plan as a sort of executive credit union, some form of deferred compensation. When one's income reaches a level where an additional $10,000 or $20,000 is somewhat irrelevant, it is easy to succumb to the temptation to tuck something away for retirement years. After all, one's tax rates will presumably be lower, and the income will be more needed then. This, however, is not a compensation decision, it is an investment decision—and one of the most complex the salaried executive will encounter. Some of the relevant considerations are discussed in Chapter 9.

There are industries and companies where spreading a bonus over three or four years will stabilize income and facilitate sound personal financial planning. This is more likely to be the case in volatile or cyclical industries, the securities business, for example. In most cases, however, "rollover" systems do not provide for any interest accrual on the bonus monies, and that is clearly a disadvantage in periods of galloping inflation when a dollar in hand is intrinsically more valuable than a dollar in the future.

A few companies provide other options in addition to deferral or payout over time. Some have adopted so-called cafeteria systems that allow the executive to choose such tax-favored forms of payout as additional insurance, special perquisites, and the like. In terms of practical application, these add up to a hornet's nest. One corporation spent over $150,000 in computer programs designed to equalize various options. It dropped the system within two years when only one out of eight executives elected anything other than cash. My own view is that there is much wisdom in the old saying, "Take the cash and let the credit go."

The incentive bonus plan is a unique pay device. No other form of compensation tells you so much about the value system and management style of a superior or a top executive team. No other vehicle can be influenced so much by top management's attitude, e.g., the degree of participative management, toughness in distinguishing between personnel, the relative emphasis that is placed on team cooperation, individuality, short-term profit results. Decision time comes with frightening regularity every twelve months. The very existence of the plan multiplies the instances when you have to evaluate the fairness of the decisions others have made about you.

Yet many incentive plans fall far short of their potential because companies that install them lose sight of the fundamental question: compensation for what? If top management fails to establish clear beacons in the form of corporate and division strategies and objectives, if it fails to appraise individual results honestly within such a framework, an incentive bonus can create confusion and generate gamesmanship in the executive ranks.

Base salary programs do not create the same environmental problems. Salary administration can be and usually is more institutionalized, and some companies are just not good candidates for an incentive compensation plan. The company's business may be poorly suited to a bonus system. Or the really important decisions may be confined to a very small group at the top. Or the top management may not have the courage, skill, or personal style to use the award process as a tool for managing the business. Adopting an incentive plan is not a guarantee of superior corporate results. Some early incentive pioneers have prospered; others have survived; still others have disappeared. Some companies have adopted plans for the wrong reasons, often as a knee-jerk response to competitors' actions. There are dozens of reasons for not adopting the device.

All in all, though, assuming good management and a company with exciting prospects, the individual is clearly better off with an incentive plan. Cash compensation will be higher in the final analysis, but more important, a mechanism will be in place for rewarding unusual contributions. Otherwise, one can suffer the fate of Frank Dorian, the $17,500 engineer at Gillette who invented the tandem or "Trac II" razor blade outside the mainstream of Gillette's product research and development. Dorian's concept was so exciting that Gillette dropped the new blade concept then under development and turned the company to the refinement, production, and marketing of Dorian's idea. Unfortunately, Gillette did not have an incentive bonus plan at the time. Asked what reward Mr. Dorian would receive, his boss responded, "He's got a damn good future with this company."[9]

CHAPTER EIGHT

Stock Options: The Great Crap Game

I f Julius Caesar had been able to incorporate, I am sure he would
have used stock in the Roman Empire to reward his key generals
and centurions. As it was, ancient armies had to rely on land
grants and captured Sabine women as incentives for key personnel.
With the growth of the publicly held company came more sophisticated motivational tools, and in the last twenty-five years the most
commonly used has been the stock option.

Executive stock plans emerged with the rise of salaried professional managers. When companies were still largely run by members of the family, there was no need for such plans. After all, "Our
Founder" or "Junior" already owned the company. But through the
century, juniors have died or concerned themselves with less taxing
activities. Corporate ownership has largely passed from private into
public hands and management into those of a new breed of
professionals for hire. Most of the latter started out owning nothing
more than their paychecks, and the way to align their interests more
closely with those of the shareholders was obvious. Give them stock,
stock as incentive, stock as reward. R.H. Macy & Company took
this direct approach in the 1930s by granting stock bonuses. Other
companies, such as Goodyear Tire & Rubber Company, offered
their executives special stock-purchase arrangements. John C.
Baker's classic 1938 study of executive compensation[1] uncovered

eight option arrangements in the 1928 to 1936 period in sampling 100 of the 450 industrial corporations then listed on the New York Stock Exchange.

These earliest executive stock plans share a common premise with their more esoteric modern counterparts: If a substantial portion of an executive's own personal net worth is tied up in company stock, he or she shares the public stockholders' interests on a long-term as well as short-term basis. The need for this closer alignment was perhaps most compelling in the depressed years of the 1930s and 1940s. Paradoxically, however, it was not until 1951, when the weekly index of Standard & Poor's composite of 500 stocks finally climbed back to early 1929 levels, that stock options began to come into broader use. And then the real reason had to do with taxes.

During the Korean War, ordinary income taxes hit peak marginal rates of 92 percent, while the maximum capital gains rate remained at 25 percent. Clearly, any form of compensation that could qualify for capital gains would have a significant appeal to the executive. For those in the top brackets, the difference swung between 75 cents and 8 cents on the dollar. At the same time, such compensation would mean less net cost to the company. In the early 1950s, therefore, a few companies such as Minnesota Mining & Manufacturing (3M) began to develop the option concept. Their experiments were favored by the 1950 tax law, which permitted companies to grant key executives the right to purchase stock in their own companies over a ten-year period. The option could be exercised at 95 percent of the market price at the date of grant, and the stock had to be held only for six months after exercise in order for proceeds from its sale to be taxed at the low capital gains rate.

Today's executive, reeling under the seemingly infinite variety of executive stock plans coming off the compensation drawing boards, may find it hard to recall that this simple type of plan, the restricted stock option, was virtually the only executive stock vehicle used for a decade and a half. Now there are qualified and nonqualified and, for a while, tandem options; there are phantom stock and unit dividend plans, appreciation rights, and performance share plans— and apparently infinite combinations of most of these.

All this is more confusing than it should be. In fact, there are really two broad types of executive stock plans: those under which any income is taxed on a capital gains basis (currently, qualified stock options) and those under which income is subject to ordinary or (since the 1969 Tax Act) earned income tax treatment. The latter plans are commonly called "nonqualified," quite a descriptive term, really, since they don't "qualify" for capital gains tax treatment. There is another basic difference in stock plans. Some are true options in that they involve the right to purchase stock in the future; others are really outright grants of stock or stock equivalents, with the recipient usually taking ownership immediately, albeit subject to certain conditions. Exhibit 10 provides a summary description of each of the stock plans used over the last three decades. It is a long list and many of the additions date to the late 1960s.

Stock Plan Evolution in the 1960s

At first and for many years, executive stock plan design turned on one simple question: to have a plan or not. Most large companies answered yes rather quickly. As early as 1955, for example, a McKinsey survey of executive compensation showed that 47 percent of the nation's leading companies employed some form of stock option plan.

And in what was generally a series of bull markets, options seemed to work. Standard & Poor's stock price index rose steadily starting in 1949, after the five ho-hum years following the end of World War II. From a 1949 close of 16.76, it rose by the end of 1964 to 84.7, rather easily digesting four short downturns. So by the end of 1964 most companies had had ten to fifteen years of steady stock price growth—with accompanying stock option success.

Two characteristics seemed essential to option plan success: favorable capital gains tax treatment and that inherent ability of the option to take a "futures" position, apparently without any real risk, in a rising market situation which presumably would go on forever. But then the market sailed into the doldrums, two key changes in the tax law were adopted, and by 1970 most companies had begun to realize their certainties were illusions.

The new, tougher era for executive stock plans started with the federal income tax overhaul in 1964. This lowered the marginal income tax rate to 70 percent and outlawed the restricted stock option. For the latter, there was substitued a pale shadow called the qualified stock option. Congress spelled out its provisions rather explicitly, mindful of widespread public criticism of windfall option

EXHIBIT 10

Summary description of the major executive stock plans used in U. S. industry.

	PLANS WHICH ENJOY(ED) CAPITAL GAINS TAX TREATMENT		
PLANS	1. Restricted Stock Options	2. Qualified Stock Options	3. Restricted Stock Plans
EXTENT OF USE	The dominant executive stock vehicle in the 1950s and early 1960s; outlawed in the 1964 Revenue Act.	First authorized in 1964 Revenue Act; used by 80 percent of large publicly held companies; still widely used.	Used for several years in the late 1960s. A series of IRS rulings and the Tax Reform Act of 1969 have severely limited its use.
BASIC TYPE OF PLAN	An option to purchase stock at a set price over a period of years.	An option to purchase stock at a set price over a period of future years.	These plans usually take either of two forms: (a) the outright award of the stock through an incentive bonus plan; or (b) executive purchase of the stock, usually at a bargain rate and with financing help.
AWARD PRICE	Market price at date of grant or 95 percent of that price.	Market price at date of grant.	Usually offered at a discount from market.
TERM OF THE AWARD	10 years.	5 years.	Usually 5 years to 10 years.
EXERCISE/VESTING PROVISIONS *(TYPICAL PLAN PROVISIONS)*	Typically only a portion of the stock could be exercised during each of the initial years. Once exercisable though, the stock could be exercised any time during the award period.	Same general approach as the restricted stock option, but limited to a 5-year term.	Stock is "restricted," subject to forfeiture and nontransferable for a period of years. After the initial restrictions, some companies add others —e.g., restricting sale of the stock until, say, a year after retirement.
HOLDING REQUIREMENTS AFTER EXERCISE OF DISTRIBUTION	6 months.	3 years.	
SPECIAL PROVISIONS		By law an option holder cannot exercise a lower-priced qualified option if he still has higher-priced options outstanding.	Under the Tax Reform Act of 1969, gains are subject to ordinary income tax unless recipient declares initial award as income in year of receipt and establishes a gains base for any subsequent capital gains.

PLANS WHICH RECEIVE ORDINARY (OR EARNED) INCOME TAX TREATMENT			
4. Nonqualified* Options	5. Tandem Options†	6. Phantom Stock	7. Performance Share Plan
Rare prior to 1969, but emerging as the most common of the "newer" plans.	Another common "solution" to the new tax environment, effectively outlawed in 1973.	Used by some larger companies in 1970s.	A very new concept used by only a few companies.
An option to purchase stock at a price over a period of years. Market price at date of grant or at a discount from market.	An option the recipient can exercise as either a qualified or nonqualified award. Usually granted at the intial market price.	In its most common version, a simulated option. No real stock is involved. Normally the recipient gets the incremental increase in the stock over the award price and sometimes accrued dividends.	In effect a longer-term incentive award made in common stock equivalents (like phantom stock) but subject to stringent vesting provisions that relate to company or division performance measures.
No fixed rules, typically 10 years.	Qualified: 5 years; nonqualified: no fixed rules, but usually 10 years.	No fixed rules; usually 5 years.	Typically 3 to 5 years.
Usually a fixed percentage exercisable each year—e.g., 10 or 20 percent annually.	Usually the option is fully exercisable by the end of the fifth year, as with a standard option	Appreciation in stock value is automatically paid out (in cash or real stock) in accordance with the term of the plan.	These plans require the executive to remain with the company during the term of the award or forfeit the entire amount. Other vesting requirements relate to company performance—e.g., earnings per share growth.
"Insider rules" may require executive to hold the stock for 6 months.	If executive exercises as a qualified option, 3 years; otherwise 6 months as indicated at left	If real stock is distributed, 6 months as indicated at left.	When vesting conditions are met usually the entire award is valued using current market price, then paid out half in cash and half in actual stock. Additional holding requirements may be imposed on stock distributed.
Plan may permit a company to make a cash award of the difference between the award and exercise price, thus avoiding any withholding or financing problems.	Most commonly a single award is granted that functions as a qualified award for 5 years and then turns into a nonqualified option.		The basic performance share unit does not have to relate to market price, although this is the most common approach. Other techniques include book value, a fixed EPS multiple.

* Also unqualified.   † A combination of qualified and nonqualified awards.

gains. Several aspects of the change evoked grumbling in executive suites: the elimination of market price discounts, for example, and stringent mandatory holding provisions (three years versus six months to qualify for capital gains). But qualified option gains still received the magic capital gains tax break, and because the stock market had resumed strong growth, the most serious constraining provision was masked. Not until the market softened did the new provision that the qualified option could run for only five years emerge as a serious problem.

At the outset, however, faced with limited evidence of flaws and no real alternatives, most companies quickly shifted to the new qualified option plans, casting only an occasional wistful glance backward. By 1969, five years after the 1964 law went into effect, 93 percent of the companies polled in the annual McKinsey Top Executive Compensation Survey were relying on qualified options as their only executive stock plan. They had simply shifted from one standardized tax-favored plan to another. More tax reform and a suddenly disastrous stock market showed up the weakness of that simplicity.

In December 1969, after protracted study, debate, and delay, Congress responded to the need to cool an overheated war economy. The Tax Reform Act of 1969 proved more effective in changing certain fundamental tax concepts than in raising additional revenue, but change for its own sake was in the air in the late 1960s. The 1969 law took a swipe at tax shelters, increased the capital gains tax, introduced the concept of preference income, and, although the plan was only indirectly mentioned in the legislation, it fundamentally changed the economics of the qualified stock option. By lowering the tax rate on earned income and increasing the capital gains tax, Congress effectively narrowed to a bare fifteen percentage points the spread between the tax on stock option gains and the tax on other income. Moreover, the interaction of the preference tax, the earned income provision, and the higher capital gains rate meant that the larger the capital gain, the higher the executive's total effective tax liability—as Exhibit 11 demonstrates.

At about the same time, the *risks* inherent in the qualified stock option became painfully obvious in a few well-publicized cases. Stuart Saunders, former chief executive of the Penn Central, was just one of those caught between the proverbial rock and a hard place. Saunders had exercised options on approximately 45,000

EXHIBIT 11

Total effective tax liability on large capital gains.

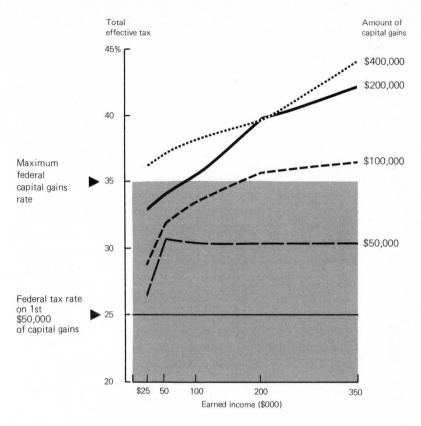

SOURCE: "Look at What's Happening to Capital Gains", *Fortune,* August, 1972.

Penn Central shares during 1966 and 1967, when Penn Central's stock ranged between $42 and $60, roughly double his option price. The stock spurted as high as $86 in 1968, yielding him nearly $3 million in paper profit. Then Penn Central's problem unfolded, and the stock began its plunge. When the price finally reached $6, Saunders had a potential loss of more than $600,000.[2] The market decline that began in 1969 brought these risks home to many other executives as well.

To add insult to injury, the prime rate began a climb to heights never imagined, sharply increasing the carrying cost of qualified stock options during a time of increased uncertainty about the economy. The senior vice president of one major corporation, a friend whose case is not atypical, exercised options on 20,000 shares in late fall of 1967, anticipating net annual carrying costs of $2,750 on his $190,000 loan after netting out dividends and the tax deduction for interest on the loan. By 1969, however, with a completely unanticipated suspension of dividends and a staggering increase in the prime rate, the net out-of-pocket annual burden had ballooned to $8,550, over three times the anticipated amount. In two years his paper profit had shrunk from $150,000 to less than $60,000. My friend finally sold out in late 1969, forgoing any capital gains. When he heard the story, the company's chief executive officer nevertheless turned down a remedial option financing plan—on the ground that a prime rate of $8\frac{1}{2}$ percent just had to be a onetime phenomenon.

At the time most corporate executives and compensation planners began to hear of such disappointments, a few innovative companies had already hit upon a new device called the restricted stock bonus. The first plans were adopted in the mid-1960s, only to be emasculated by the IRS in June 1969. While it lasted, the restricted stock plan was an unusually attractive pay device. Under the most common version, the company granted key executives an incentive bonus in shares of "restricted" common stock, usually at an attractive discount from the market. When the "restrictions" were lifted, any gain was taxed on a capital gains basis. In some cases, corporations devised means of deferring the executive's tax liability far into the future by using a sequential series of restrictions. The stock might be subject to forfeiture for five years, for example, then another restriction activated to prevent sale until two years after retirement. The plan bypassed the financing problem of the option, while permitting the recipient to collect dividends during the period while the stock was subject to forfeiture.

Just as the restricted bonus began to get wide publicity, the government started issuing regulations to diminish its appeal. In late 1968 it was announced that plans adopted after July 1, 1969, would not qualify for capital gains treatment; executives would probably be taxed at the time of receipt rather than when restrictions lapsed. Many rushed to get under the wire before June 30. A few companies granted extraordinary awards at that time. But like any compensation arrangement whose primary motive is to reduce taxes, many of these eleventh-hour restricted stock plans went sour for the recipients. One giant oil company, for example, encouraged its top executives to take a portion of their 1969 bonuses—which would have normally been paid in early 1970—in special restricted stock awards. In addition to offering the lure of one last award under favorable tax rules, the company sweetened the pot by increasing the award by 35 percent. For example, the executive with a normal $20,000 bonus got $27,000 worth of restricted stock. By mid-1970, however, the stock price had dropped by more than 60 percent, and the $20,000 bonus was worth about $11,000.

With the further crippling of the qualified stock option and the emasculation of the restricted stock bonus, business entered the 1970s in a quandary about which direction to take in the executive stock area. The financial press predicted a shift back to cash. While that happened to some extent (see Chapter 7), the near avalanche of esoteric new stock plans, unique in the annals of corporate pay programs, was spectacular.

Developments since 1970

Pacesetting, growth-oriented companies provided the first clues of what was to come. In March 1970, stock-plan innovator ITT unveiled a triple-threat package consisting of a qualified stock option, a new unqualified option, plus something called a "stock unit plan." The last was actually a form of deferred phantom stock award. One month later Ford Motor, another compensation pioneer, asked its shareholders to approve a new twin-element plan consisting of qualified and nonqualified options.

The nonqualified, or "unqualified," option is central to the ITT and Ford programs, and evidence suggests that more and more executives are going to be rewarded with this type of device. It has several advantages over qualified plans, even though it is not eligible for capital gains treatment. With a nonqualified plan, the company has virtually unlimited flexibility in tailoring the plan to fit its motivational needs. The stock can be offered at a discount from market, the option can run for ten or even fifteen years, and so on. Moreover, recipients do not have to worry about long-term financing. After six months they can sell a portion of the stock to repay loans taken out to finance the options. The recipients are liable for the tax at exercise, of course; under Revenue Ruling 67-257, this has to be withheld. But some companies overcome even this problem by "loaning" the executive the amount of the tax during the six-month holding period.

The standard nonqualified plan does not begin to exhaust the range of possibilities for equity incentives. Several imaginative companies developed so-called tandem arrangements, under which the traditional qualified option could be either exercised or, after five years, converted into an equal number of units of nonqualified stock, which were then available for another five years. The theory was that if the stock price soared the qualified plan's tax advantage could still be very valuable. In 1970 and 1971, many companies assumed that the stock market would soon renew its long, sustained climb. The validity of the assumption became moot in January 1973 when, with Revenue Ruling 73-26, the IRS pulled the rug out from under the tandem concept.

Another imaginative stock technique was the so-called phantom stock plan, actually the refinement of a plan quietly initiated years ago by the Campbell Soup Company. Most phantom plans in effect simulate options on paper. The executive is awarded a certain number of "share equivalents," usually at market price. No actual stock is involved at this point. In time, say five years later, the individual is paid the difference between the award price and the going market price, provided that vesting conditions have been met. The final payment can be in either cash or stock. An arrangement Supermarkets General set up for its three senior officers illustrates the phantom concept.[3] The chairman, vice chairman, and president were each awarded 4,000 stock equivalents at a base price of $39.32. The company undertook to pay them "the aggregate appreciation" on these shares over a period of not more than five years. In this deal, unlike some phantom arrangements, the executive had some choice on when to realize the gain. The initial 2,000 phantom units could be "exercised" after three years, for example.

A few companies combined qualified options with a form of phantom stock. Richardson-Merrell adopted a plan under which contingent stock units were awarded simultaneously with qualified stock options on a one-for-one basis. These phantom units had the same base price as the qualified option shares but they increased in proportion to dividends, so the executives had a double shot at profiting from their options. If they exercised the qualified options, the phantom units canceled. On the other hand, if they didn't exercise the options, they got the difference between the aggregate initial award value and the average actual price at the end of the agreement. Thus an executive getting a 5,000-share option at $40 in 1968 would receive another 5,000 phantom units at the same price. Assuming the stock is worth $60 a share five years later, and that dividends entitled him to another 640 phantom shares at an average price of $50, by the fifth year the executive has the choice of exercising the qualified option, on which he has a $100,000 paper profit, or keeping the phantom shares, for a gain of $106,400.

One of the most esoteric variations of the nonqualified option is the variable price or "yo-yo" option. The yo-yo option fixes the option neither at market price nor at a set discount. Instead the option price *decreases* as the market price *increases*, thereby multiplying the impact of stock price change. Among the companies that adopted some form of the variable price option was 3M. In May 1971, it modified its qualified stock option plan to permit nonqualified awards with a "stock appreciation incentive" feature. Under the 3M plan, the "credits" that lowered the exercise price were automatically canceled if the recipient did not buy the stock under the normal exercise schedule. Other variations include Kaufman & Broad's "merit options," under which the exercise price drops 20 percent per year after a 2½-year waiting period, down to a par value of $1.

Other companies stayed faithful to qualified options in the early 1970s, perhaps encouraged by expert advice.[4] Too, many stock prices seemed abnormally low in this period. Some companies saw in the market downturn an attractive opportunity to grant new rounds of qualified awards, thereby positioning their key people for the "inevitable" market upturn. In April 1971, for example, LTV's new board chairman, Paul Thayer, received 200,000 option shares at $12.62 a share, only $5 above the stock's low for that year and well below the LTV high of $169 in 1967.

Other companies like Burroughs went even further, permitting executives to cancel outstanding options that were "under water," or below current market prices. One large West Coast electronics company, whose stock was trading at $24 a share, permitted an executive to cancel qualified options priced higher than $40 a share. Some 75 percent of the stock freed in this transaction (more than 100,000 shares) was used later in the year to grant new qualified awards at the current lower price. Legally, the executive still had to wait for the five-year term to elapse on the original options. But at least the new stock options were likely to be worth something by 1975.

While most companies were still driving down the option road, experimenting with ways to turn 1970-model options into something as rewarding as the sleek pre-1964 versions, a few were looking for more revolutionary vehicles. Some even abandoned the option concept, with its ultimate returns inextricably tied to market price. In its place they instituted something called a performance share plan. The gimmicky nonqualified and phantom arrangements were designed primarily to beat the tax collector. The new plans returned to one of the very first principles of executive stock plans: motivating the executive to better performance on behalf of the company. Under the performance share concept, the executive is granted a certain number of common stock share equivalents, all or a portion of which will ultimately be paid in a combination of cash and real stock. But that ultimate payout depends heavily on company performance results. Most plans set a high earnings-per-share requirement: 10 percent compound growth during the three-to-six-year term of the award. The executive who leaves during this period usually forfeits the entire amount. This contrasts with most option situations under which the executive can exercise at least a portion of an award and then leave the next day.

The performance share plan was pioneered by such companies as PepsiCo, CBS, Chubb & Sons, and J.C. Penney. Since one of the fundamental design concepts of this plan is to tailor provisions to specific profit and growth goals, as well as to the overall compensation system of a company, the details vary quite widely. The Chubb plan generates "growth segment awards" from an overall incentive formula each year. Under the pro forma example shown stockholders in the proxy material, 7,376 units, or $396,512, would have been available in 1970.[5] Other plans set aside a stated number of shares for the entire term of the plan. The five-year plan CBS adopted in 1971 authorized 750,000 performance share units, worth slightly over $30 million.[6]

A performance share plan can provide a substantial capital accumulation opportunity for the executive. Over ten years, a participant in a representative plan might realize pretax gains between $45,000 and $1.7 million, depending on the corporation's performance against a 10 percent EPS target and the individual's position and cash compensation. See Table 8–1.

Table 8-1. Potential Value of Ten-Year Total Payouts under a Representative Performance Share Plan
(Unit: $000)

Participant	1974 salary	Award as multiple of salary	Total pretax payout over ten years assuming annual EPS growth of			
			10%	9%	8%	7%
Chief executive	$145	1.5x	$1,755	$1,290	$840	$410
Group vice president	90	1.2x	770	565	365	180
Division manager	40	0.6x	200	145	95	45

NOTE: Numbers are approximations for a representative case and are intended for illustrative purposes only. In practice, payouts depend on several interacting variables, including price-earnings ratio, salary increases, and the individual's performance. Plans vary significantly from company to company.

The cost of a performance share plan to the corporation can be significant. While stock option payout depends wholly on increases in the market price of the stock, payout under performance share plans involves actual full shares from the company treasury. Also, under current accounting practices, the entire value of the payout must be charged to company earnings spread over the term of the plan. On the other hand, the well-designed performance share plan, administered with a demanding performance target, ensures that the participant receives no benefits unless the shareholder also gains through increased earnings. And in most cases the after-tax costs to the company are below 2 to 3 percent of total projected earnings.[7]

Future Developments

Wage and price controls put a temporary stop to further stock plan development in 1971 and a bad bear market kept the damper on after controls were lifted. But there is no evidence at all that companies are quitting the executive stock arena permanently. Almost all the arguments that got stock plans started in the first place are still valid. And as a practical matter, options do not have the same proxy statement visibility that an extra $50,000 or $100,000 in cash would. So the stock option and variations on its theme will be with us for the foreseeable future.

For the latter half of the 1970s, the trend is already clear. We will see a period of experimentation with plans that do *not* qualify for capital gains treatment. The qualified stock option may well persist as a core plan, but more and more it will be supplemented by nonqualified plans—and that is where the action will be. From the company standpoint, the search will be for ways to reduce the risks and inequities that the bad stock market of the early 1970s exposed in the plans of the past. As a case in point, stock plan innovator ITT went back to the drawing board in 1974 to revise radically the phantom stock plan it had developed only four years earlier. Rather than continuing to value its award units in terms of increases in the company's drifting stock price, ITT asked its stockholders to permit valuation in terms of per-share increases in *consolidated book value.* Plan details will continue to evolve this way, with new wrinkles being tried every couple of years or so, and combination plans will become increasingly prevalent.

The new awareness of stockholders will be a greater factor in plan design. More and more stockholders are going to demand a full reckoning on compensation matters, including executive stock plans. It is my judgment that stockholders are also going to insist more on sustained profit results. Both trends augur well for the acceptability of performance share plans.

And from the individual executive's standpoint, all this says he or she is going to need to be considerably more financially sophisticated than even a decade ago. The plans presented executives—the various options under them, the tax complications inherent in wisely balancing income and deductions from company and personal sources—all argue for more understanding of concept and attention to the fine print. More specifically, there are a number of key factors the executive should analyze carefully in order to evaluate any given stock package properly and manage intelligently his or her participation in the range of programs that are available.

The Company Stock Itself

Fortunately for the U.S. economy, most executives are much better at their jobs than at forecasting the price performance of their company's stock. Down-the-line managers especially, but often their superiors as well, regularly show a total lack of realism in assessing the stock of their own companies. Younger people often shift jobs, lured largely by their first stock option opportunity, without carefully assessing the intrinsic and potential value of their prospective employer's shares. Relying on the enthusiastic forecasts of those hiring them, or the performance of the stock over the last few months, they generally overvalue the option element of the pay package being offered. The same myopia afflicts the executive already in place. Otherwise capable people seem to be incurable optimists about the company with which they've cast their lot. Perhaps it's a species of loyalty, the godlike prospect of affecting the profit performance and ultimately the price and even the multiples awarded by the investment community. But the blinders are there.

Some realism is in order. Only the truly exceptional company can sustain high earnings growth over a substantial period of time. The executives of those exceptional companies that do can fare very well, of course, as Table 8–2 shows. Some became millionaires, even during generally depressed market periods.

Rather than being dazzled by the records above, however, the thinking executive is better advised to consider the more normal pattern set forth in Table 8–3: The majority of large companies are simply unable to sustain an earnings per share growth rate greater than 6 to 7 percent a year over a ten-year period.

Obviously, in a special situation or during a bull market, average stock prices can grow more rapidly than 6 to 7 percent a year. The market is likely to anticipate earnings or strengthen overall price-

Table 8-2. Executive Stock Option Gains in Representative High-Performing Companies, 1968–1972
(Unit: $000)

Company	Average 1972 cash compensation of top four executives	EPS growth rate 1962–1972	Stock option gains*		
			Five-year total	Average annual	Percentage of 1972 compensation
Johnson & Johnson	$489.2	20.61	$3,667.5	$733.5	150
Xerox	323.0	29.40	1,954.2	390.8	121
Dow	239.0	11.53	1,326.0	265.3	111
IBM	352.0	17.13	1,936.0	387.0	110
Procter & Gamble	318.0	10.03	1,383.0	277.0	87
Merck	234.0†	16.03	1,006.0	201.0	86
General Mills	207.0	12.41	466.0	93.0	45
Beatrice	256.0	10.10	269.0	54.0	21
Honeywell	211.0	8.94	148.0	29.0	14

*Pretax gain from all executive stock plans, using 1972 average stock prices for each company. Includes both exercised and unexercised stock options.

†Three executives only.

SOURCE: Proxy statements.

Table 8-3. Analysis of "Fortune 500" Companies' EPS Growth* over Successive Ten-Year Periods

EPS growth	Percentage growth in ten-year period ending								
	1965	1966	1967	1968	1969	1970	1971	1972	1973
Upper quartile	9.75	9.58	10.18	13.02	10.85	10.50	11.18	11.79	13.77
Median	5.72	5.71	5.83	7.93	6.48	4.99	5.45	6.93	9.04
Lower quartile	1.23	1.74	1.36	3.29	1.53	(2.04)	(1.99)	2.14	4.35

*Average annual growth rate, compounded. The companies having losses are not included.

SOURCE: *Fortune Double 500 Directory, 1965–1973*, Time, Inc., New York, 1974.

earnings ratios. But over a long period of time, stock prices will follow the earnings record of a company, as definitive studies at the Center for Research in Security Prices at the University of Chicago confirm. The pioneering study of Professors Lorie and Fisher on total stockholder return from 1926 through 1965 found a return rate of 9.3 percent, when both stock price increases and dividends were included.[8] This is a far cry from the returns one is led to expect from the 20 and 30 percent annual earnings improvement in the really outstanding companies. And the fact is there aren't that many key jobs lying around in the outstanding companies. The right job in one of their executive suites is much easier to contemplate than accomplish: As Chapter 2 discussed, those that are established tend to promote from within; it requires rare foresight to identify those that will be the winners of tomorrow. For most executives, therefore, the chance of catching a high flyer at the right time is pretty slim.

Nevertheless, since stock option gains are the primary hope for executives who aspire to substantial capital accumulation, one should get in the game. One sensible way to cut down the odds is to seek out the corporations that have properly designed stock programs, an aspect of a company's "compensation philosophy" that deserves much more attention than it typically receives during employment discussions.

One technique occasionally used by the large established company involves granting options on the stock of subsidiaries. Although such options typically carry repurchase agreements to guard against equity dilution, a small, rapidly growing division can well have more dramatic short-term earnings potential than the stable parent company. One public Wall Street firm uses this technique for its real-estate subsidiary, for example. Several years ago it granted nonqualified options to key personnel, with the provision that subsidiary shares could be converted into parent company stock over ten years on the basis of book value equivalents. Other companies try to protect the recipient from stock market vagaries by granting "unit" awards whose value relates to something other than stock price, e.g., earnings-per-share growth or book value. The performance share plan has this among other virtues to recommend it.

In the final analysis, however, it comes down to the parent company and its stock. You can't make a Xerox out of a U.S. Steel, and there simply isn't enough leverage in option design features, whether discounts, yo-yo options, or stock bonuses, to match what the star company can achieve through sheer performance.

Few executives can afford to change jobs because of stock analysis alone; other more fundamental choices are generally involved. There are instances where a large potential gain is a major factor in a career decision, as when an ailing company appears about to turn around. Undoubtedly, the executive who does have a range of choices should take potential option gains into account in evaluating alternative career moves. My point is simply that a good deal of hard realism in such calculations is in order, particularly for the executive jumping from a stable, known situation to the kinds of ventures where option gain is the principal lure. The ex-IBMers who jumped to Memorex, University Computing, Recognition Equipment, and scores of other peripheral manufacturers and software firms in the 1960s can attest to that. When all the analysis is done, it may still be a crap shoot, but at least the analysis improves the odds.

Beyond the company and the stock itself, three factors bear particular scrutiny by the individual: (1) the size of the award; (2) the time period over which it will take place; and (3) the financing arrangements, if any, that accompany it.

The Amount of Stock

Most executives have very little control over the size of their option grants. Usually there are only one or two key people in an enterprise with enough influence to force serious consideration of new option techniques or to negotiate individual arrangements beyond the company's normal award pattern. This means that the average executive is probably at the mercy of the existing system when it comes to option awards. Most studies show that the "going rate" of an award ranges from one to two times pay at the lower participants' levels, to awards with an initial value of six to eight times pay for senior management.[9]

Awards of this magnitude surely are not going to produce a new generation of "superrich," particularly at the entry levels. The $30,000 executive granted options equivalent to one year's pay will have a pretax paper gain of about $18,300 in five years if the stock grows at 10 percent a year. Even with a rapid price growth of 30 percent, the before-tax gain would amount to about $81,400, good but not spectacular.

The larger the award, the better shot one has at substantive capital accumulation, obviously. Shrewd executives bear this in mind in negotiating those compensation arrangements in which they have the upper hand. When Michael Bergerac was recruited from ITT Europe as the new president of Revlon in 1974, he reportedly got close to $1.5 million in stock—in addition to a five-year contract at $325,000 a year. Bunkie Knudsen's going-in option as president of Ford in 1968 was 75,000 shares, worth over $4 million—a healthy step toward independence, even if it caused a good deal of resentment among career Ford executives. When John Burke resigned from the chairmanship of Howmet in February 1970, he insisted upon a large stock position as he sorted out job offers. He finally settled on becoming president and chief executive officer of Automation Industries. In the bargain, he was permitted to buy 200,000 shares from founder Corwin Denney, and he received a 30,000-share option. Burke remarked, "I think it's a lot more interesting if you have an appreciable interest of your own." True enough. The problem for most of us is getting an interest that's appreciable enough.

The Term of the Plan

Those who remember the golden days of the 1950s and their ten-year options can attest to the impact of time on the value of a stock award. The longer-term option has a distinct advantage that is evident as soon as one compares relative price appreciation for successive five- and ten-year option awards starting in 1954.

In this fact lies another major reason for the new popularity of nonqualified options. Not only can the nonqualified option be set up for extended time periods; there are other timing advantages as well. Nonqualified options can be exercised without reference to any other options the individual may hold, at whatever price. In that this further increases the individual's flexibility, it is a significant advantage in uncertain times. Moreover, with a six-month as opposed to three-year minimum holding time, the executive has much more latitude on when to cash in. An executive who must hold shares for three years almost always misses several opportunities to sell at attractive stock prices. Moreover, he or she risks seeing hard-won holdings materially shrink in value.

The Financing Arrangements

More and more, the net cost of money is a key variable in the option game. Here too there is a wide range in the extent to which companies will help the option recipient with the financing burden. For years the standard practice of blue chip companies was to arrange a loan source at a friendly corporate bank, at something close to the prime rate. The interest was deductible, of course, and dividends on the stock reduced the net out-of-pocket cost to modest levels. The upward spiral in the prime rate, however, has conspired to make this traditional arrangement considerably less satisfactory. For one thing, banks are increasingly reluctant to tie up scarce loan funds for years at low rates, even for favored customers. Thus even old-line companies have begun to look afresh at a formerly taboo approach, direct company financing of options. The Federal Reserve has cooperated, issuing its Regulation G, which sets forth modest repayment requirements in the event of substantial stock price appreciation.

Suppose, for example, that an executive is granted an option at a total price of $100,000. Five years later the value of the shares has increased to $150,000. Not surprisingly, the executive decides to exercise the option. The company provides a loan for the full sum required to take advantage of this grant. Under the Fed's Regulation G, repayment requirements are established by calculating the value of the loan at $52,500 (a 35 percent margin requirement times the value of the option at exercise), then establishing a "deficiency value" of $47,500, i.e., the option price minus the loan value. Over the next three years, the executive is required to repay 60 percent of the deficiency value, or in this case $28,500. Thus the executive's annual repayment for each of the next three years is only $9,500, or one-third of $28,500. The greater the appreciation of the stock, the lower the deficiency value, hence the lower the annual repayment required. Companies also are permitted considerable latitude in setting interest rates; some have granted loans at 4 percent.

Financing is not an issue with the stock bonus or phantom stock, of course. While there are usually strings attached in the form of forfeiture clauses, performance requirements, and the like, this type of stock plan is usually a surer deal than options. The president of one of the ten largest banks in the country, for example, has accumulated 3,500 shares of restricted stock (worth some $232,000 at the award price) under a plan first approved in 1968. As was common under pre-1969 restricted stock plans, the stock must be held until the president retires. Even though the company has the right to repossess the stock at the original price in the event of certain types of termination (thus eliminating any gain), the odds against this eventuality are far more favorable than against a leveraged loan.

As the old saw has it, it's getting harder to make a buck every day. This is certainly true for the salaried executive who aspires to wealth through participation in the executive stock program of a publicly held company. One after another, the IRS has eliminated or crippled the most attractive features of executive stock plans— cutting back capital gains treatment, the restricted stock option, and the restricted stock bonus. Each had a good run; fortunes both modest and immodest were made. In the new stock era of the 1970s some fortunes will be made as well, undoubtedly. We are going to see more venturesome arrangements, regardless of the state of the stock market. In today's environment, however, the stock game increasingly will be a risky game. Outright stock grants, longer-term option awards, more effective financing—all can reduce the risks, and negotiating really sizable awards will almost always make the risks worth while. Picking the right company will continue to be the best hedge of all. But these are increasingly difficult times for the corporate insider. A passion rampant in the land equates disclosure with good, and this clearly constrains the executive's flexibility. Understandably enough, the press has focused a harsh public eye on the political mistakes and public relations gaffes of ITT and the outright fraud of Equity Funding. Stockholder suits are increasing.

In this climate, many executives are asking themselves whether the option game is worth the candle. They can see themselves locked into a situation with exercised stock, writhing while their personal net worth deteriorates. They hear of unanticipated increases in option financing costs, or envision themselves forced to forgo capital gains as the market turns down. There are fewer and fewer guarantees. Finally, the executive who does realize some stock free and clear must worry whether it has been at the cost of committing the deadly investment sin of having too many eggs in one tightly covered basket; for most chief executive officers still view the sale of stock by key company executives as a demonstration of extraordinarily bad judgment.

Withal, until someone changes the rules entirely, today's executives still must expect to accumulate most of their capital through participation in one or more executive stock plans. Doing it right will take wisdom, fortitude, and luck. But for some time to come, the executive stock plan will remain the principal game for those whose talents and ambition can carry them to the top. It's going to be a game with many variations and rule changes in the 1970s. But for many it will be the only game in town.

CHAPTER NINE

Deferred Compensation: Two Plus Two Can Also Equal Three

Back in the late 1950s when William Holden was approached to star in a new David Lean film, he insisted on a percentage of the profits, to be deferred and paid out over time. Many of Hollywood's troubles were already apparent; the era of blockbuster productions and lucrative star contracts had already started to wane. With the help of a prestigious Los Angeles law firm, Holden negotiated a contract with Warner Brothers that would pay him $50,000 a year out of his share of the profits. At the time, the guessing was that this deferred compensation could provide him with a good source of income for at least five years, perhaps even ten. The picture, *The Bridge on the River Kwai*, went on to win three of the top five academy awards and shatter box office records. It has been estimated that Holden will have to live well over a hundred to exhaust his share at $50,000 a year.

Few deferred compensation arrangements in business are as exotic or lucrative as the Holden plan. But the concept of deferring income has long had great appeal for those with large current incomes or those fortunate enough to come upon sudden windfalls of cash. The basic concept is quite simple. An executive in a high tax bracket defers receipt of a portion of his or her earnings until a period when, it is expected, income and therefore the applicable tax rate will be considerably lower. For most people, this means deferral to retirement. Our tax laws permit this, of course; no one is taxed on income until he or she has "constructive receipt." If both employer and employee are willing, therefore, flexible timing in the receipt of compensation offers significant potential advantages. From this basic idea, deferred compensation has grown to become the third most prevalent special executive pay device, after stock options and bonus plans.

Prior to 1964, when the marginal federal income tax rate could go as high as 92 percent, the motive for deferring income was both obvious and compelling. One could often "halve" the tax bite, at least on paper, by postponing effective receipt of income until after retirement. In theory at least, the same effect could be achieved if the company simply increased the size of the executive's pension. But the long arm of the tax law precludes that straightforward approach. Pension and profit-sharing plans cover broad groups of employees and by law must not discriminate in favor of executives. Raising pensions for the top management group would therefore require a commensurate increase across the board, a costly proposition indeed.

Increased executive mobility has also spurred the popularity of deferral schemes, particularly at the CEO level. When a top executive is recruited by another firm, he or she is often forced to sacrifice substantial accrued pension credits with little likelihood of recouping. Under such circumstances, a deferral scheme with the new employer is indispensable to the executive's future financial security. Moreover, since the executive usually negotiates his or her new salary at a level significantly above current needs—thereby making Uncle Sam the largest potential beneficiary—some deferral provision is frequently built into the package. For example, when Floyd Hall left TWA in 1963 to pull Eastern Air Lines up by its bootstraps, he negotiated a 15-year employment contract. It included a base salary of $80,000, annual retirement income of $25,000 a year, and a retirement consulting fee of $40,000 a year for twelve years after retirement.[1] In fact, Eastern offered deferred-compensation contracts to lure close to a dozen experienced professionals from other airlines during the early 1960s.

The mushrooming popularity of incentive bonus plans in the 1950s had the side effect of extending the deferral concept down below the top two or three executives. Many companies followed the lead of General Motors and rolled out their cash incentive awards over a period of years, or even mandated that a portion of the bonus be deferred until retirement to "lock in" key personnel. Other companies saw bonus deferral as a way to build the executive's net worth. Du Pont was one of the first to hit upon the idea of paying part of the bonus in deferred stock equivalents, a conceptual forerunner of today's phantom stock plans.

The whole idea of deferred compensation was thus well attuned to the corporate values of the times. During the period following World War II, American industry was obsessed with the idea of holding onto key executives. Withholding current income seemed a powerful retention tool, since the accrued amount was subject to forfeit if the key executive left to join a competitor. In the classic case of Bunkie Knudsen's shift from General Motors to Ford, he had to walk away from about $1 million in deferred compensation and other pay "futures."

Many of the factors that made deferred compensation such a sensible device in the 1950s and 1960s have changed. Yet American business is responding only slowly to the new situation. In fact, the use of deferred compensation is almost as prevalent today as it was ten years ago. Approximately one out of five of the largest companies in the country uses deferred compensation for one or more of its top officers; and, as Table 9-1 shows, the device is still quite common in industries characterized by high mobility in the officer ranks.

Ironically, deferral arrangements are even more prevalent in smaller companies, despite their much lower compensation levels. A 1972 McKinsey survey of 795 companies with average sales of $76 million showed that 46 percent deferred some CEO pay, even though the average cash compensation of the presidents was only $84,000.[2]

Of course, "deferred compensation" is a broad term covering a multitude of plans that serve a variety of motives and circumstances. Some schemes apply to the entire executive group, some are negotiated individually. Some provide cash payments, others pay out in stock, and some combine the two. Some plans provide fixed-sum payments over specified periods of time; others link the amount of payout to years of service or to the corporation's performance. Most progressive plans now stipulate that the compensation deferred be invested on behalf of the executive, so that it

Table 9-1. Industries with a High Prevalence of Deferred Compensation Plans

Industry	Percentage of major companies with deferral arrangements
Air transportation	58
Textiles	47
Apparel	40
Retail trade	32
Utilities: electric and gas	29
Retail food chains	25

SOURCE: 1974 McKinsey Top Executive Compensation Survey, McKinsey & Company, Inc., New York.

earns interest during the term of the deferral. Investment "vehicles" can vary widely. Often the terms of the deferral agreement are set forth in an employment contract negotiated during a recruitment negotiation. Many such contracts include clauses that void the corporation's obligation to pay if the executive later goes to work for a competitor or starts a competing business. And some require that the executive provide consulting services following retirement.

Take the example of Seymour Rosenberg. He signed an agreement with Mattel in May of 1972, shortly before he resigned as the company's executive vice president for finance and administration. It guaranteed him $60,000 a year for twenty years, in exchange for which he agreed to "provide consulting services during this period." He also agreed to refrain from working for competitors through 1975.[3] Obviously the contract involved some risk on Rosenberg's part. Mattel could go bankrupt, for example. But events to date proved it was a lot less risky than the stock option that Mr. Rosenberg traded for the deferred-income guarantee. Mattel estimated that these options—40,000 shares exercisable at $6.34 a share—had a value of about $750,000 when he signed the new agreement in 1972. Twelve months later, Mattel stock had dropped to $4.50 and the option shares were worth half a million dollars less.

Some form of guaranteed future income or minimal employment term is only prudent in certain situations, such as when a company is trying for a turnaround or has record top-level changes. Since 1969, for example, troubled MGM has had three presidents. Two of them, Robert O'Brien and Louis Polk, were still collecting under the deferred portion of their contracts when James Aubrey was brought in to try his hand.[4]

Weighing the Inherent Risks

Clearly, the Mattel and MGM type of negotiated compensation can be advantageous for the individual. But how advantageous are the more traditional deferral schemes generally available to executives? In weighing their value, one must remember that the amount being deferred has been or is being earned *currently*. The only justification for taking payment in the *future* is if the compensation will be *worth more* to the individual then. Whether it actually is or not depends on the circumstances, of course, as with any special pay plan. More often than not, however, these plans add up to a risky and relatively unattractive form of *investment*, rather than compensation.

Deferred compensation is risky, first, because it involves a fixed commitment of a portion of earnings, with no guarantee that the tax assumptions motivating the deferral will be valid in the payout years. The fact is the government has already made one serious effort to impose a type of retroactive tax on deferred compensation when it is paid out. Early drafts of the Tax Reform Act of 1969 contained provisions which, in essence, would have taxed deferred income at the rates applicable when the money was earned.

Moreover, in most cases the IRS doesn't view deferred compensation as "earned" income at all, which means that it probably will be subject to a maximum 70 percent rate instead of the earned income rates, which have a 50 percent maximum. In practice, the retired executive's annual taxable income rarely puts him in the 70 percent bracket; but theoretically, deferred compensation can be taxed at a higher rate than current compensation.

Even if the current tax rules on deferred compensation don't change, some relevant provisions in the tax code almost certainly will. Who can predict the tax bite five, ten, or fifteen years from now? Federal tax rates on ordinary income have dropped since 1964, but this trend could be reversed. Or there could be a special surtax in effect at the time of payout. Finally, state income tax rates obviously have not peaked as yet.

There are other forms of risk, too. Any compensation that is deferred is only a general obligation of the corporation, in essence a bookkeeping entry. Most companies use the deferred funds in the normal course of doing business. In the event of a bankruptcy, these deferred compensation "commitments" can evaporate or be cut back by court trustees. If this seems a remote risk in a large corporation, remember that it did happen to a group of Penn Central executives. And there is the United Mine Workers case. The union had established special unqualified retirement benefits for several of the top officers, essentially a deferral scheme. When W. A. (Tony) Boyle lost a government-mandated special election in January 1973, the new UMW hierarchy eliminated a $34,000-a-year payment that Boyle was accruing and later canceled a $2 million fund set up for the three top officers. In short, the old adage that "a bird in the hand is worth two in the bush" often applies in a deferral decision.

Benefits illustrate this too. Most life insurance and retirement benefit plans are geared to cash compensation. Therefore, a decision to defer can very easily reduce the value of one or more of these benefits. If the group life insurance policy provides coverage at three times current pay, a $20,000 deferral can reduce the coverage by $60,000. Companies do have considerable flexibility in developing life insurance schedules and this coverage need not be lost, but it often is. The more serious problems come with pension, profit-sharing, and savings plans, in which the amount of retirement accrual or annual contribution is also normally related by formula to current compensation. Take the case of a chief executive invited to choose between a pay package of $150,000 in salary and one composed of $100,000 in salary and a deferred accrual of $50,000. By choosing the latter, and deferring $50,000 a year for ten years, the person would reduce the annual pension by as much as 55 percent.[5] Ten years ago, when pension maximums were fixed and companies rarely included bonuses in the pension calculation, this wasn't an issue. Now it is an obvious one. Yet some companies have been slow to adjust deferral ground rules.

Finally, there is the risk of lost investment income. Too few executives recognize that a deferral decision is really an investment decision, rather than a compensation or tax decision. It should be obvious that $10,000 paid ten years from now is worth less than $10,000 paid today; one loses the interest that could be realized during those intervening years, and inflation continues to erode the

Table 9-2. Value of $10,000 Current Income Deferred for Ten Years

Assumed earnings rate (%)	No inflation	At 3.7 percent inflation rate*	At 7 percent inflation rate
5	$6,140	$4,267	$3,119
7	5,080	3,531	2,581
9	4,220	2,933	2,144

*Average annual cost-of-living increase, 1964–73.

purchasing power of the dollars ultimately paid out. Table 9–2 illustrates this.

In spite of the obvious conclusion that emerges from these figures, many individual deferral schemes in effect today still do nothing to provide an "investment gain." In fact, it is not at all unusual for an individual deferral contract to require proportional reductions if the executive leaves the company prior to the end of an employment contract. Most *group* deferral schemes, particularly those tied to bonus plans, have some modest provision for interest, but one can still encounter plans where this is not the case. Several years ago, the chief executive officer of a drug supply company in the East asked me to discuss compensation terms with the president of a small company it was acquiring for $3 million stock. This gentleman, who was to stay on for five years, was interested in deferred compensation. I mentioned some alternatives, including one which involved a $25,000-a-year deferral that would appreciate in relationship to his division's earnings. The approach appealed to him, but when I reported it to the chief executive officer the next day I met with dead silence. For six years his company had been deferring the bonuses of top executives without any provision for investment buildup.

Actually it doesn't cost a company anything to credit gains each year so long as the rate of gain doesn't exceed the cost of capital to the company. Deferred payment obligations are a form of debt like bank loans or bonds, in that they represent future obligations of the company. There is no tax advantage to either the company or the individual in segregating the money in a special fund.

The growing awareness that deferred compensation is really an investment decision has spawned an almost bewildering assortment of new deferral plans. To guarantee an investment gain, some companies have used a variety of theoretically stable outside investment yardsticks. One bank uses the rates paid on AA corporate bonds. Many companies use the prime rate, although this has hardly been very stable recently. Some companies fix a rate, usually between 4 and 6 percent. The more venturesome, seizing the chance to add yet another incentive element to their compensation packages, use some measure of company performance. One major oil company uses return on stockholders' equity; a diversified Midwest manufacturer uses profit-center return on investment; a large food company uses annual EPS growth. To my knowledge, rather few companies have used broader industry stock indexes, and those that have often regretted it. In a deferred compensation scheme adopted by one mutual fund management company in 1968, investment appreciation was pegged to the composite return of its three largest funds. The company abandoned this concept in 1971 after the deferred fund had shrunk to about 60 percent of its original value.

Analyzing the Economics of Deferral

Fortunately, one can analyze all the variables affecting the economic wisdom (or folly) of a deferred compensation investment decision. Like any investment decision, of course, the results of this one are only as good as the underlying assumptions. Those that need to be forecast carefully are:

- What is the individual's marginal tax rate at the time of the deferral decision? In other words, how much would he or she have to pay in taxes if the entire amount due were paid immediately in cash?
- What could the recipient earn, net after taxes, on those funds during the time the income is being deferred? What is the rate of appreciation expected over this period?
- Finally, what is likely to be the individual's marginal tax rate during the period of payout?

Exhibit 12 illustrates the interrelation of these factors in schematic form and shows how the results vary when one of the assumptions changes.

A careful analysis of these calculations suggests a series of guidelines. First and most important is the differential between the current and future tax rates. In the case shown in the exhibit, for each $1,000 deferred every 10 percent increase in tax spread adds

EXHIBIT 12

Relative impact of various factors on the return from deferred compensation.

FACTOR TO BE VARIED	Marginal tax rate at deferral	Rate of deferred fund appreciation	Years between deferral and payout	Marginal tax rate at payout	Net after-tax opportunity cost to employee	Net value of deferred cash options
	%	%		%	%	$
Base case: $1,000 deferred	50	10	10	30	10	523
Marginal tax rate at deferral	**30**	10	10	30	10	0
	60	10	10	30	10	783
	70	10	10	30	10	1,042
Rate of deferred fund appreciation	50	**7**	10	30	10	80
	50	**11**	10	30	10	690
	50	**15**	10	30	10	1,534
Years between deferral and payout	50	10	**5**	30	10	322
	50	10	**15**	30	10	838
	50	10	**20**	30	10	1,346
Marginal tax rate at payout	50	10	10	**40**	10	263
	50	10	10	**50**	10	3
	50	10	10	**60**	10	(257)
Net after-tax opportunity cost to employee	50	10	10	30	**7**	838
	50	10	10	30	**12**	268
	50	10	10	30	**16**	(385)

about $260 to the return. In my judgment, no one should participate in a deferral scheme unless there is apt to be at least a thirty-point difference between his current and future tax rates. Theoretically, a lower differential still makes economic sense if the deferred amount appreciates rapidly; but in most cases the risks outweigh the potential gain. To put it another way, deferred compensation is a very dubious proposition if you are not in at least the 60 percent tax bracket (combined federal and state). Moreover, anyone who is still moving up through an organization and whose compensation is therefore likely to increase would be foolish to defer current income. People in this situation find it particularly difficult to forecast accurate postretirement income; they simply can't predict how high advancement and inflation will push their salaries.

On the investment return side, the "spread" is again the key. The wisdom of deferral turns on the difference between potential after-tax income from independent investment and potential after-tax income from money left with the company. Suppose one takes $10,000 now, pays the income tax due, and invests the remainder in tax-free municipal bonds paying 5 percent. If one is in the 50 percent tax bracket, the proceeds at the end of ten years will be $8,144.45. On the other hand, if one defers the $10,000 for ten years, and assumes a 30 percent applicable tax rate at time of payout, one would have to earn slightly more than 1.5 percent compounded on the deferred funds to achieve the same results. If the company doesn't pay that level of interest or higher, it is clearly better to take the money as soon as it is available.

One aspect of the deferral mathematics subject to real argument is the ideal deferral period. The longer the deferral period, the greater the *apparent* potential advantage of the deferral decision. Obviously the compounded effects of the initial tax advantage will be greater over twenty years than ten. To my mind, however, there are real questions as to whether one should make a locked-in investment of this type for more than ten years. The risks discussed earlier obviously multiply over time, and other unknowns can arise. Personally, therefore, I get increasingly uncomfortable as the deferral period stretches out beyond five years. Actually, deferred compensation makes the most sense for executives in the fifty-five to sixty age bracket, who can see ahead clearly to a retirement period. Their children are probably educated; more likely than not, they are committed to their current employer; and they can forecast their pension and other retirement income fairly accurately. Even these executives need to do some careful calculating to make sure a deferral doesn't cost them more in company benefits than they save in taxes. The whole interrelation of deferral payout and other retirement income should be balanced carefully.

Such executives and, even more, their younger brothers and sisters should remember that certain tax shelter investments provide an altogether different alternative for the salaried executive with a surplus of current cash and a high tax burden. Accepting a company's deferred compensation scheme without considering alternative investment options is just plain silly.

On the whole, then, the great popularity of deferred compensation is harder and harder to understand in today's environment. As my associate George Foote wisely observed, "Few compensation devices have been more enthusiastically received and more widely overrated."[6] As a general rule of thumb, if a company's deferral scheme has not been thoroughly analyzed within the last few years, the odds are that it is marginally attractive at best.

Be that as it may, deferral schemes are likely to be with us for some time, since the concept involves some legitimate tax advantages and fits well with every company's desire to retain key executives. In some cases, deferred compensation is of tangible value to the individual and he or she is fortunate to have the option. But the accent should be on "option," since the value of deferral depends heavily on the individual's personal circumstances. A few innovative companies, recognizing this, are thinking in more flexible and individual terms in designing executive compensation packages. They focus on the value to the company of a given position, conceiving it in terms of net worth—say $250,000 to $1,000,000 in ten years, depending on performance. Having determined this, they then design the most cost-effective total package from the standpoint of the company *and* the individual.

While a few companies are beginning to plan along such lines, however, most still offer a hodgepodge of plans and provisions set up at different times for different purposes. The burden of planning and choice thus falls on the individual, where some would argue that it should remain. In any event, for the foreseeable future the individual executive will have to choose from a smorgasbord of compensation methods, some of which are classic but dull. Deferred compensation is likely to be one option, but not necessarily one of the most attractive.

CHAPTER TEN

Perquisites: From the Company Car to the Executive Sauna

Over the years, *Playboy* has unveiled many a bare bosom and beautiful backside. When its parent corporation, Playboy Enterprises, first sold a small slice of its stock to the general public in 1971, the prospectus in turn revealed some of Playboy's own secrets, including the pay of Playboy prototype Hugh Hefner. It seems that the founder, chairman, and president of the bunny empire was generously rewarded indeed: a yearly salary or "direct remuneration" of $303,847 plus $806,151 in annual dividends from his 71.7 percent of Playboy Enterprises stock.[1] Mr. Hefner's compensation didn't end with cash. For $650 a month he leased a "portion" of the fifty-four-room Playboy Mansion in Chicago, which had cost $1.49 million with improvements. The company provided Hefner and other Playboy executives with a sleek $5.8 million DC-9 airplane staffed with "jet bunnies." More recently, a twenty-nine-room mansion was acquired in Los Angeles. According to Playboy Enterprises, these corporate expenditures establish public recognition of "its role in promoting a particular style of urban living."

Subsidized executive housing, the company jet, and, I guess, bunnies are called perquisites in compensation parlance. I doubt there's a business in this country that doesn't provide its owners or key executives with some perquisites. From General Motors to Sam's Delicatessen, the perks that go with the job range from a personal Cadillac to free sandwiches. Many perks have considerable monetary value—cars, club memberships, travel privileges. Others have more psychological than material worth: large corner offices, plush carpets and other luxurious furnishings, executive washrooms, and the like.

As an eclectic observer of the perks scene over the years, I have often noted an inverse correlation between the company performance and the generosity and range of the perk package. Most very successful companies are perk-lean, and those that are offered are clearly tied to business requirements rather than personal status trips or competitive practices. In fact, many profit-minded CEOs have a bias against perks, convinced that they foster a hedonistic environment and aren't performance-based. Nevertheless, perks abound.

The old compensation drive wheel of taxes is one reason, of course.[2] Properly designed perks do offer a way to add to an executive's rewards without adding to his or her taxes. But I suspect humankind's innate fascination with the pecking order is even more of a factor. Most perks are, after all, highly visible manifestations of status; their allocation often defines the hierarchical nature of an organization more pointedly than direct money rewards. Eligibility for a given perk is invariably tied to salary or position level; gradations in the value of perquisites correspond to successive levels in the organization. Corporate executives take it all very seriously, naturally, but it's a shame to forgo the entertainment value. Take the company car program, for example: the sales force drives Fords or Chevys; vice presidents drive Pontiacs or Buicks; Cadillacs and Lincolns are reserved for the top management group; the chairman drives a Mercedes. Company drivers and parking space locations can provide further important distinctions. At one company in Minneapolis, indoor versus outdoor parking is considered the swing perk. No wonder. The weather gets so cold in the winter that the outdoor parking lots have to be equipped with electrical starting posts. A delegation of junior officers once made a half-serious proposal to take salary cuts if the company would construct additional indoor parking.

Careful planning has introduced the tiering concept into other benefit areas as well. Executive physical examinations provide just one example. The senior executives of a large East Coast manufacturing company are sent to the Mayo Clinic for physicals every year; the bulk of the officers go to Executive Health Examiners; and junior managers are examined by the company's own medical staff. Health and age, which might seem logical factors to take into account, do not enter into the picture at all.

Some perquisites are byproducts of the industry that offers them: free travel in the airline industry, merchandise discounts in retailing, special car benefits in the automotive industry. These can be a real element in the compensation package, particularly at the upper levels. Most airlines, for example, give their board members and officers unlimited free personal travel privileges on their own routes on a reserved-seat basis. The levels below officers are likely to be restricted in the number of trips a year and further by rules that relate to seniority. They fly "space available" and pay a small service charge.

The ultimate form of perk, those in the "rank has its privileges" category, is likely never to show up in the rulebook at all. These are the privileges of the very top group and are governed by chief executive officer philosophy, gentlemen's agreement, and precedent. The category includes the use of company airplanes, company reimbursement of spouse travel, control of expenses in the gray area of business entertainment, and the use of company personnel to perform personal services. The *Wall Street Journal* recently described a running battle between a company president and his legal advisers over two employees on the company payroll. One was the president's full-time horse trainer; the other was the gardener on his estate. Fortunately for shareholders, this sort of thing is rare.

Good Reasons and Sound Value

Despite occasional glaring abuses, most perquisites have a very sound business rationale behind them. The executive dining room is valuable for outside visitors and facilitates executive communication. The company physical helps protect valuable executives. The company car can save executive time. It would be naive to deny that the perk is also a major way of paying a person on a tax-free basis. If the company can provide $20,000 worth of perks to a top executive in the 50 percent pay bracket without creating any imputed income, that is the equivalent of $40,000 or more of additional salary. And it generally does cost the company less to provide a perk than to increase cash rewards, so long as the perk involves legitimate business deductions. The corporation, with a tax rate of 52 percent, incurs an earnings charge of only $9,600 for the $20,000 package, meaning it can usually provide perks for less than their "retail value."

The Internal Revenue Service has an obvious interest in ensuring that these special benefits and perks are in fact legitimate business expenses and not tax dodges. Over the years, an elaborate body of precedent and regulations has built up in this area, although it is continually changing with specific new rulings and court cases. For example, IRS regulations permit a company to deduct the cost of entertaining business associates at "quiet business meals." In one of a seemingly endless stream of "clarifications" as to which places are appropriate for a quiet meal, the Tax Court recently excluded the "19th hole" and "gin rummy table."[3] The tax aspects of most perks are not explicitly covered in the tax code, but rather are examined on a highly individual basis and special circumstances can be controlling.

Several generalizations can be made about the tax system that governs perquisites. First, legitimate business purpose is the primary tax consideration for both the company and the individual. If a perk has no business relevance, a company cannot deduct it. "Business relevance" has therefore had a pronounced effect on perk evolution. The business relevance doctrine affects the individual too, since there is strong legal precedent against taxing the person involved in a legitimate business activity (e.g., business entertainment, relocation, a luncheon club membership), even though the individual may also enjoy the activity. In situations where business relevance is debatable, individuals and companies can often forestall IRS objections and avoid large imputed income consequences by paying the portion of the costs that theoretically cover the personal aspects of the service or benefit. Thus, some companies charge their executives a modest monthly fee for the executive dining room, say $20 or $30, or suggest that executives report some income for use of a company car, say 10 cents per mile driven for personal purposes.

The tax consequences of a particular perk obviously influence its income value to the individual. But there is an even more basic determinant of the value of a perk: its subjective worth to the individual. If an executive is indifferent to the benefit and would never buy it personally, then it is essentially worthless. Many perks originated in the dim reaches of corporate antiquity. They may have been modified to be more responsive to the needs of the current executive group, but only rarely are they more than indifferently tailored to the requirements of an individual executive. This is particularly true in large companies. As a result, any specific perk, regardless of cost, can range from an idle privilege never exercised to an indirect money reward well worth its cost even in after-tax dollars, or something in between. I know one executive who refuses to participate in the company's annual physical program because she thinks the doctors are incompetent chauvinists. She forgoes a perk that costs the company about $500 a person but has no value to her. An airline executive who has a propensity to keep records told me that he and his family have chalked up air travel worth $4,600 in the last three years. In the same company there is another executive who hates to fly. He has used this travel privilege only once in that same period.

By and large, the true money value of perks is something far short of total replacement cost. This is particularly true of status-symbol perks. There may be considerable psychic satisfaction in moving from the tenth floor to the executive wing at the top of the building but, as the saying goes, you can't spend satisfaction. The perk with tangible monetary value, however, certainly deserves to be taken into account when calculating the total value of a compensation package. Obviously it is difficult to be precise in comparing one perk program with another. The range of perks is incredibly diverse and their replacement cost is affected by a host of factors. There are about a dozen perks, however, that have a fairly definite monetary value, and these *can* be evaluated with some degree of accuracy. In analyzing them, the individual executive should keep several important questions in mind. Which are most important in building personal net worth, the executive's ultimate passport to independence? Which can trigger imputed income and problems with the IRS? What other risks, if any, are involved in accepting the perks? What are the key provisions to look for? And, of course, what's the value for me?

Loans for Executives

The perk with the most obvious money and net worth value is the loan of capital to key executives. Generally, the loan is made for investment purposes. The practice originated in small, privately held companies where stock options are often not a practical compensation vehicle. In order to provide competitive capital accumulation opportunities to the top professional managers, such companies devised alternative plans to facilitate the building of net worth. The most important of these is the low-interest loan. For example, one small mutual fund management company created several special limited partnerships for investing in venture situations; then the president loaned several junior executives enough money to participate. A closely held electronics firm loaned some $300,000 to a limited partnership of seven of its principal officers; they promptly invested the funds in tax shelters of one kind and another. And I know of one wealthy entrepreneur who lured a coveted executive with the offer of a $500,000 personal loan for investment purposes.

More recently, a few large publicly held corporations have begun granting loans to key officers, usually to finance stock options. Whether this will become common practice remains to be seen, but early evidence suggests a trend may be developing. A 1970 survey uncovered five loan plans in a group of 160 large blue-chip corporations. All but one of these companies had initiated its loan program since 1968. Since 1970, such companies as Dow Chemical, Xerox, and Gillette have followed suit with similar arrangements to help finance stock option exercise.

Company loans for investment purposes have inherent risks, of course. The money must be repaid sooner or later, and if it has been invested unwisely the executive could find himself in a difficult predicament. On the other hand, leverage is a key ingredient in many investments, and the availability of instant investment capital at favorable interest rates can be valuable indeed. The experience of an executive in a West Coast real estate firm illustrates one way such a loan can be worked. He negotiated a $200,000 personal loan from the wealthy founder at 4 percent interest. Since the interest was tax deductible and he was in a 50 percent plus tax bracket, his "cost" was under $4,000 a year, or under 2 percent.

Beyond the nature of the investment itself, one should understand clearly the repayment terms and timetable, and know what happens in the event of a termination of employment.

Financial Counseling

One of the hottest new perks for senior executives is company-paid personal financial counseling services. So complicated was the Tax Reform Act of 1969 that it immediately made obsolete the informal system of providing executives with part-time financial advice from an assistant treasurer on such matters as option exercise decisions and bonus settlement choices. Difficulties in personal financial planning were compounded by newer types of executive stock plans. Some forced the individual to make tough choices involving qualified and nonqualified options, phantom or performance share plans, all of which can create large potential "earned income" gains. Finally, most companies became increasingly aware that personal asset management was competing with company matters for the time of their top professional managers. The answer they came up with was the company-sponsored personal financial counseling service provided by outside experts at "group" rates of $3,000 to $5,000 per year per person.

Like company loans, this perk is linked to the building of personal net worth. The counselor helps the executive to analyze his or her current assets and liabilities to forecast future income. Then, after exploring the executive's investment philosophy and risk orientation, the counselor develops a specific financial program covering such matters as insurance, securities, and tax reduction opportunities. In some cases, usually at the option of the executive, the counselor follows up annually at a reduced charge.

To date, this perk has been reserved for the privileged few in top management who have the income and assets to make it worthwhile. A good rule of thumb is that current income should be at least $50,000 and the executive's personal net worth $100,000 or more. A few companies, however, have extended the service downward, prompted in part by the fact that the counseling fee is considerably lower for this group. Counselors themselves agree that executives in the $30,000 to $40,000 range can benefit from a onetime diagnosis and plan but probably do not require yearly guidance.

The costs and payment arrangements for personal financial

counseling vary widely and depend on the scope of the services and the number of executives covered. In a fairly representative group plan for fifteen to twenty executives, each is allotted twenty hours of counseling time for the initial year of the program at a charge of $2,500 per person. This charge is split between the company and the individual. In subsequent years, the individual pays the entire fee, which ranges from $600 to $1,200 depending on the service provided.

Since this type of service is relatively new, the tax regulations governing it are still evolving. For a while it appeared that the company could deduct the full cost, with no income imputed to the executive. But when the perk mushroomed, IRS issued Revenue Ruling 73-13 requiring that the value (i.e., the cost of the service) be considered as taxable income. (As such it is subject to withholding, of course.) Since the expense is deductible for the individual taxpayer, however—as are other charges for tax and investment advice—the ruling didn't impose too severe a cost. Such plans have therefore continued to grow. A 1973 Conference Board study indicated that 20 percent of the top 500 industrial corporations now offer financial counseling.[4]

In the final analysis, the value of personal financial counseling depends on the caliber of the advice received, of course, and the caliber varies from excellent to mediocre. The financial counseling business has expended rapidly since 1969 when the AIMS group of New York devised the first group counseling plan for General Mills executives. In the last few years a number of specialized firms have been formed in response to the growing demand, and several banks and securities firms are also moving into the market. It is worth noting that some of these organizations may not be altogether impartial in their advice. Many of them package their own tax shelters, real estate investments, oil drilling ventures, etc., which one can presume they tend to promote. On the whole, however, the service is generally worth the cost. It could be worth a great deal more.

The Company Automobile

Every weekday morning, Alexander Farkas, president of Alexander's Department Store, arrives in downtown Manhattan by private helicopter. In demonstrating the ultimate in transportation one-upmanship, Farkas is not alone but he is still ahead of his time. The company car remains industry's No. 1 transportation perk, be it a chauffeur-driven Rolls-Royce Corniche worth $48,500 or a humble Ford Pinto. At the chief executive officer level, the automobile is an extremely common fringe benefit. In fact, in Los Angeles 88 percent of the chief executives drive company cars, and 54 percent of them park in special spaces.[5] Below the top officer level, company practice begins to diverse. A few companies provide cars for several layers of management, particularly in areas where public transportation is poor. More often, though, companies limit the privilege to those who clearly need a car for business reasons.

The company car is the type of perquisite that titillates the design instincts of perk planners. Not only do they have a range of cars with different status implications to play with, there are such other variables as chauffeurs and built-in bars. Opportunities for developing procedures abound. I know one company that devotes sixteen pages of its policy manual to dos and don'ts regarding automobiles. Radio repairs and wax jobs are nonessentials and therefore are *not* reimbursable; tire and tube replacements, however, *are* legitimate expenses and paid for by the company.

Leaving the status value aside, just what is a company car actually worth? After all, if one uses a personal car for business purposes, it is possible to deduct any expenses from one's tax return even if the company doesn't allow the item on a monthly expense report. The answer is, company cars are worth quite a bit for several reasons. To cite one, with its fleet purchasing power the company can generally negotiate a lower price for the car, insurance, and servicing. More important, the individual with a company car avoids the cash outlay and monthly expenses of automobile ownership. At the sales or middle-management levels, such a program may be the only way the individual can afford to have a second car.

The specific value obviously depends on make, replacement timetable, and the like, but a rough rule of thumb holds that the value is equal to 25 percent of the cost of the car if it were bought privately. For a specific estimate, you have to work up itemized costs: so much for the monthly lease rate ($250 a month for a Cadillac in Manhattan, for example), insurance, operating costs, and parking. Then determine how much of this amount you could recoup as a business expense on your tax return. Even where there is no private use of the car intended, it's hard to persuade the IRS to allow more than 90 percent of the cost as a legitimate deduction—and any amounts reimbursed must be subtracted, of course. For example: If the total monthly cost to the executive were $500 and he could support a deduction of 90 percent ($450) and was reimbursed only $50, he would have a tax deduction of $400 a month, or $4,800 annually. In the 50 percent bracket, this cuts his "real cost" to $2,400. The "real costs" after tax deductions are a good measure of the real value of the company car, and they can have the effect of eliminating any cost at all for the executive.

Special Medical Benefits

I once asked a company medical director why he had given up private practice for a career of running first aid facilities, examining employment candidates, and giving annual physicals to lower-level executives. The doctor was quite candid. He said he was willing to accept a lower income ($50,000) and a humdrum routine for the nine-to-five hours, the company benefit package, and the Miami location. He may be a very fine doctor for all I know, but he was not highly respected by the senior executives. They were all examined by outside physicians with incomes closer to theirs. This is a fairly typical pattern. The company medical facility serves the lower-level workers, while the executive group receives special medical treatment from private physicians or organizations like Executive Health Examiners that specialize in providing medical checkups on a contract basis.

The extra medical benefits provided by a company can be quite extensive. They may include free flu vaccines and cold remedies, free immunization for foreign travel, even thorough annual physicals at such prestigious institutions as the Mayo Clinic, where the tab can run to $500 or more. Moreover, some companies provide their executives with additional medical cost reimbursement beyond the group medical program. One company reimburses its officers for up to $5,000 in family medical expenses, including checkups and normal medical and dental expenses not covered by the company insurance plan. The officers of a large engineering firm have extra guaranteed life insurance coverage of $100,000 after retirement, from which they can draw up to $5,000 a year for five years for medical expenses. Ingenious.

The value of such extra medical benefits obviously depends to a large degree on the general health of the executive and his or her family, as well as on the adequacy of the company's basic medical insurance. Given the rising costs of medical care, however, these privileges may well be worth several thousand dollars a year.

The Executive Dining Room

While on a consulting assignment in the United Kingdom a few years ago, three of my colleagues and I were confronted with a delicate problem. We were serving a fine old British company, rich in tradition and rigidly stratified. This client had not one, but three executive dining rooms, and there was no mixing of people among them. Our principal contact in the company had weathered the tests of time and fortune and now dined in the most exclusive of the three rooms. When time for luncheon came, we sensed from his embarrassed hesitation that two members of our consulting team were somewhat young to eat in this sacred room; their presence undoubtedly would cause comment. We solved his problem by expressing a desire to eat in the common dining room, where we might gain some insight into the company by talking informally with the junior managers.

In the years since, I have eaten in many an executive dining room and have concluded that they embody much of the spirit of an organization, particularly its employee relations philosophy. Some chief executives feel quite strongly that the special dining room creates artificial barriers and actually impedes communication between various levels of the organization. Not long ago, one chief executive described his decision to eliminate the executive dining room in these terms: "I have a hard enough time getting those big shots out where they can learn what's really happening without encouraging executive isolation. We now have a program of active lunch fraternization." Banks often illustrate the other extreme. Business-related luncheons among banking officers are a prevalent practice, but the two and three classes of dining rooms I have observed in some banks do encourage status-conscious and insular organizations.

Executive dining rooms—*all* employee lunch facilities, for that matter—are expensive propositions for the company, even though most of them charge a dollar or two for the meals. Utilization inevitably peaks around noon and there are real pricing constraints;

yet the demands for quality and variety are relentless. If a major rationale for the dining room is to entertain important guests, a certain elegance is required. Even when the facility is justified as a time-saving convenience for the company's own executives, the food must be at least moderately appetizing. Under the circumstances, it is not surprising that few company dining rooms are self-supporting. One company estimates the per-meal cost at its executive dining room at about $15. In a recent study of federal executive lunchrooms, the General Accounting Office discovered that the average meal cost ranges from a modest $3.53 at the Interstate Commerce Commission to $16.05 at the Department of Transportation.[6]

I seriously doubt that the average executive would view $16 a day multiplied out as an accurate measure of the income value of this particular perk. On the other hand, it does have some monetary value. If the executive saves $2 to $3 a day by eating in the company dining room rather than the restaurant down the street, the privilege is worth $600 per year: $2.50 times 240 lunches. That is equal to a $1,320 annual raise for the executive in the 50 percent tax bracket.

Memberships in Clubs

When it comes to income value, the downtown luncheon club is another story, particularly when the club offers such additional facilities as squash courts, card rooms, libraries, a pool, exercise facilities, and even satellite beach facilities and golf courses outside the city limits. And most clubs do offer more than mere eating. Companies in suburban areas are more apt to finance memberships in country clubs, since the club may be the only decent and convenient facility for business entertaining. Of course, there is an added benefit for the golfers.

Data on the prevalence of this perk are somewhat sketchy, perhaps understandably. In a survey of fifty companies in the Los Angeles area, I found that only ten provided country club or yacht club memberships, and these were often limited to the top few men. On the other hand, about 80 percent provided luncheon club memberships for their officers, often on a tiered basis, with the junior officers slotted into the relatively modest University Club or the Los Angeles Athletic Club, and the senior officers assigned to the more prestigious California Club.

Most companies that provide club memberships pay the initiation fee, and often the monthly dues are reimbursable. Some companies limit their dollar commitment by level of officer. Others provide a luncheon club and one other club, again with a dollar limit. In terms of tax implications for the individual, there is generally no "imputed income" associated with luncheon clubs, but country club membership and expense reimbursements must often be reported as taxable income.

Housing for Executives

Another perk with obvious status overtones is the executive apartment or hotel suite, a device used by about one out of five companies. Like most perks, this one has a legitimate business rationale. The executive who lives in the suburbs occasionally has to work late in town. The company with multiple locations often requires executives to spend a good deal of time away from their home base. To cushion the inconvenience, many companies provide special accommodations of one sort or another. One oil company has permanent reservations for about 100 suites in luxury hotels thoroughout the world. A New York corporation with operations in Fort Lauderdale provides personal apartments there for all its senior vice presidents and higher officers. Many companies own apartments that function more or less like executive dormitories, with internal reservation systems.

Such accommodations have an obvious practical value, as anyone who has visited a major city during an American Legion convention can attest. But their chief value is perhaps symbolic. I sat next to a young executive on a late-night flight to New York recently. The weather was bad, and the plane was forced to circle for some time before landing. I mentioned that I hoped my hotel would hold my reservations. My companion smiled happily and said that he was staying in the company's suite, which happened to be located in the same hotel. He added that he had just been promoted to vice president and this would be his first stay there. Unfortunately, when we arrived at the hotel there was a snag in the arrangements. The clerk was not expecting him and could not find

EXHIBIT 13
Range of perk values.

	Chief executive $200,000 level		Junior executive $50,000 level
Company car	$ 3,000– $ 5,000		$1,000– $2,000
Chauffeur	8,000– 10,000		. . .
Executive physical	500– 1,000		250– 500
Downtown luncheon club	2,000– 3,000		500– 1,000
Executive dining room	1,000– 1,500		500– 800
Personal financial counseling	3,000– 5,000		2,000– 3,000
Loan	5,000– 10,000		. . .
Country club	5,000– 8,000		. . .
Spouse travel ⎫ Use of company aircraft ⎬	2,000– 4,000		. . . . . .
Company apartment	6,000– 8,000		. . .
	$35,500–$55,500		$4,250–$7,300
Pretax value as a percentage of salary	17.75 to 27.75%		8.5 to 14.6%

his name on the master !ist of eligible executives. Like most lists, it was out of date. The hotel management finally allowed him to use the suite, but by that time all the pleasure was gone. Still, he was luckier than I. At 10:00 P.M. they had given my room to a hardware salesman from Peoria.

Although such accommodations generally have little income value, in some cases they can be worth a substantial amount. The apartments in Fort Lauderdale are a case in point, and even a weekend in San Francisco at the Fairmont is worth having.

The perquisites discussed above are among the most common, but they by no means exhaust the range of possibilities.[7] I've also encountered an executive exercise room, a company-maintained ranch in Texas, free shoeshine service, a private masseur, free newspapers, company yachts, personal stationery, special checking account privileges, more family travel privileges, annual conferences at spa locations, home telephones, and my special favorite, the company barber housed in his own suite of offices.

One seeks a distillation. It's easy enough to snicker at some of the bizarre subspecies but perks have become a reality of business in virtually every size and type of organization, and their cumulative value is impressive. Exhibit 13 itemizes the perk packages and their approximate equivalent value in salary for a junior executive and a chief executive officer. The values are simply too large to ignore.

Nor should one dismiss the psychological value of the perk. Abraham Zaleznik, professor of social psychology at the Harvard Business School, claims that "people with authority and power should have certain recognition symbols to remind themselves that they carry weight and responsibility. Besides, it's unhealthy to deny the fact that you deserve these little pleasures. Life would be very gray without them."[8]

"Little" is hardly the word to describe some elements in the perk package fostered by our tax environment, corporate precedent, and that old motivator of compensation, "competitive practice." Certainly perk recipients should analyze what they have in dollars-and-cents terms, particularly when contemplating a change of jobs. What the perk package tells one about the value system of an enterprise, however, is as important as dollar values, if not more. Large companies in particular can be hierarchical societies, and the splendidly tiered array of perks defines them more clearly than any packaged philosophy of management.

CHAPTER ELEVEN

Entrepreneurmanship: Getting There on Your Own

An entrepreneur is defined as a person who organizes, manages, and assumes the risk of an enterprise or a business. But the word is used more loosely. The aggressive product development manager, the corporate acquisition specialist, the general manager of the new division in a large company, even though they are salaried, often think of themselves as entrepreneurs. One school of thought even considers the modern breed of mobile manager as a new type of business entrepreneur whose equity reward comes in the form of stock options.

Still, despite the demands and complexities of modern business society, there's hardly a shortage of classic entrepreneurial types— the individual men and, to a lesser but growing extent, women who start a company, build it into a viable business, and, in the prototypical denouement, sell all or part of it for major financial reward taxed on a capital gains basis. Each year in this country thousands of individuals go into business for themselves. Many thousands more dream of doing it but never seem to find the right opportunity, or perhaps they just lack the originality, inner drive, or that last measure of courage it takes to strike out on one's own. Of those who do take the plunge, many are employees of established companies, émigrés from IBM, General Electric, ITT, and hundreds of lesser enterprises, who turn their backs on the security and steady career paths of stabler companies to become builders of new ventures. Some found their own companies; others, whom I call secondary entrepreneurs, take their gambles by getting in on the ground floor of new enterprises recently founded by someone else.

There are others, call them mavericks if you will, who never spend very long in the commonplace world of corporations but are stirred early by some consuming passion to build a successful business. Many try again and again until something "clicks," as it did for Ray Kroc, the builder of the McDonald's hamburger chain. Even when he was regularly employed, Kroc hustled for thirty-five years at one venture after another. At fifty-one he stumbled across a small drive-in restaurant in San Bernardino, California: it seemed to be doing an incredibly large volume of business. At the time, Kroc was trying to build a business based on sales of a patented product called the Prince Castle Mixer, for which he had the exclusive rights. His original idea was to franchise McDonald's outlets in order to sell more mixers. Kroc soon raised his sights. Today, McDonald's is a $600-million giant with over 2,800 outlets, and Ray Kroc has incorporated the following words into "Press On," the official McDonald's creed: "Nothing in the world can take the place of persistence."[1]

The motives of the men and women who go independent are as many as their numbers—and often money has rather little to do with it. For the New York City taxi driver who foresakes the fleet and buys his own cab and medallion, for the Sears, Roebuck buyer who becomes a manufacturers' representative, the motive is more likely "to be my own boss." Others see themselves as happy with a decent current income so long as they can live where they want; this can mean running a machine shop in a Chicago suburb, owning and operating a McDonald's franchise in New Hampshire, or something as romantic as opening a ski lodge in Aspen, Colorado. Many of these small local businesses can yield cash incomes of $50,000 a year and up. They also provide an opportunity to use, on one's own behalf, many of the compensation techniques we've discussed in earlier chapters: insurance, pensions, bonuses, and especially perquisites of all types. The people who take this route would probably only smile at the No. 2 man in an Atlanta software company who told me recently: "I promised myself I'd be a millionaire by the time I'm forty." "I've got seven years and two months left," he said, after checking the calendar on his desk. My own view is that there are likely to be more and more talented people thinking like my friend from Aspen and fewer like my friend from Atlanta.

The focus on the quality of life will increase, but there will always be those entrepreneurs whose real obsession is to prove the worth of a new product or a new piece of technology. Often such men care very little about building a company or making a fortune. That's one reason, incidentally, why the original inventor is so often eased out of a new venture early. For even if they don't conceive the idea or are not present at the creation, there are always, waiting in the wings, men who *do* want to build companies and fortunes. They know full well that one of the few remaining avenues to real wealth lies in founding a company—preferably one centered around a new product or concept of service—building, through several successive periods, an earnings growth that is as spectacular as possible, then selling a part of it through a public stock offering. Those who are able to continue earnings-per-share growth are then in a position to acquire other companies with their highly priced stock. By repeating the process, they and the secondary entrepreneurs who get on the bandwagon early can rejoice exceedingly as personal net worth multiplies in a matter of months.

The swinging 60s provided many examples of this phenomenon. Ray Kroc's net worth was under $100,000 as late as 1962. Today he is one of the two dozen wealthiest men in the United States, with a personal fortune approaching $200 million even after McDonald's stock fell to the low 20s in 1974. His secretary, who accepted McDonald's stock in lieu of salary in the early years, wound up a multimillionaire. An investor who had bought $5,000 worth of McDonald's stock in 1965, when it was first publicly available, would have an investment worth $300,000 nine years later. Companies like Winnebago, Kentucky Fried Chicken, and Electronic Data Systems also spawned dozens of millionaires among the secondary entrepreneurs who joined them early instead of waiting the twenty or twenty-five years it would have taken for them to climb the compensation heights at General Motors or IBM.

The swinging 60s gave birth to legends and heroes as well as fortunes. No one illustrates that phenomenon better than Ross Perot, the onetime (for two years) IBM salesman who founded Electronic Data Systems. Perot used virtually no capital to start EDS, a Dallas-based computer software firm providing programming, systems design, and facilities management services. The stock had a book value of about 20 cents when he first took it public in 1968 at $16.50 a share. Within two years EDS stock had increased a thousand percent, hitting a high of $162 in March 1970, and Ross Perot was a paper billionaire. That same year, touted as a wunderkind and flushed with his success at EDS, the wily Texan galloped to the rescue of the floundering brokerage firm of Francis I. duPont. He was heralded by some as the hope of the free enterprise system, and his $5 million initial investment in Wall Street was described in many quarters as a sound, even brilliant diversification that would benefit EDS in its own right. He received the ultimate accolade: a feature article in *Ramparts* magazine that denounced him as a "hard core free enterprise freak."[2]

But the swinging 60s gave way to the sagging 70s. By 1974, when Perot closed down what had become duPont-Walston, he and his partners stood to lose most of what had swollen to a $100 million investment. EDS stock itself had long since peaked and started down. By October 1974 it had dropped to $12 a share, Perot could count his paper losses in $100 million increments, and he was no longer described as a business genius.

Suddenly the papers were making household words out of a different kind of entrepreneurial venture, spelling them Four Seasons Nursing Homes, National Student Marketing, Performance Systems, Equity Funding. The colorful venturists with unusual backgrounds had suddenly become shady wheeler-dealers. Take Stanley Goldblum, the former chairman and president of Equity Funding. For a time Equity Funding was the hottest insurance company around, whose shares (listed on the New York Stock Exchange, no less) were bid up to some $600 million. Goldblum was wined and dined by the establishment, too. But then a securities analyst named Ray Dirks got wind of what was to be the greatest insurance scandal of the century, at least to date. Much of Equity Funding proved a sham. Over 64,000 insurance policies and $100 million in underlying assets simply didn't exist. In April 1973, Mr. Goldblum resigned as the scandal mushroomed, and people sneered at his early business experience at the Cherry Meat Packing Company, as a swimming and gym instructor, and as a scrap dealer, ignoring the fact that his experience wasn't any more typical of the entrepreneur than that of Ross Perot, the account representative and salesman from IBM.[3]

As the stock market slumped badly—far worse, in fact, than such traditional indexes as the Dow-Jones made it appear—the losses and subsequent doldrums were worst among the companies that a short time before had seemed so glamorous. Executives who had joined them suddenly discovered that instead of being part of exciting new growth ventures they were just working for relatively small companies. Instead of harvesting stock market fortunes over a "reasonable" period of five years or less, they found they were working for closely held companies whose stock had little liquidity. The new issues market, the arena for so many coups of the 60s, all but collapsed. The 1960s had seen the number of new issues soar from a norm of several hundred a year to 887 in 1968 and 1,026 in 1969. In the first six months of 1974 there were only ten, and they went at prices that brought joy to practically no one.[4] In all, spirits sagged even lower than paper losses piled high.

Yet if the people who believed that "you can't lose" have been straightened out and sobered a bit, the entrepreneurial instinct has hardly died. The new value systems, in fact, are a good guarantee that it won't. More and more Americans are simply going to insist on greater control over their own destinies, on earlier financial independence, on more "quality" in their lives. The flame still burns, therefore, and many a large-company manager is now simply biding his time for the auspicious moment. And so, from the more cautious perspective of the mid-1970s, it is perhaps an ideal time to take a hard look at the real compensation implications of the new venture.

How do the founder entrepreneurs really make their money? Over what time period, and at what risks? Is the payoff shared very broadly in most of these companies? What does it take to succeed, and how much is success influenced by events outside the founder's control? How does the founder cash out? And what about the professional managers drawn to the new venture after the initial stock offering? What compensation vehicles does the new company have that are not available to the established large corporation? And what are the prospects for the founder-entrepreneur in the late 1970s, a period that promises to be vastly different from the 1960s?

To provide sound perspective one should look at a broad cross section of firms. After all, several thousand companies went public in the 1960s. Many of them are impossible to trace, having merged or gone bankrupt. Of necessity, then, one has to focus on those that survived. Early in 1970 I started to research companies that had gone public in the preceding decade, pinpointing those that were under $20 million in sales in 1965 and had at least doubled in size by 1969. The New York, American, and National Over-the-Counter Stock Exchanges listed some 240 companies that met these criteria. To get a factual dimension on the reward structure and risk profile of the new venture, I researched a cross section of forty of these companies, tracing their evolution from their founding to the first public offering, and then following their development through 1974.[5] They are listed in Exhibit 14.

Unlike earlier waves of new ventures, few of these companies were in basic industries. Less than 40 percent were even in manufacturing, and many of those that were dealt in some form of higher technology, such as computers. In general, it was the decade of "concept companies"—some with special strength in marketing, e.g., fast-food chains and other franchisers, some offering new or expanded services, e.g., computer software. For specific illustrations, I have chosen five companies. They are not so colorful as some of the decade's ventures, but they engage in several of the more representative of today's new businesses. They include both successes and near failures; on one or two of them the vote is still out.

Marion Laboratories is one of the success stories of the decade so far. The company was founded by Ewing Kauffman in 1950 in Kansas City, Missouri. Kauffman's early experience was as a salesman in a small Midwestern drug company where his career was meteoric. He was made sales manager in four months and two years later was making more than the president. When the company tried to cut his commissions he quit and started his own business, working out of his basement. Instead of developing new drugs, Kauffman decided to focus on selling specialty drugs to doctors on a door-to-door basis, and he developed a well-trained and highly motivated sales force. One of his first real winners was Os-Cal, a calcium supplement made of ground oyster shells. The business grew slowly and even by 1965, when it went public, Marion Labs was only a $7 million company. But it was profitable, and its high multiple enabled it to grow and prosper through acquisitions and internal development. In 1973 it netted an incredible $10 million profit on $63 million in sales.[6] (Never mind what that tells you about the price of medicines.)

At the other end of the spectrum is an Amarillo, Texas, venture

EXHIBIT 14

Profile of selected new ventures.

Number	Type of business	Examples: 40 companies and year they went public
Manufacturing/industrial		
21	Computer products and systems	California Computer Products (61) Systems Engineering Labs (66)
15	Other high technology	Recognition Equipment (65) National Semiconductor (66)
6	Packaged products, pharmaceuticals	Marion Labs (65) ICN Pharmaceuticals (63)
20	Recreational and entertainment	Larson Industries (67) Winnebago (67)' Craig Corporation (68)
13	Other consumer-oriented	Franklin Mint (66) STP Corporation (68)
15	Industrial manufacturing	International Controls (66) Marathon Manufacturing (69) Guardian Industries Corporation (68)
90/	37.5% of total	
Nonmanufacturing		
23	Real estate and construction	U.S. Financial (64) Shapell Industries (69) Alaska Interstate (66)
9	Fast food and other restaurant	Pizza Hut (69)
8	Computer services	Electronic Data Systems (68) Computer Technology (68)
16	Other commercial and industrial services	Wackenhut (66) Planning Research (64)
15	Leasing	Rockwood National (65) Sea Containers (68) ITEL (68) Leasco (65)
11	Other financial services, insurance	Equity Funding (64) Donaldson Lufkin & Jenrette (69/70) American Financial (61)
8	Medical care facilities	Hospital Corporation of America (69) Beverly Enterprises (66)
7	Publishing and broadcasting	Corinthian Broadcasting (67) Downe Communications (68)
7	Distribution	Telecor (69)
8	Oil and gas exploration, development, servicing	ProChemco (69) Dearborn Storm (67)
24	Retailers	Levitz Furniture (68)
3	Personal services	
11	Miscellaneous	Western Union International (63) Sandgate (66) Equity National Industries (64)
150/	62.5% of total	
240	**Total**	

Source: Special analysis of listed stocks which went public in 1960s, were under $20 million in revenue in 1965, and had doubled in size by end of decade and were still independent at that time. Exchanges screened were NYSE (produced 46 companies), ASE (144 companies), and National Over-the-Counter (50 companies).

that combined some oil wells, an oil and gas well servicing business, a cattle ranch, and a pecan farm. *ProChemco* went public at the end of the decade in the so-called garbage market of 1969. The prospectus showed it had made $730,000 on revenues of $11.6 million in fiscal 1968. But profits would have been only $350,000 without a couple of acquisitions made just before the company went public. Even that didn't tell the whole story. The prospectus reveals that certain accounting assumptions were changed at this same time. If the books had been kept the old way, fiscal 1968 earnings would have been $10,689 instead of $350,000.[7] ProChemco has since gone into and gotten out of a number of businesses, never making much money and reporting a $3.42 million loss in 1972. It recently sold its oil and gas properties and now is concentrating on custom cattle-feeding and ranching operations. Revenues were $48 million in 1973, profits $774,000.

STP Corporation was a spinoff from Studebaker-Worthington in 1968. STP makes an oil additive, of course: "the racer's edge" that a promotional genius named Andy Granatelli made synonymous with high-performance cars, including the pioneer turbine racers that he entered in the Indianapolis 500. The STP emblem became instant Americana between 1966 and 1973, as upwards of 250 million STP decals were distributed all across the country. Granatelli was a bona fide entrepreneur who made his first million in his early thirties with a company called Grancor. He started another venture, Paxton Products, which he sold to Studebaker-Worthington. At the same time he talked that company into letting him run its STP Division. Run it he did, building it from an $8.7 million to a $30 million business in five years through shrewd advertising and promotion.[8] Up until 1972, STP grew rapidly, largely through acquisitions, but revenues peaked at about $95 million. Sales dropped 8.1 percent in 1973 under a barrage of criticism of some of the company's products.

Wackenhut Corporation is an interesting product both of our service economy and of our times. The service it provides is protection. Wackenhut started in Miami as a group of "private eyes" and soon diversified into guard services. The founder, George Wackenhut, is a former FBI agent. Early on the new company landed some important government contracts that enabled it to build a large, people-intensive organization with 4,000 employees, operations in twenty-two states, and $17.7 million in revenues when it went public in 1966. Wackenhut has continued to grow and diversify within its field since then; revenues hit $90 million in 1973. The margins in the protection business evidently aren't as high as they are in drugs—1973 net income of $2.26 million was only about one-fifth of Marion Labs'—but the company has been consistently profitable.

It is hard to select a "typical" high-technology firm in a period of such high-flyers as Recognition Equipment, Systems Engineering Labs, Memorex, and Potter Instruments. But *CalComp* is an interesting example. A manufacturer of special digital graph plotters, it emerged early in the decade (1961) and found a niche that enabled it to survive when so many others failed. The company is still run by one of its founders, Lester Kilpatrick. After losing money in 1972, it seems to have turned back into the black, registering a modest profit on $63 million sales in 1973.

These five companies provide useful perspective on the prospects for great rewards and unusual "compensation" in the new company.

One must begin by understanding the realities of any new venture. The first trick is simply to survive. There aren't any hard statistics on the survival rate, but most experts estimate only a small proportion of the new businesses founded each year—perhaps only one in five, certainly less than half—will survive their first few years. The venture capital firms that back the new enterprises testify to the casualty rate by their practices. The professional financiers of new businesses almost never provide money to *start* a company. They don't like the odds. Most demand a track record of several years before they will even consider investing in a new company. Then they accept only about one deal for every 200 or 300 they reject. And even then, the venture capitalists claim, "two out of every ten investments are successful, six are mediocre, and two are failures."[9]

This sort of record can effectively block a new venture, particularly one requiring substantial capital, from getting the expansion money it needs. Only rarely—in the best of stock market times and with the most seductive of company stories—can the new enterprise go straight to the market. In order to get public investors to buy promise rather than performance, it certainly helps to be in an exciting business with theoretically unlimited potential. That's one reason why so many high-technology companies were able to get started in the 1960s. CalComp, for example, rode the crest of the new issues boom of 1961, going public only three years after its founding team left the Autonetics Division of North American to make a business out of an invention.

But even if a company gets started, and in the best of times, it is usually a long hard road up. The median time between founding and going public was seven years in our forty-company sample. New ventures that do survive their first seven years can lose money in one and be pushed to the brink of bankruptcy. Going into the red or even sustaining a big drop in earnings usually wreaks havoc with the stock price, after the public has bought in. Over half of the forty ventures in Exhibit 14 have lost money in one or more years since going public. And while Marion Labs and Wackenhut have consistently increased their earnings, ProChemco and CalComp have both sustained sizable loss years.

During CalComp's first ten years as a public company, it managed to avoid the huge write-offs that plagued other high-technology firms. But when the founders diversified out of the business they knew best, to reach for a larger market in disk drives, they drastically increased their vulnerability. IBM, CalComp's direct competitor in products that account for about 41 percent of the small firm's revenues, finally reacted to the inroads made by the independents by redesigning its peripheral products and cutting its prices. CalComp was forced to write off millions of dollars of deferred R and D, as well as other development costs, and to write off an inventory that was abruptly obsolete. This cost the company a whopping $12.8 million loss in 1972. CalComp's experience is far from unusual. My associate Donald Clifford did a study of 795 somewhat larger but still evolving "threshold" corporations. It showed that even at an average size of $61 million, close to one out of five loses money in a year like 1970.[10] More significant from the standpoint of potential investors, only about a third have relatively stable earnings-per-share growth.

Even when a new company has begun to achieve the financial muscle and stability that let it weather periodic disasters, vulnerability remains a chronic condition. The threat can be as direct as IBM's new pricing thrust or as bizarre as the series of events that nearly did in STP. In the July 1971 issue *Consumer Reports* came out with a story claiming that any good grade of multiviscosity motor oil could achieve the same effect as STP (which stands for "scientifically treated petroleum"). The magazine charged that Granatelli's product "may violate a new car warranty."[11] In two days STP stock dropped $19.50 a share, beginning a year-long slide. The attacks began to multiply. *Automotive Cooling Journal* criticized one of the company's hot new products, STP Keep Kool, a radiator cooling additive, and *Business Week* picked up *ACI's* research and gave it a broader audience. Around this time a group associated with Ralph Nader filed a petition with the Federal Trade Commission to declare STP oil additive a worthless product. By 1974 STP common stock had plunged from its peak of $58.75 to $4 a share. In October 1973, Andy Granatelli was ousted by the board of directors and his successor, John J. Hooker, Jr., soon followed. The average new venture hardly travels a straight, smooth road to success.

What does all of this mean for the founder of the new enterprise? First of all, it often means years of fairly low pay. I would estimate that more than half of the chief executives of companies going public in the 1960s still earned less than $30,000 after ten years of long hours and hard work. Lester Kilpatrick, the president of CalComp, was paying himself only $16,600 in 1961, the year his company went public. Through most of the rest of the decade he continued to draw under $30,000, and he was still under $40,000 in 1969. His story illustrates the fact that low cash compensation can continue long after the initial stock offering. Even at Marion Labs, a profitable company in a well-paying industry, owner Ewing Kauffman paid himself only $75,000 after fourteen years; none of his executives got salaries over $30,000.

Inflation has pushed founder-president salary levels up some lately, but even after the company gets to the $20 million to $30 million level the president rarely draws down more than $50,000 before the company goes public. (For a public company of this size cash income would be $68,000, about 30 percent higher.) In effect, of course, the owners are "capitalizing" their salaries by holding them down to perhaps one-half to two-thirds of the pay levels for comparable responsibility in publicly held enterprises. The salary implications for lesser executives is obvious, of course.

From the founder's viewpoint, this can all prove worthwhile *if* he can retain control of the company until its first public offering. Marion Labs' founder Ewing Kauffman did it; he controlled 60 percent of the company at the initial offering. George Wackenhut and his wife owned more than 70 percent. But not all founder-builders have the skill or luck to hold on to 50 percent or more of the stock. It's particularly difficult for those in capital-intensive busi-nesses because of the pressure to give up ownership shares for the capital needed. It is also tough when there's a group of founders rather than just one. Les Kilpatrick was only one of a group of founder-directors, each of whom owned about 15 percent of the company when CalComp went public. Over the years he held on to most of his stock but by 1973 his shares represented less than 5 percent of those outstanding. Andy Granatelli, though, again provides the saddest example of all. Although he didn't start STP, more than anyone else he built the business. Unfortunately for Granatelli, he built it as a hired hand for Studebaker. Although he got a free hand, a handsome salary of $125,000 plus deferred compensation, he owned only a token 15,000 shares out of 5.7 million outstanding after the first public offering. You could say he had less to lose when the stock went down, except, as noted earlier, he couldn't stop himself from being fired.

But even if the founder does own a significant amount of stock, he or she is hardly home free. Many new public offerings flutter for a while and sink. Over half of the forty companies listed in Exhibit 14 now sell for below their offering prices. Some, like ProChemco, have never won market acceptance; its stock declined steadily from $13.00 at offering to $1. Other stocks do modestly well for a while but suffer badly in doldrum markets such as we have recently experienced. Wackenhut is an example of this group. And some stocks like Marion Labs and STP win great acceptance and promise to meet the grandest expectations of the founders, only to fall in response to some mysterious roller-coaster law.[12] A bare handful of the spectacularly successful new issues have escaped the roller-coaster in the last fifteen years, in fact, as Exhibit 15 shows with its picture of eight of the highest flyers of the 1960s.

Well, isn't the answer obvious? The founder should sell some portion of his or her stock, if possible at or near the peak. This is easier said than done, unfortunately. The founder (and other key early executives, for that matter) usually owns unregistered securities, or what is generally called "letter stock."[13] The owners of such securities are under very tight constraints from the Securities and Exchange Commission on how and when they can sell their stock once a public market is established. To protect the general investing public, letter stock can only be sold in very small amounts. Selling a large block requires registering the shares with the SEC as a public offering and publishing a prospectus, with all the detailed disclosure that involves. Getting SEC approval can take twelve to eighteen months and cost $40,000 in fees. Moreover, the underwriters must also agree and they are generally much happier when the founder

EXHIBIT 15

The rise and fall of eight new issues' share price.

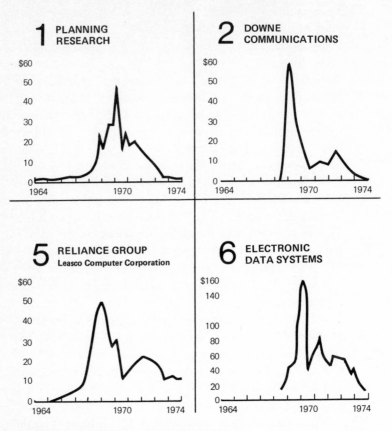

SOURCE: *Security Owners Stock Guide,* Standard and Poor's Corp.

hangs in there as an act of faith. The founder's selling off also requires, as a practical matter, acceptance by potential investors themselves. Finally, the fledgling company simply may not be able to afford an offering the proceeds of which do *not* go into its treasury. Present and future cash needs may be too pressing to permit the founder the luxury of cashing out big.

Because of these constraints, only about four of ten new offerings provide the founders with an opportunity to sell, and the *prevailing* bull market was of real help to those who did pull it off. Even when founders begin to "liquidate" early, they usually have to wait for their major gains. In the initial public issue, George Wackenhut and his wife got $1.3 million after underwriter discounts and commis-

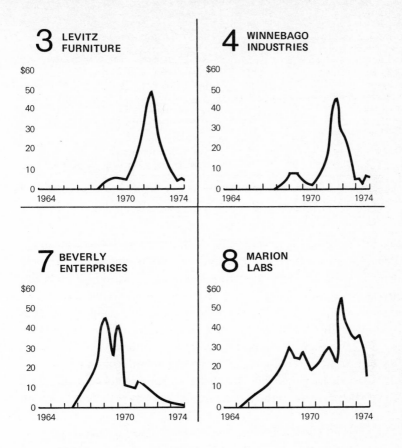

sions; Ewing Kauffman got $1.8 million. In each case the sellers disposed of less than a quarter of their holdings. Kauffman waited until 1968 for a secondary offering to bring him $12.9 million more. Many other entrepreneurs are forced to settle for selling off in the small amounts the SEC permits through normal brokerage channels. With such hurdles it's no wonder that many founders choose to sell their companies outright to larger enterprises whose stock is theoretically more stable and liquid. Some new ventures do this without ever going public. Other companies go public and then merge, some with superb timing, some less fortunately. There are no easy answers, and luck is often a disproportionate factor.

Under such circumstances it is obviously very difficult for any

Table 11-1. Range of Founder Rewards

Magnitude of reward	Distribution of 40 survey companies	Representative founder executive
Minimum gain or a loss	9	Andy Granatelli, STP Corporation
Under $1 million	10	Paul Engler, ProChemco
$1–5 million	9	Lester Kilpatrick, CalComp
$5–20 million	5	George Wackenhut, Wackenhut Corporation
$20–50 million	4	J. H. Whitney, Corinthian Broadcasting
$50–100 million	2	Ewing Kauffman, Marion Labs
Over $100 million	1	Ross Perot, Electronic Data Systems

SOURCE: Company proxies and prospectuses. Gains from the sale of stock were considered as well as stock holdings valued at mid-1974 levels.

outsider to know the actual rewards that accrue to these founder-entrepreneurs, who have invested up to twenty years in their businesses. In the forty companies, however, I would estimate the founders' "rewards"—measured in current stockholdings plus pre-tax gains from sales of stock—to be as shown in Table 11–1. It is apparent from these estimates that one can still make a very large amount of money founding a company, despite all the problems. The question is whether the payoff is worth the sacrifice and risk. Most of us would find the odds against big success very long indeed. But it is the nature of entrepreneurs to see the odds as on their side.

What about those who join the venture at some early stage in its evolution—the relatives, the old school friends, the former colleagues at Big Company X, the individuals simply recruited—how do they make out? Their hands clearly are not on the tiller, yet they face many of the risks of the founder. What is their potential for really major gain? Much, much less than most people suppose, I'm afraid.

If overoptimism is rampant among those who found companies, the disciples of the founders are even less realistic. The problem seems to start with a widespread misconception about how the new venture rewards its people. The harsh reality is that the newly public company does not have any unique pay missiles in its compensation arsenal. It has the same tools as General Motors or PepsiCo. In fact, in the early years the average new venture actually uses fewer types of rewards. Few privately held companies have pension plans, or incentive bonus schemes, or much in the way of tax-saving perquisites. A surprising number have not even adopted stock options. Only some twenty-five of the forty companies I surveyed used options, and my conclusions check with those of a confidential survey of twenty-six companies founded around Boston's Route 128, which showed that over a third didn't offer any options at all prior to going public.[14]

Cash compensation levels in the new venture are low and often remain below competitive levels, even for key executives, for years after the company goes public. The average No. 2 executive in the new venture is likely to make about 50 percent of the founder's salary, which itself is low, as we've seen. This compares with the more normal pattern of 75 percent in the established company. Other executives' salaries are usually scaled down as well, of course. When Marion Labs went public in 1965, most of the key executives under Ewing Kauffman were earning not much more than $20,000 and the second highest paid man, J. Warren Perryman, drew only $30,000, or 40 percent of Kauffman's earnings. By 1973 the three top Marion lieutenants still averaged only $47,750.

The executive joining the new venture probably doesn't really expect a large salary and generous benefits. He or she is banking on dramatic stock gains. Occasionally, the bet pays off, of course, but it's a mistake to assume that the important insiders in the new venture will necessarily do well in the stock area. To reap sizable gains the secondary entrepreneur must acquire a significant amount of stock at an attractive price, then have the flexibility and insight to sell at the right time. Few executives manage to execute all the elements in this formula.

To start with, it isn't easy to get stock at bargain-basement prices. The most attractive time to buy, of course, is during the company's early days when it is still privately held. At this stage, most companies value their stock conservatively, using book value or a fixed multiple of earnings. As a result, even after ten years of operation the value placed on the company may be a good deal less than the market value would be. But very few new ventures have proprietors who are openhanded with their stock. Most reserve it for the founder group, their relatives, and their direct investors. Moreover, it appears to be especially difficult to join the inner club, to say nothing of getting stock, without sharing the founder's background. For example, Ross Perot quite logically turned to IBM alumni when he founded and staffed EDS; George Wackenhut had turned to the FBI for twenty-one of his forty-eight key managers and executives by the time he went public in 1965. According to my research, 37 percent of new ventures offered no stock at all to executives or employees before going public. The odds are somewhat better among high-technology firms and in such talent-intensive businesses as real-estate development, consulting, or computer software firms. But many companies don't have to share ownership, and they don't. Even though he was president of the STP Division of Studebaker-Worthington, Andy Granatelli had to wait seven years before he got his first shares, which equaled .003 of the stock outstanding. Later options came at prices much above that of the initial offering.

Andy Granatelli's experience always seems a little extreme, but those new ventures that do offer prepublic stock usually offer it to only a limited number of executives and the amounts involved are usually quite modest. CalComp was built with a cadre of engineers who were recruited in the early years for their technical expertise in some facet of electronics. Many were given stock. But while the core founder group owned 86 percent of the company at the time of the initial offering, the nine others had less than 10 percent among them. And Wackenhut's No. 2 man, Executive Vice President John Ammarell, got his stock early (in 1962) and at an attractive price ($2.52 per share); but his 10,000 shares were less than 2 percent of the amount held by the founder and his wife and, although stock dividends and splits increased his shares to over 35,000, at the 1974 price his total gain would be under $250,000.

One of the few companies that don't fit this general pattern is Marion Labs. By the time Marion went public in June 1965, 48 percent of the company's employees owned stock, much of it acquired in the early 1960s for from 91 cents to $1.33 per share. But for many the real kicker was in the company's retirement plan. Founder Ewing Kauffman, with a great deal of foresight, set up a qualified profit-sharing plan in 1954, a few years after the company was founded, arguing that "those who produce should share in the profits." Over the years he sold or gave Marion stock to the profit-sharing trust for about 15 cents a share. By the time the company went public, the profit-sharing trust was the second largest stockholder. Even though the fund's managers began to diversify its holdings and pay retirees, the fund mushroomed to $30 million by 1972. The plan was so successful that the trustees decided to limit each individual participant to $1 million (there were nine participants at this level in 1969) with the excess amounts used to reduce future company contributions. This entirely justifiable ruling spared the company from making any contributions for several years and still left the fund with a $5.2 million reserve as of June 30, 1973. Kauffman described it as "the first [profit-sharing trust] to our knowledge in the history of American industry to be completely self-supporting."[15]

There are other ways for the secondary entrepreneur to get stock at an attractive price. At the time of the public offering, companies usually set aside up to 10 percent for the employees to purchase if they want to. This employee allocation is usually oversubscribed, however, and often has to be rationed out in relatively small parcels. Five out of ten companies adopt stock option plans at the time of their first issue and keep adding plans in the period immediately afterward. Of the forty companies we've been following, thirty-eight have instituted a total of 120 separate stock option plans since they went public. But, on average, 80 percent of the first stock plan shares are actually granted in the first year, even though the plan may have set aside a block for grants over ten years. By the time more stock is authorized, or the second and third plans are approved by stockholders, the price has often been bid up to ridiculous levels.

Our five representative companies illustrate this phenomenon when you plot the dates, amounts, and exercise prices of stock options against a backdrop of overall stock price trends. Options were never valuable, of course, for ProChemco, and there have been only modest paper gains at Wackenhut and CalComp. Both STP and Marion Labs, on the other hand, had spectacular runups but dropped sharply from their peaks. Their experience demonstrates the advantage of the early option holder. In the case of Marion Labs the really sizable gains (a potential of $19.5 million at the peak price of $54) came from options granted before the company went public. At 1974 stock prices, over 80 percent of the total potential gains in the last ten years are attributable to the first plan. In fact, options granted in 1970–73 are "under water." So are those of most public companies in these disastrous days for that matter, but the newer company has proved particularly vulnerable.

Ironically, it is during the latter stages of the big stock runup and the high-priced options that most secondary entrepreneurs are recruited. Only an occasional key man will have been brought in before the company goes public, e.g., a new financial vice president to replace the old bookkeeper controller. But the real executive recruiting takes place later on, as the company struggles with new functions and tries to cope with growth. Within five years of the initial public offering, most new ventures will have replaced a third to a half of the first executive team or created a real management structure for the first time, even though the founder remains.[16] These later executive arrivals not only have less chance for great gain, they face great personal financial risk when they commit themselves to a highly volatile stock (see Chapter 8). When the new venture stock falters, the market tends to overreact badly. Those who've exercised options at high prices can be very nearly wiped out before they have time to put in a sell order. Two-thirds of newly public companies use qualified stock options, and there are other special dangers that are a product of the 1964 and 1969 tax laws. Even when a special deal has been set up, the spread may not be wide enough to guarantee gain. When Walter Heinze served as part-time chairman of STP, he was given a chance to buy 36,000 shares of stock on an installment basis at $25 a share. His underlying contract was terminated in October 1972, when STP was selling for about $20 per share. Heinze had purchased 24,000 shares by that time.[17]

If disaster is always lurking in the wings, so is the temptation for those who have enough stock at a good price to hold onto it too long. Knowing when to sell isn't all that easy. The executive in the new venture is generally an optimist about the company's prospects and inclined to hold on. He or she may also see the shadow of the founder over the left shoulder. The latter is likely to be obsessed with the stock market at this juncture and quite dyspeptic about "unwarranted" sales.

Again ironically, the executives that make out best are often alumni from the initial cadre who proved inadequate for the next phase of growth. I remember one such case vividly. The new venture started in the early 1960s and had astonishing early success in computer peripherals. But troubles developed and suddenly the company registered an $18 million loss. From its high of $104 in the early 1960s, the stock had plummeted to around $3 a share.

Everyone's options were under water and rapidly sinking deeper. At least four different key executives wistfully told me the story of the company's first vice president of marketing who was fired in the mid-1960s near the height of the company's market value. He cashed in his holdings and walked away with more than $1 million. That was far more than the founder's stock was (and is) worth. Oh, well.

Despite the difficulties, when all is said and done some secondary entrepreneurs do indeed make money, particularly those who get in on the ground floor. But I believe that relatively few secondary entrepreneurs make as much money as they had expected when they joined the venture. My analysis shows that our forty selected companies have to date produced about 150 *paper* millionaires—out of some 1,500 secondary executives. And of the 150 new millionaires, the luckiest probably made $5 million. To gain more than that, you have to stumble onto a McDonald's, a rare bird indeed.

Within five or ten years of going public, the vast majority of new ventures begin to slow down, that is, they reach their natural economic levels. The men and women who run them still hope for additional stock action, of course. And they may get it. But generally, during this period, the compensation profile begins to change, as illustrated by Exhibit 16. There is more and more pressure to raise cash compensation as new executives have to be recruited at high salaries and the president begins to feel secure enough to increase his own pay. Often the first formal cash bonus scheme is adopted. As the management group gets older, fringe benefits begin to improve. Where only 24 percent of the new companies had a pension or profit-sharing plan when they went public, 62 percent had them by the end of 1973. In short, the venture company gradually takes on the characteristics of the established company, and its compensation program mirrors this trend. It may still offer its executives an exhilarating environment, greater promotional opportunity, and, with luck and sustained good earnings, excellent stock gains. Now the very volatility of the stock can create opportunities to offer newly recruited or promoted executives attractive stock options at artificially depressed prices. But on the whole, within ten years after the initial offering the compensation program takes on the dull gray paint of the "established company," and the compensation questions become more classic.

204

EXHIBIT 16

Typical compensation program evolution.

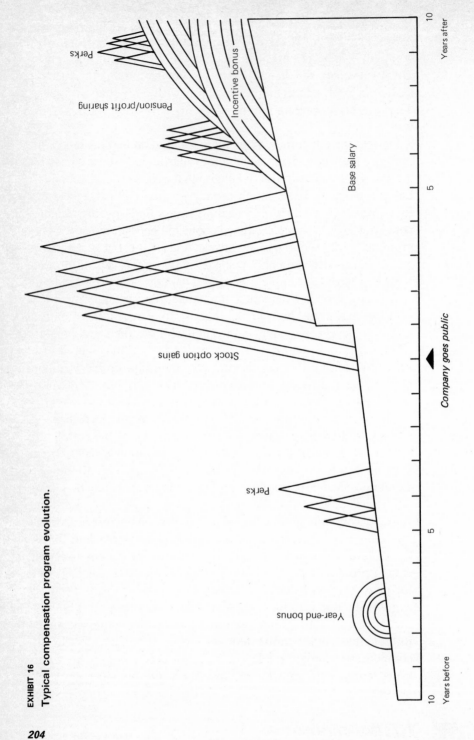

That's been the pattern to date, anyway, but we should look at the future. What are the prospects for founder entrepreneurs and their lieutenants in the 1970s? Will the stock market come back? It has in the past, and many astute observers even predict a rebirth of the new issues garbage market of 1969. But what about the solid new companies, currently becalmed unfairly in the new issues doldrums? Are the Marion Labs of the 1970s doomed to sell forever at book value until they ultimately merge into some faceless conglomerate?

Ask the entrepreneurs of the 1960s. Lester Kilpatrick's CalComp prospered in the early new issues boom of the decade, and by 1971 he had already gone through several stock market booms and busts. Kilpatrick says: "I think the opportunity for people to start new companies and have them grow to be successful is as high as, if not higher than, it has ever been."[18] Ross Perot, one of the big winners—and losers—is even more ebullient. The man who became a billionaire in eight short years after founding EDS has been quoted as saying: "Somewhere in the United States there's a young man or woman who will break every financial record I've set. That's the amount of opportunity that exists in this country."

CHAPTER TWELVE

Compensation and Financial Independence

Some time ago, three young men from Newport Beach, California, took a hard count of their lives and came up short. By most standards, they were successful: college graduates, well employed. Hugh Kelly was already a partner in an established law firm at thirty-two. Jay Carlisle, twenty-five, had become the youngest member of the Pacific Coast Stock Exchange a year earlier. Dan "Mok" McCullum, a contemporary of Kelly's, was a hustling sales representative. But all three felt tired of the race. For over a year they had been talking about chucking it and setting sail for Tahiti, where it would be cleaner, less harried, without smog or freeways. Ah, the coconut palms, lazy green lagoons, and Gauguin's beauties. Unlike most of us, who dream of James Michener's South Pacific and board the 7:20 train, these men sailed for their Bali Hai. Within a year, all three were lazing on Tahitian beaches and the California rat race was a blue ocean away.

For a while, the Californians dabbled in vanilla growing, fishing, and Tahitian vahines on the island of Moorea, a short sail across the Sea of the Moon from the Tahitian capital of Papeete. But they tired of sunshine and flowers and began to study the curious state of the Tahitian economy, which the jet airplane was just beginning to open to thousands of tourists. Just as a game, they thought, why not open a small, informal hostelry right on Moorea? As a source of income, too. A group of locals had started out with just such an idea but ran out of funds and courage. After considerable haggling with the French authorities, Kelly & Co. bought their unfinished building. They called their modest Moorean outpost the Hotel Bali Hai, since the island had, quite literally, been Jim Michener's model. The "hotel" had a small central house, four bungalows, and a dining room. It opened for business in June, 1962. In part because of the roistering personality of Tahitian-speaking Kelly, it soon became a happening. The tourists flocked to Moorea, and Bali Hai grew to twenty-two bungalows, then forty. The group started a second hotel, on Raiatea near Bora Bora. They expanded their farming operation to provide more food for the hotels. Other deals kept coming up. When I was first there in 1968, the group was starting to execute an entirely plausible scheme to corner the Society Islands market for eggs, 90 percent of which were still imported. By 1969 that idea had turned into another flourishing business—after 10,000 baby chicks and a California chicken farmer were flown in from the States.

Soon the whole complex had become a major enterprise and the trio was working much harder than in California. But Kelly, Carlisle, and McCullum were "in control" of their destiny, which was leading them to even greater freedom if they wished: already there had been several multimillion-dollar offers to buy them out.[1]

I think of this story whenever someone talks about chucking it all for a life of leisure in Tahiti—or, for that matter, immigrating to Australia or New Zealand. What they are really saying is that they feel trapped, that their lives are empty. But sailing into the sunset to find peace is likely to prove a voyage into illusion rather than a new life. After all, one takes one's self along. Two of the Tahiti trio, incidentally, are already back in the United States.

The fact is that the odyssey each of us makes in our careers can be as adventurous as a Tahitian voyage, if one remains reasonably in command during the trip. Those of us fortunate enough to be living in America, if you'll permit me the observation, have the greatest chance of all to exercise that command. No other country in the world offers the individual so much choice. We have the largest higher education system in the world. Unlike our European cousins, we face few social and hereditary barriers to the better jobs. Our advanced technologies are continually creating new career opportunities; the computer alone has spawned thousands of companies and some three million new jobs. We complain about taxes and, as Chapter 3 demonstrated, they are complex, irritating, and even burdensome. But they are not confiscatory. Taxes take only 30 percent of the gross national product in the United States, compared with 34 percent in Germany, 37 percent in France, and 42 percent in Sweden.[2] It is still possible for new wealth to be created in the United States; the top ranks of business and the professions are filled with self-made men and women. We have the most advanced system of job mobility the world has ever seen. And since the end of World War II, we have enjoyed thirty years of general prosperity interrupted only by short pauses or very mild dips.

It has been popular for some time to question our future viability. Our troubles have been, and are, real: double-digit inflation, a seemingly unmanageable economy, resources that are being depleted, stubborn and costly pollution, and political corruption on a massive scale. Some say the most discouraging fact of all is our changing value system. Some say no one wants to work today, that the incentive isn't there, that this country is gradually sliding into economic stagnation from lack of spirit. Poppycock! (One is tempted to a more modern expletive.) Certainly values are changing. Individuals are increasingly impatient with meaningless jobs. They are demanding much more of a say. Even a majority of one of the Roman Catholic Church's strictest monastic orders, the Capuchins, are dissatisfied with their lot, as a recent survey revealed.[3] The average employee in New York or Los Angeles is perhaps even more restless. As part of the whole thing, individuals from workers to top executives want to be fairly rewarded. People are already much more aggressive—and precise—in the way they measure their rewards. Personally, I think that's a good thing. People are simply happier and more productive when they feel they're being properly rewarded. But withal, Americans today are as ambitious and as risk-oriented as their forefathers. One shouldn't be thrown off by the fact that their priorities and timetables are different.

There is ample evidence that the opportunities for self-fulfillment are as great as they ever were both for the young men and women who get their first jobs in the 1970s and for those whose careers are already well along. At the same time, the world is getting far too complex for a laissez-faire approach to one's career. There have been times in this country when all success took was the right education and hard work. Those times are gone for good. A college degree is no longer that exclusive. And ironically, while opportunities exist today, the competition is much more severe. This is going to be particularly true for the group that has had it easiest for the first couple of hundred years of this republic, the white male. He has had an unfair share of the jobs, a good three-quarters of the professional and middle-management jobs, and probably 95 percent of the top-management jobs. Not only were minority groups shut out from most of the opportunities, so were women. Even today, women constitute less than 10 percent of full professors in colleges, only 7 percent of doctors, and 3 percent of lawyers.[4] The record in business is even more shameful. A *Fortune* survey of 1,220 large U.S. corporations showed that men outnumbered women among top officers and board members by 600 to one![5]

But signs of change are here, no mistake about that. In 1974 the world's largest commercial bank, the Bank of America, settled a job discrimination class action suit brought by some of its women employees. Among other things, the bank agreed to increase the proportion of women officers to 40 percent by 1975, guaranteed that 45 percent of trainees will be women over the next five years, and set up a $3.75 million trust fund for training and educational reimbursement for women! Clearly, the rules of the game are changing.

The increasingly competitive career environment goes far beyond new opportunity for women. The character of the economy itself is changing continually. While the greatest growth in the last few decades has been in the private business sector and in government, the shift toward a service economy suggests the greatest future opportunities could be in knowledge-based institutions. One forecaster, Harvard sociologist Daniel Bell, thinks the research-based university will replace the corporation as the key organization in the next hundred years.[6] Such fundamental shifts only underscore the need for thoughtful, solid career planning.

What is required in this environment, for men and women, for majority and minorities, is a lot more intensive, long-range personal planning, in the context of honest specific goals. The most important goals will be, and should be, qualitative and intensely personal. As psychologist Alfred Adler said, "What an individual feels is success is unique with him." But everyone's private and unique definition requires some translation into the tangible practicality of daily work. We simply have to decide what we are going to do with our working lives; work consumes most of our waking hours. And, inevitably, part of that decision turns on what financial rewards we really expect from our work.

Yet setting money goals doesn't come naturally to most of us. Articulating our financial goals seems crass. We are reluctant to push. Most of us, in fact, are more comfortable accepting less pay for "really interesting work." In a stimulating discussion of the "prosperity psychosis" in America, Princeton Professor Eric Goldman had this to say about the attitudes toward money of today's generation: "It assumes good living. Beyond that the pursuit of big money, or at any rate the too direct pursuit, smacks of the gauche, even the corrupt. How much you make has to be constantly weighed against a variety of status concerns: how you make it, what sense of 'identity' and 'creativity' it gives you, how much it removes you from 'the middle-class syndrome.'"[7]

I'm convinced that most men and women need to face off with money much more directly. Whatever the mix of their motives, by and large people do a poor job of pay management. They typically undervalue their compensation "worth" and, I've found, are usually poor negotiators. The result is they often go through life burdened by the nagging suspicion that they are somehow being taken advantage of and arrive at retirement anxious about whether they have "enough" to last them the rest of the way. Neither emotion is conducive to happiness. Part of the solution lies in being much better informed about the structures of careers and taxes (discussed in Chapters 2 and 3) as well as acquainted with all the special forms of pay covered in the body of this book. But knowledge isn't enough. People need to integrate pay "goals" effectively into their career plans and the overall objectives they have set for their lives. Long-range personal financial goals are essential whether one is just starting out or well on the way. They not only force one to think through what one really wants, they also provide useful reference points for measuring progress along the way. For most of us, money is not the primary objective; but there are money consequences flowing from virtually every decision in one's life. Those consequences themselves inexorably add up to very major decisions that profoundly affect our futures.

In my judgment, two kinds of specific objectives are required: cash income targets, which should be looked at in a time framework, and a net worth goal, which should be met by retirement, or earlier if some sort of second career is part of your view of life.

Then, with these goals, and the forecasts that attaining them requires, one should focus on the negotiating process through which they can be achieved.

Cash Income Objectives

Coming to grips with current income is an obvious necessity in these inflationary times. Every family should have a budget and at least a current-year forecast of income and cash flow.[8] But the individual who wants to control his or her destiny or even, on a more mundane level, meet personal and family "needs" must go further. For that you need to set annual income goals that reach out for at least ten years.

Rather than pulling figures out of the air (e.g., "I want to double my salary in five years"), the most practical way is to start with a forecast of what is most likely to happen. Experts call this a "base case" projection, and giving birth to such an animal can be made to seem very complex. In fact, most financial counselors, accounting firms, and banks use computer models. To cite one example, Price Waterhouse's system INFORM (for *In*dividual *For*casting *M*odel) provides a series of ten-year forecasts, including detailed printouts of: (*a*) income; (*b*) deductions, expenses, and tax liabilities by year; (*c*) a projection of assets, liabilities, and net worth; and (*d*) a ten-year source and application of funds analysis. With a pocket calculator and a quick review of the old Accounting I textbook, though, most of us can do a reasonable forecast more simply and by ourselves. And as you begin the process, you quickly reap the first benefit you would get if you were paying a counseling firm several thousand dollars: you can collect all of your records in one place. You'll need them because the typical financial questionnaire calls for a great many facts and runs twenty to twenty-five pages—yes, you still dig up all the records for the professionals, too.

Your first conclusion is likely to be rather startling: you are probably not even sure of your present compensation, at least in all the particulars. Form 1 in the Appendix is a work sheet to be used in documenting just what you are paid. It is organized into current income, income equivalents, protection benefits, and net-worth-building vehicles. (This work sheet and the other forms referred to in this chapter are also reproduced as a separate pamphlet, which is included with the book.)

With this analysis completed and before turning to the future in detail, it is well to pause for a moment to reflect on a few of the basic realities of your situation. What is your present and probable "value" to the society—in strictly financial terms? Some lines of work are and will continue to be valued much more highly than others. Unless you have the golden touch of a Norman Vincent Peale, for example, you can't expect to be paid too much as a minister of the cloth. On the other hand, when Vida Blue of the Oakland Athletics amassed a 24–8 won-lost record in his first season, he promptly picked a contract squabble with Oakland owner Charles Finley. Blue's attorney offered the following rationale for an immediate pay boost from $14,750 to over $90,000: "The fallacy in baseball is that a salary has to be based on number of years in the game. We think he [Blue] should have a salary somewhere around the average of what the top ten pitchers are making. We know some salaries and $92,500 is about the average."[9]

Star athletes always seem to be paid "above the average," by almost any standard. But knowing the average, or the going rate, for jobs similar to yours is pretty important. That's one reason top executives read each other's proxy statements so avidly, and why there are so many surveys on compensation levels. Geography also has an influence on one's going rate, as we discussed in Chapter 2: "average" executive salaries are likely to be 20 to 25 percent higher in the Northeast and 10 to 15 percent lower in the South. Only when one's salary gets above $30,000 or so does it become easier to rise above the average. A uniquely developed skill can help. So, it is important to realize, can visibility. The individual who is active in industry associations, or who speaks or writes publicly with some frequency, is more likely to be sought out by other potential employers and likely to get more pay when he is hired away from his current one.

The most important influence, though, is the old familiar law of supply and demand. When a new professional area is just evolving, as the electronic data processing function was in so many companies in the 1960s, experienced people can command very handsome premiums. The same applies to whole industries. There was a period recently when mutual fund management companies were all bidding outlandish salaries for a very limited supply of experienced people. Real-estate development companies went through a similar phase. This sort of phenomenon tends to be short-lived, however. It is likely to last no longer than four or five years, which increases the premium on a keen sense of timing if one is going to capitalize on a

EXHIBIT 17

Fluctuations in executive demand, 1954–1973.

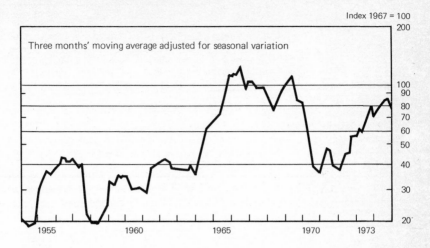

Index 1967 = 100

SOURCE: Heidrick & Struggles *Executrend* ® survey and analysis of display advertising in major markets across the country.

temporary disequilibrium in the job market. Timing affects *all* jobs as well as specific professions, moreover, since demand rises and falls with the economy. The prestigious executive search firm of Heidrick & Struggles has measured this phenomenon for twenty years now and the cyclical patterns are dramatic, as Exhibit 17 shows.

Having calculated your current compensation—and weighed it against the objective factors that determine your market value—it is time to look at the future in more detail. Your first task is to figure how to at least "stay even" in cash income terms, and at first glance the future salary levels required to achieve that may appear down-right ridiculous. To be sure, cash income levels have escalated sharply, particularly since the inflation that began in the late 1960s. But even in "normal" times the combined effect of inflation and increasing taxes, particularly the graduated income tax, makes very significant salary increases necessary even to maintain one's present status. The Conference Board recently did a study on what a family of four needed to earn in 1974 to equal its 1949 income. The amount proved more than double at all income levels. The family with a 1949 income of $25,000 needs $54,300 to live as well today; at the $50,000 level, the equivalent gross income is $112,700.[10] If inflation continues at the rate it has averaged so far in the 1970s, the rates of

Table 12-1. Increase in Salary Required to Maintain Equivalent Spendable Income over Ten Years

	$25,000 executive		$50,000 executive		$100,000 executive	
	1974	1984	1974	1984	1974	1984
Salary	$25,000	$54,732	$50,000	$112,820	$100,000	$211,930
Taxes	3,540	12,517	10,790	35,688	30,560	75,332
Net spendable income	21,460	42,215	39,210	77,132	69,440	136,598
Net spendable income in 1974 dollars	21,460	21,460	39,210	39,210	69,440	69,440
Percent increase in salary required						
Over 10 years		118.9%		125.6%		111.9%
Per year		8.2%		8.5%		7.8%

ASSUMPTIONS: Married taxpayer claiming four dependents. Itemized deductions equal 20 percent gross income. Income all earned income. Inflation 7 percent a year.

increase given in Table 12–1 are going to be necessary over the next ten years just to stay even.

These kinds of numbers make one realize how important it is to have goals against which to measure actual progress in real income terms. If your "base case" forecast indicates you are likely to fall behind inflation—or your own goals—it can and should trigger serious career reassessment. As we discussed in Chapter 2, for example, the key to more rapid salary progress is rapid promotions. This is likely to prove even more important in the 1970s since many companies will not be able to afford increases in *real* income for their work forces as a whole. Similarly, incentive bonus plans, discussed in Chapter 7, provide the opportunity for significant jumps in income based on performance; they too will be even more valuable in the years ahead. All these factors should be taken into account when evaluating cash income, current and future, and assessing whether some fundamental course changes are advisable. Such calculations are particularly advisable during the first twenty years or so of one's career. For, despite the federal laws against employment discrimination on the basis of age, there is no question that one's "value" to a prospective employer peaks out at about age forty-five.

In any job move that does come up, one should look hard at the net income consequences of the offer—considering changes in taxes, potential deductions, cost of living, and the like. Form 2 in the Appendix is a current income/cash flow analysis work sheet that will facilitate this comparison. But one should also total up and compare *all aspects of compensation,* as Form 1 permits, and forecast net worth as well as cash income.

Net Worth Objectives

It is in the area of net worth analysis and forecasting that the really tough soul-searching comes in. For net worth, not cash income, is the key to independence and personal financial security.

Despite our great wealth as a country, the average American today is almost totally dependent on current income and has little in the way of net worth. The Urban Institute estimated recently that only five million taxpayers, or 4.4 percent of the adult population, had a net worth of $60,000 or more.[11] Those five million, incidentally, held two-thirds of all the outstanding common stock and three-fourths of the privately held municipal bonds. By contrast, if the bottom half of the adult population sold all their assets and paid all their debts, they would be worth an average of about $3,000.

Obviously, one needs to get into the upper group, and well past the $60,000 entry level, to achieve any degree of personal financial independence. This is not easy, and the old saws don't have the answer. The average rate of savings in this country is about 7 percent. Most experts estimate that it takes three to four times that rate to achieve any kind of independence. As one put it recently, "A man has to save 25 percent of his *after-tax* income before he eats if he ever expects to become financially independent."[12] This implies a regimen of greater sacrifice, particularly considering that huge expenditures loom on most families' horizons. Four years at a private college already costs an average of $14,000 and is expected to increase to $20,000 by 1978 and to $26,000 by 1984.[12] Major savings are also required for such other personal or family goals as a second home, or early retirement to permit one to spend more time on long-deferred personal projects.

One of the big advantages of setting net worth goals is that it forces some realistic thinking about the balance between current and future needs, or, as John Maynard Keynes put it, between "jam today and jam tomorrow." If achieving a degree of financial independence is important to you, then a specific goal must be defined, as well as the means for getting there, in realistic, candid terms. Starting with a "base case," which should include an accurate projection of the capital accumulation potential from various company plans, is again the way to begin. The Appendix provides a work sheet (Form 3) for this purpose, too. As you will see, company-aided net-worth accumulation comes from four types of compensation plans:

First, a *pension* (Chapter 5) is technically an asset that increases net worth, even though under most plans there is no opportunity for lump-sum settlement and no benefit if one dies before retirement. It is usually more helpful, therefore, to consider the pension in terms of its contribution to one's future income flow. But remember, if there is no pension, then clearly other plans have got to produce more.

Second, a *profit-sharing or savings plan* (Chapter 6) provides the best vehicle for straight personal savings (up to 10 percent of pay) although the investment options and withdrawal privileges require careful study. If the company contribution is meaningful, the profit-sharing or savings plan can contribute six-figure amounts to net worth.

Third, the *stock option* (Chapter 8) or some variation on it should provide the salaried executive with his or her best chance to increase net worth in a big way. All the evidence points to the continued use of such plans, you'll recall, and a long-term view argues that substantial gains are still possible despite the experience of the early 1970s. Form 4 in the Appendix is a work sheet for estimating potential stock option gains; it will also prove useful in weighing alternative job offers.

Fourth, *deferred compensation* (Chapter 9) is a form of savings. As it is structured in nine out of ten companies today, however, it is a bad investment and therefore a comparatively poor vehicle for building net worth.

There are other types, of course, which are likely to come and go with the fashions of the times. A few years ago the hottest new compensation scheme was the company-sponsored tax shelter. Most of these cropped up on the West Coast, following the example set by Litton Industries, and most involved real estate. A few pioneering companies actually organized executive syndications, but if they had worked out better more firms than the eight I know of would surely have joined the parade. Even in the more conventional vehicles, however, there is risk. Don't forget Stuart Saunders and the legions of others trapped with options exercised at top prices, when the only thing moving faster than the carrying cost was the price of the stock—except it was headed down.

What can one expect from all these plans in a modern corporate environment? What kind of net worth is possible from company sources? Circumstances vary widely, of course, but a common goal of large companies is to provide their handful of very top executives with a net worth between $1 million and $2 million. Such companies also aim for $500,000 to $750,000 or so for other officers, and between $100,000 and $200,000, at the most, for middle managers. In most companies, these amounts are intended to be accumulated over a ten- to fifteen-year period, which can begin as early as age thirty. Most relevant survey findings confirm that many corporate chieftains, at least, do reach these target levels—or at any rate have in the past.

Getting there in the future may prove a good deal harder. Congress has stiffened the capital gains tax and there are proponents of even tougher legislation. A lid has been placed on qualified pension benefits and, for the first time, on total dollar contributions from profit sharing. The qualified stock option is certainly a lot more restrictive than its predecessors. Ever since the income tax, however, Congress and the IRS have been repeatedly surprised by imaginative new schemes of compensation. And the more we complicate the tax law, the more new loopholes we seem to open up. Motivating key individuals with longer-term incentives remains an important objective, and I doubt it will be subverted.

If one's objective is to join the ranks of America's 120,000 millionaires, however—and the possibility is still there—it will require even more initiative and risk than in the past. Those who want substantial wealth will find the quickest route involves a big gamble indeed: starting one's own company, as did the men described in Chapter 11. For such ventures, the sky can indeed be the limit.

The Negotiating Process

Unfortunately, it isn't enough to know where you are, what you are "worth," and where you want to be. Equity in compensation has to be negotiated. Most of us are actually in negotiating situations a couple of dozen times in our careers. Moving from one company to another obviously is one such occasion, but so is every decision to accept or decline a promotion, or transfer to another division. Even talking over one's performance and prospects while staying in the very same job is really a negotiating situation. But since we often fail to recognize these occasions for what they are, or handle them badly even if we do recognize them, most of us wind up being inadequately compensated or, as John Connally would say, badly paid in relation to what we are really worth. There are a number of reasons, some having to do with the nature of companies, some having to do with the way we as individuals approach these critical points.

Many aspects of the way companies run conduce, however innocently, to underpayment. Some are obvious: stinginess or, if you prefer, trying to get the most for the least; a superabundance of compensation rules, procedures, and preoccupation with precedent, all of which tend to constrict; a traditionalist reluctance to "spoil" an up-and-coming talent with too much money or too rapid advancement. The net of the inhibitions is this: unless one is fortunate enough to work for a senior executive who understands the dynamics of money motivation and, at the same time, has the courage and authority to make bold moves, one will almost inevitably be pushed toward some arbitrary average. That average exists in every compensation plan, from stock option grants to simple salary. Companies instinctively think of people in terms of their job titles, apparently, and categorize them in terms of current income. Thus, even when a man or woman is being hired away by a new employer, he or she will likely be thought of as a $25,000-a-year plant manager, say, and a new company will be reluctant to give its new recruit a raise of more than 20 percent over the salary he or she is currently making.

But in my opinion the real blame for inadequate compensation belongs on the shoulders of the executive who accepts less than he or she should. After all, corporations are not eleemosynary institutions and it has been written that the Lord helps those who help themselves. So it behooves each of us to beware of certain negotiating pitfalls and learn how to manage rather than be managed by them.

To begin with, most executives simply underestimate their worth. At the root of this is not only the failure to have clear goals, but also the fact that most of us are severely constrained by our prior experience. The financially successful man or woman, if the truth be known, is usually making a lot more money than he or she ever expected to; ironically, therefore, we may even feel overpaid. Underestimating current worth is therefore likely to be a self-perpetuating state of affairs. Current compensation thus not only conditions what prospective employers want to pay, it has a tendency to "psych" us as well. Students of negotiation theory will tell you the combination is fatal. To negotiate effectively one needs a strong self-image and unashamedly high aspirations. Understandably, people tend to raise their aspirations after success and lower them after disappointment or failure. We are therefore most likely to be good negotiators after a success, a lesson that Vida Blue applied. Conversely, one is least likely to negotiate well when unemployed or after a severe disappointment in one's personal life. It's hard to avoid negotiating for a new job when confronted with a mounting stack of unpaid bills, but reminding one's self of the objective criteria defining one's real market value is doubly important at such a time.

Unfortunately, many people have a sense of timing that is either poor or nearly nonexistent. In contrast to Blue's modus operandi, two Boston Bruins superstars, Bobby Orr and Phil Esposito, signed long-term contracts just before the World Hockey Association began raiding the National Hockey League, thus driving up salaries astronomically. As we discussed earlier, certain jobs, and individuals too, are worth more at some times than others. But good timing is vital not only in knowing when to initiate a negotiation, it can also be critical in the negotiation itself. Thus it is particularly important to sense just when first to discuss money in detail. (My advice, incidentally, is to establish the outside compensation parameters very early, while simultaneously emphasizing that money is not the primary consideration.) Equally, one should sense the right moment to press hard for a higher offer, a moment that usually comes after the basic commitment has already been arrived at by the other party. In my opinion, this is no time for a reluctance to haggle a bit.

As I suggested earlier, one very common mistake the individual makes is failing to understand the company's motives and manners. For example, personnel people are often trained to talk in negative terms, and so they create the impression that the executive being recruited really has very few choices. The fact is most companies actually have considerable freedom, and the higher the position one is negotiating about, the more room for maneuver actually exists. While companies won't often create a whole new compensation plan (except occasionally for a new president) they can and will *bend* almost every administrative rule if a good negotiator has leverage, a clear definition of what he or she wants, and some degree of courage. One can get an amazingly accurate picture of the possibilities even before an initial meeting by studying a company's proxy statements. These spell out top management pay, from which one can extrapolate the whole compensation structure. They usually explain even the intricacies of such special plans as bonuses, stock options, deferred compensation, and any other available vehicles. At this time the individual should also have a pretty solid idea of the "mix" of vehicles that will enable him or her to best attain interrelated cash income and net-worth objectives.

Finally, the question often arises in changing jobs whether to ask for an employment contract. It is probably wise to protect one's self legally in a turnaround situation or where one distrusts the other characters involved. (If the latter case pertains, why take the risk in the first place?) But by and large an employment contract won't guarantee that the board or president will support you, and it certainly doesn't guarantee one against summary dismissal. There is a correlation between the kind of company willing to give an employment contract and the degree of risk. When in doubt get legal counsel, of course, but when possible some discreet interviews with members of senior management, or even the board, can be quite useful.

I believe these do's and don'ts of negotiating can be of real help. Applying them can enable the executive to do significantly better when a negotiating occasion arises. I hope they will also make it possible for the executive actively to welcome such occasions, perhaps even to seek them out when the circumstances are right. After all, each occasion is a potential step along the road one has decided to travel.

In the last analysis, however, skill and good timing in the negotiating process can be at best an adjunct to the essentials of self-knowledge and compensation planning I have been preaching throughout this book. In *Desiderata*, Max Ehrmann[13] articulated a thought we might all subscribe to: "Keep interested in your own career," he wrote. "It is a real possession in the changing fortunes of time." I have repeatedly confessed my faith that this is a time of great opportunity as well as great complexity and challenge. To me, the fundamental question is how each of us responds to opportunity or, better yet, shapes it in highly personal terms.

Compensation Planning Forms

Form 1

TOTAL COMPENSATION SUMMARY FORM
FOR _____

CURRENT INCOME _____

HISTORY

| Year | Salary | Bonus Award | | Cash Profit Sharing | | Total Cash Compen-sation | Percent-age Change | Comment |
		Dollars	Percentage of Salary	Dollars	Percentage of Salary			
____	$____	$____	____%	$____	____%	$____	____%	_____
____	____	____	____	____	____	____	____	_____
____	____	____	____	____	____	____	____	_____
____	____	____	____	____	____	____	____	_____
____	____	____	____	____	____	____	____	_____

PROJECTIONS

Year	Salary	Dollars	%	Dollars	%	Total	%	Comment
____	$____	$____	____%	$____	____%	$____	____%	_____
____	____	____	____	____	____	____	____	_____
____	____	____	____	____	____	____	____	_____

SALARY RANGE   Minimum $_____   Midpoint $_____   Maximum $_____

SALARY INCREASE POLICIES

Merit increases   Size range____% to____%   Time guidelines_____

Promotion increases   Size range____% to____%   _____

BONUS AWARDS

Payout options   ☐ Current   ☐ Over____ years   ☐ Deferred_____

Comments:_____

_____

| Projected Bonus | Size | | Assumptions/Requirements |
	Dollars	Percentage of Salary	
Minimum	$____	____%	_____
Most likely	____	____	_____
High	____	____	_____

Form 1

PERQUISITES/INCOME EQUIVALENTS _____

Type	Estimated Value	Imputed Income	Comment
Company car	$	$	
Parking			
Personal financial counseling			
Tax preparation assistance			
Excess medical			
Luncheon club			

Country club			

Executive physical			
Company dining facilities			
Housing benefit			
Spouse travel			
Tuition reimbursement			

PROTECTION _____

Type	Coverage	Personal Contribution Required	Imputed Income
Basic group life		$	$
Supplemental life			
Accidental death and dismemberment			
All-risk accident			
Travel accident			
Comprehensive personal liability			
Long-term disability			
Hospital/surgical			
Major medical			
Dental			

Form 1

NET WORTH BUILDING _____

VEHICLES AVAILABLE

☐ Stock options
   ___ Qualified
   ___ Nonqualified

___ _____

☐ Performance share
☐ Phantom stock
☐ Loan program

☐ Deferred compensation
☐ Pension
☐ Qualified profit sharing
☐ Thrift/savings
☐ Qualified stock purchase
☐ _____
☐ _____

EXECUTIVE STOCK

	Current Outstanding Awards				Exercise Provisions	
Award Date	Number of Shares	Type	Award Price	Exercise Price	Earliest Date	Latest Date
_____	_____	_____	$_____	$_____	_____	_____
_____	_____	_____	_____	_____	_____	_____
_____	_____	_____	_____	_____	_____	_____
_____	_____	_____	_____	_____	_____	_____
_____	_____	_____	_____	_____	_____	_____

Comments _____
_____
_____

LOAN

Date	Amount	Terms	Repayment Schedule
_____	$_____	_____	_____
_____	_____	_____	_____
_____	_____	_____	_____
_____	_____	_____	_____

Comments _____
_____

Form 1

DEFERRED COMPENSATION

Source	Current Status			
	Amount Deferred/ Earned Yearly	Total Deferred Account	Basis of Appreciation	Payout Schedule
☐ Bonus deferral	$_____	$_____	_____	_____
☐ Individual contract	_____	_____	_____	_____
☐ Group deferred compensation plan	_____	_____	_____	_____
☐ _____	_____	_____	_____	_____

Comments: _____

PENSION

Eligibility provision _____

Date entered plan _____

Retirement	Age	Date
Normal	_____	_____
Early	_____	_____

Earnings base   ☐ Salary   ☐ Bonus _____

Assumed earnings current year $_____   Formula earnings _____ $_____

Formula _____
Vesting schedule _____
Other benefits   ☐ Spouse pension _____
                      ☐ Disability pension _____
                      ☐ _____

PROFIT SHARING/SAVINGS

Eligibility provision _____
Date entered plan _____

Retirement	Age	Date
Normal	_____	_____
Early	_____	_____

Contribution history

	Previous Three Years			Current Year 19__
Individual contribution				
Mandatory	$_____	_____	_____	_____
Voluntary	$_____	_____	_____	_____
Company contribution	$_____	_____	_____	_____
Allocated forfeitures	$_____	_____	_____	_____
Total company	$_____	_____	_____	_____
As percentage of pay	_____%	_____%	_____%	_____%

Investment options and results _____

Withdrawal privileges _____

Vesting schedule _____

Form 2

CURRENT INCOME/CASH FLOW ANALYSIS WORK SHEET
FOR _____

	Current Position	Option A	Option B
Title			
Company			
Location			

CASH INCOME

1. Salary	$_____	$_____	$_____
2. Bonus			
3. _____			
4. Subtotal—cash income	$_____	$_____	$_____

IMPUTED INCOME

5. Life insurance	$_____	$_____	$_____
6. _____			
7. _____			
8. _____			
9. Subtotal	$_____	$_____	$_____
Taxable income (4 + 9)	$_____	$_____	$_____

TAXES

10. Federal taxes	$_____	$_____	$_____
11. State taxes			
12. City/county taxes			
13. Social security tax			
14. Subtotal taxes	$_____	$_____	$_____
Income after taxes	$_____	$_____	$_____

CONTRIBUTIONS

15. Life insurance	$_____	$_____	$_____
16. Medical insurance			
17. Disability insurance			
18. All-risk accident insurance			
19. Pension			
20. Profit sharing			
21. Savings/thrift			
22. Stock purchase			
23. _____			
24. _____			
25. _____			
26. Subtotal—contributions	$_____	$_____	$_____

SPENDABLE INCOME

27. Income after taxes and contribution	$_____	$_____	$_____

ADJUSTMENT FACTORS°

28. Cost of living			
29. Commuting costs/time			
30. Job security			
31. Location/life style			
32. State income tax rate gradation			
33. Promotional opportunities			
34. Company environment			
35. Moving reimbursement			
36. Perquisites			

° Indicate +, −, or no impact.

Form 3

NET WORTH FORECAST WORK SHEET

FOR _____

Item	19__	19__	Period 19__	19__	19__	19__	19__	Period 19__	19__	19__	At Age 55 19__	At Age 60 19__	At Age 65 19__
Assumed cash income	$												
Pension													
Accrued pension to date	$												
As percentage of pay	__%												
Vested pension	$												
As percentage of total pension	__%												
Pension payable immediately	$												
Pension payable at permanent disability	$												
Spouse pension	$												
Profit sharing/savings													
Company contribution	$												
As percentage of pay	__%												
Employee contribution	$												
As percentage of pay	__%												
Account status at year-end													
Company contribution and earnings	$												
Percentage vested	__%												
Individual contribution and earnings	$												
Total	$												
Deferred compensation													
Amount deferred/earned this year	$												
Appreciation rate amount													
Rate	__%												
Amount	$												
Account status at year-end	$												
Stock options													
Market value of stock owned/exercised	$( )										( )	( )	( )
Net carrying cost to date	$( )										( )	( )	( )
Amount owed	$( )										( )	( )	( )
Estimated net value	$												

Form 4

STOCK OPTION PLANNING WORK SHEET
FOR _____

REFERENCE OPTION

Type	Number of Shares	Date Awarded	Award Price	Exercise Price
_____	_____	_____	$_____	$_____
_____	_____	_____	_____	_____

Exercise provision/choices _____

_____

STOCK PRICE CONSIDERATIONS

	Previous 3 Years			Forecast		
	19___	19___	19___	19___	19___	19___
Market price						
Low	$_____	$_____	$_____	$_____	$_____	$_____
Average	_____	_____	_____	_____	_____	_____
High	_____	_____	_____	_____	_____	_____
Actual/assumed earnings per share	$_____	$_____	$_____	$_____	$_____	$_____
Implied price to earnings multiple						
Based on previous year earnings	_____	_____	_____	_____	_____	_____
Based on current year earnings	_____	_____	_____	_____	_____	_____
Actual/projected yield	_____%	_____%	_____%	_____%	_____%	_____%

FORCAST OF NET GAIN

	Exercise Date	Financing Period			Sale Date	Shares Retained
	/ /	19___	19___	19___	/ /	
1. Per share price	$_____	$_____	$_____	$_____	$_____	$_____
2. Number of shares	_____	_____	_____		_____	_____
3. Market value	_____				_____	_____
4. Cost at exercise	_____					
5. Original investment	_____					
6. Amount financed	_____					
7. Yearly financing cost (net)	(_____)	(_____)	(_____)	(_____)	(_____)	
8. Dividends (net)	_____	_____	_____	_____	_____	
9. Accumulated cost basis (4 + 7 − 8)	_____	_____	_____	_____	_____	
10. Pretax paper profit (3 − 9)	_____	_____	_____	_____	_____	
11. Assumed tax						
a. Minimum tax on preference income	_____	_____	_____	_____	_____	
b. Earned income offset	_____	_____	_____	_____	_____	_____
c. Capital gains tax	_____	_____	_____	_____	_____	_____
d. State/city tax	_____	_____	_____	_____	_____	_____
e. Total tax	$_____	$_____	$_____	$_____	$_____	$_____
12. Net gain	$_____	$_____	$_____	$_____	$_____	$_____

Notes
and
Bibliography

When one surveys the literature on compensation it is quickly apparent that quantity isn't a problem. There is a vast and continuous outpouring of writing and data on pay levels, on new tax wrinkles, and on what the notables of the world make, from rock musicians to corporate chieftains. You can find articles dealing with pay or taxes in perhaps a dozen magazines. Much of the writing is purely topical, however, and, as I noted in the preface, some subjects are researched and dissected frequently while other forms and aspects of pay are addressed only rarely. Pay, for example, is only occasionally discussed from the individual's perspective; and it is even rarer to find solid material on careers and their money implications.

Selecting a bibliography in this subject area is therefore a frustrating endeavor, and I certainly don't pretend that the product which follows is the last word. I have therefore made no effort to be all-inclusive. Rather, I have tried to provide a sound starting point for those who wish to pursue a particular topic in more depth. The bibliography consists of numbered references organized by chapters in the book, as well as a list of other books and articles that have been of particular interest or help to me. When I felt inclined to offer a comment on a work I have done so.

Chapter 1

1. "Phase II: How It Will Work," *Business Week*, Oct. 16, 1971, p. 21.
2. For an excellent survey and analysis of this trend see Richard John Pietschmann, "Salaries in Professional Sports," *Mainliner Magazine*, December 1973, p. 18.
3. See the series of articles by Fabian Linden in *The Conference Board Record*: "Age by Income—1980," June 1971, p. 25; "The Characteristics of Class," October 1973, p. 61; "Income by Age—1985," February 1974, p. 54; and "Reshuffling the Age-Income Mix," March 1974, p. 58.
4. Herman P. Miller, "Profiles of the Future," *Business Horizons*, April 1971, pp. 5–16. Updated by the Census Bureau in its Current Population Reports Special Studies, Series P–23, No. 47, February 1974.
5. Arch Patton, *Men, Money and Motivation*, McGraw-Hill Book Company, New York, 1961. A classic.
6. David Kraus and David J. McLaughlin, *Current Trends in Executive Stock Plans*, McKinsey & Company, Inc., New York, 1970.
7. Albert Cantril and Charles W. Roll, Jr., *Hopes and Fears of the American People*, Basic Books, Inc., New York, 1971.
8. For further discussion see Thomas J. Murray, "The Revolt of the Middle Managers—Phase Two," *Dun's*, August 1973, p. 32.
9. "Commuter Income Study," Pitney Bowes, Stamford, Conn., August 1974, p. 2.
10. William R. Galeota, "Most Law Grads Seek High-Pay Jobs Despite Rise in Their Social Concern," *The Wall Street Journal*, Sept. 13, 1971, p. 15.
11. John W. Gardner, *Self-Renewal: The Individual and the Innovative Society*, Harper & Row, New York, 1963 (Perennial Library Edition, 1971, p. 20). Stimulating.
12. John W. Gardner, *Excellence*, Harper & Row, New York, 1961.

Other Sources

Ardrey, Robert, *The Territorial Imperative*, Dell Publishing Company, Inc., New York, 1966.
Best, Fred, ed., *The Future of Work*, Prentice-Hall, Inc., Englewood Cliffs, N.J., 1974.
Drucker, Peter F., *The Age of Discontinuity*, Harper & Row, New York, 1969.
———, *The Effective Executive*, Harper & Row, New York, 1967.
———, *Technology, Management and Society*, Harper & Row, New York, 1970. The Drucker books are must reading.
Galbraith, John Kenneth, *The New Industrial State*, Houghton Mifflin Company, New York, 1967.
Gellerman, Saul W., *Management by Motivation*, American Management Association, New York, 1968.
Lewellen, Wilbur G., *Executive Compensation in Large Industrial Corporations*, Columbia University Press, New York, 1968.
Reich, Charles A., *The Greening of America*, Random House, Inc., New York, 1970.
Terkel, Studs, *Working*, Pantheon Books, a division of Random House, Inc., New York, 1974.
Toffler, Alvin, *Future Shock*, Random House, Inc., New York, 1970. A controversial analysis of change.

Chapter 2

1. J. Fisher, R. H. Haas, and G. Rogers, "Where Are They Now, What Do They Think," *Forbes*, Sept. 15, 1973, p. 107.
2. Eugene E. Jennings, *The Mobile Manager*, University of Michigan Bureau of Industrial Relations, Ann Arbor, Mich. 1969. Crammed with research data and insights.
3. John A. dePasquale and Richard A. Lange, "Job Hopping and the MBA," *Harvard Business Review*, November/December 1971, p. 4.
4. Walter Guzzardi, Jr., *The Young Executives*, New American Library, Inc., New York, 1964, p. 181.
5. *Profile of a President*, Heidrick & Struggles, Inc., Chicago, 1962, 1967, and 1972 studies. Contain much useful data.
6. U.S. Department of Commerce, *Statistical Abstract of the United States*, 93rd and 94th Annual Editions, 1972 and 1973. Deserve more attention than they get.
7. *Los Angeles Times*, March 5, 1972.
8. "The Road to the Top: Jim McFarland Takes the Traditional Path, a Long, Arduous Climb" *The Wall Street Journal*, Sept. 14, 1971, p. 1.
9. Robert Townsend, *Up the Organization*, Alfred A. Knopf, Inc., New York, 1970 (Fawcett World Library Edition, February 1971, p. 53). Iconoclastic, oversimplified, fun.
10. See Heidrick & Struggles' 1972 study, *Profile of a President* (ref. 5 of this chapter), a survey of 470 of the *Fortune* 500 largest industrials and 50 largest utilities, life insurance, finance, transportation, and merchandising firms.
11. Harry Levinson, *The Great Jackass Fallacy*, Harvard University Press, Cambridge, Mass., 1973, p. 52. Insightful.
12. Richard Dougherty, *Goodbye Mr. Christian*, Doubleday & Company, Inc., Garden City, N.Y., 1973, p. 11. Delightful book.
13. *Los Angeles Times*, July 3, 1971.
14. Personal conversation. For a good discussion of Crow's successful enterprise see Wyndham Robertson's article, "Trammell Crow Succeeds Because *You* Want Him To," *Fortune*, November 1973, p. 113.
15. Special analysis of proxies 1964–73. Earnings per share growth used as basis for identifying best and worst performers.
16. Rush Loving, Jr., "The Automobile Industry Has Lost Its Masculinity," *Fortune*, September 1973, p. 187.

Other Sources

Argyris, Chris, *Applicability of Organizational Sociology*, Cambridge University Press, New York, 1972.

———, *Integrating the Individual and the Organization*, John Wiley & Sons, Inc., New York, 1964.

Drucker, Peter F., *Management: Tasks, Responsibilities, Practices*, Harper & Row, New York, 1974.

Endicott, Frank S., "Trends in the Employment of College and University Graduates in Business and Industry," an annual survey, Northwestern University, Evanston, Ill. The authoritative survey of graduates' starting salaries.

Herzberg, Frederick, *Work and the Nature of Man*, New American Library, Inc., New York, 1973.

Jennings, Eugene E., "The Co-Worldy Executive," *Management of Personnel Quarterly*, Summer 1971.

————, *Routes to the Executive Suite*, McGraw-Hill Book Company, New York, 1971.

Likert, Rensis, *Human Organization: Its Management and Value*, McGraw-Hill Book Company, New York, 1967.

The MBA Executive: A Survey of Accomplishment in Business, MBA Resources, Inc., New York, 1973. Based on a comprehensive survey of graduates from 12 of the nation's leading graduate schools.

McGregor, Douglas, *The Human Side of Enterprise*, McGraw-Hill Book Company, New York, 1960.

————, *The Professional Manager*, McGraw-Hill Book Company, New York, 1967.

RIA Pooled Intelligence Division, *Executive Compensation: An RIA Survey*, Research Institute of America, New York, July 28, 1969.

Chapter 3

1. Randolph E. Paul, "History of Taxation in the United States," in *The History and Philosophy of Taxation*, College of William and Mary, Williamsburg, Va., April 1955.
2. J. Fred Bateman, "Taxes: Who Benefits and Who Pays?" *Business Horizons*, February 1972, p. 51.
3. "Tax Report, Inflation's Bite Means Steady Tax Increase for the U.S. Taxpayer," *The Wall Street Journal*, Jan. 23, 1974, p. 1.
4. Mortimer M. Caplin and J. Robert Moskin, "14 Ways You Can Legally Cut Your Taxes," *Look*, Mar. 23, 1971, p. 15.
5. Benjamin Grund (interviewed by Gerald R. Rosen), "The Booby Traps in Executive Taxes," *Dun's*, February 1971, p. 10.
6. Joseph A. Pechman and Benjamin A. Okner, *Individual Income Tax Erosion, by Income Classes*, Brookings Reprint 230, The Brookings Institution, Washington, D.C., May 1972, p. 22.
7. *Ibid.*, p. 23.
8. "The Expanding World of Tax Shelters (Oil to Cattle Feeding)," *Business Week*, May 12, 1973, p. 45.
9. U.S. Department of Commerce, *Statistical Abstract of the United States*, 94th Annual Edition, 1973.

Other Sources

Childs, William C., "Compensating the Executive After the Tax Reform Act with Stock Options, Restricted Stock, Deferred Pay—and Even Cash," *Taxes—The Tax Magazine*, December 1970, p. 801.

Diogenes, *The April Game: Secrets of an Internal Revenue Agent*, Playboy Press, New York, 1973. Interesting reading with insider stories.

Eisenstein, Louis, *Ideologies of Taxation*, Ronald Press, Inc., New York, 1961.

The Executive Compensation Journal, a monthly publication of Tax Management, Inc., Washington, D.C. Authoritative source for current developments; many good examples.

Explanation of the Tax Reform Act of 1969, Commerce Clearing House, Inc., New York, 1969.

Rustigan, Edward C., "Compensation Planning Techniques That Can Be Used in the Present Tax Climate," *The Journal of Taxation*, April 1972.

Smith, Dan T., *Tax Factors in Business Decisions*, Prentice-Hall, Inc., Englewood Cliffs, N.J., 1968.

Stern, Philip, *The Rape of the Taxpayer*, Random House, Inc., New York, 1973. Provocative.

Surrey, Stanley S., *Pathways to Tax Reform*, Harvard University Press, Cambridge, Mass., 1973. Scholarly.

Wood, Ernest O., and John F. Cerny, *Tax Aspects of Deferred Compensation* (2nd ed.), Prentice-Hall, Inc., Englewood Cliffs, N.J., 1969.

Chapter 4

1. *1973–74 Source Book of Health Insurance Data*, Health Insurance Institute, New York, 1974, p. 53. U.S. Department of Labor statistics.
2. *Ibid.*, p. 27.
3. George L. Berry, "The Challenge of Dental Insurance," *Best's Review*, October 1972, pp. 10, 15, 16.
4. For a fuller discussion of the amount of insurance required, see Jeremy Main, "How Much Life Insurance Is Enough?" *Money*, January 1974, p. 31.
5. *Shopper's Guide to Life Insurance*, Pennsylvania Insurance Department, Harrisburg, Pa., April 1972.
6. *Consumers Union: A Guide to Life Insurance*, 3 parts, Consumers Union, Mount Vernon, N.Y., 1973.
7. Robert J. Klein, "The Wages of Disability," *Money*, April 1974, p. 57. Well worth reading.
8. John C. Perham, "The Hottest Thing in Executive Insurance," *Dun's*, February 1974, p. 72.
9. George W. Hettenhouse, Cost/Benefit Analysis of Executive Compensation," *Harvard Business Review*, July/August 1970, p. 114.
10. George W. Hettenhouse, "Compensation Cafeteria for Top Executives," *Harvard Business Review*, September/October 1971, p. 113.

Other Sources

Bogen, Jules I., *Financial Handbook* (4th ed.), Ronald Press, New York, 1968. Comprehensive discussion.

The Consumers Union Report on Life Insurance (rev. ed.), Consumers Union, Mount Vernon, N.Y., 1972.

Duarte, Alfonso, Jr., *Long-Term Disability: A Report to Management*, American Management Association, New York, 1966.

Employee Benefits 1973, Chamber of Commerce of the United States, Washington, D.C., 1974. Good source on costs.

Foegen, J. H., "The High Cost of Innovative Employee Benefits," *California Management Review*, Spring 1973, p. 100.

Gordon, T. J., *A Study of Potential Changes in Employee Benefits*—3 parts: *Volume 1: Summary and Conclusions; Volume 2: National and International Patterns; Volume 3: Delphi Study*, The Institute for the Future, Middletown, Conn., April 1969.

Gordon, T. J., and R. E. LeBleu, "Employee Benefits; 1970–1985," *Harvard Business Review*, January/February 1970, p. 93. Comprehensive discussion.

Gregg, Davis W., and Vane B. Lucas, *Life and Health Insurance Handbook* (3rd ed.), Dow Jones-Irwin, Inc., Homewood, Ill., 1973. Completely revised and updated recently and quite comprehensive, with 123 contributors.

Huebner, Solomon S., and Kenneth Black, Jr., eds., *Life Insurance* (8th ed.), Appleton-Century-Crofts, New York, 1972.

Magee, John H., *General Insurance* (5th ed.), Richard D. Irwin, Inc., Homewood, Ill., 1957.

Pickrell, Jesse Frederick, *Group Health Insurance*, Richard D. Irwin, Inc., Homewood, Ill., 1958–1961 (3d printing, August 1963).

Sutcliffe, Jon D., "Group Insurance—Where Do We Go From Here?" *Financial Executive*, March 1973, p. 34.

Chapter 5

1. Jeffrey G. Madrick, "The Case for Spending It Now," *Money*, October 1973, p. 38.
2. Richard C. Keating, "Private Pension Plan Performance," *Financial Executive*, August 1971, p. 36.
3. Officially called the Employee Retirement Income Security Act of 1974.
4. Abraham Epstein, *Insecurity: A Challenge to America*, Random House, Inc., New York, 1933, p. 142. A classic.
5. Gilbert Burck, "That Ever Expanding Pension Balloon," *Fortune*, October 1971, p. 100.
6. George H. Foote and David J. McLaughlin, *Corporate Retirement Programs*, McKinsey & Company, Inc., New York, 1965, p. 17.
7. *1973 Interim Survey of Trends in Corporate Pension Plans*, Bankers Trust Company, New York, 1973, p. 12. Comprehensive, regularly updated survey.
8. Shirley Scheibla, "Anti-Social Security," *Barron's*, Jan. 21, 1974, p. 3. The statistics are shocking!
9. For a comprehensive explation of the new law see Donald G. Carlson, "Responding to the Pension Reform Law," *Harvard Business Review*, November/December 1974.
10. "The Hidden Cost of Early Retirement," *Business Week*, Aug. 18, 1973, p. 81.
11. Burck, loc. cit.
12. Epstein, loc. cit.

Other Sources

Ellig, Bruce R., "To Remain or To Retire Early . . . That Is the Question," *Pension & Welfare News*, February 1972, p. 21.

Ellis, Charles D., *Institutional Investing*, Dow Jones-Irwin, Inc., Homewood, Ill., 1974.

Financial Executive, May, 1973. A special issue on pensions; contains 7 substantive articles on pensions.

Melone, Joseph J., and Everett T. Allen, *Pension Planning* (rev. ed.), Dow Jones-Irwin, Inc., Homewood, Ill., 1972. A fundamental text recently updated.

Nader, Ralph, and Kate Blackwell: *You and Your Pension*, Grossman Publishers, New York, 1973.

Paul, Robert D., "Can Private Pension Plans Deliver?" *Harvard Business Review*, September/October 1974, p. 22.

Pension Adjustments for Retired Employees, Life Office Management Association, New York, November 1970.

Pension Reform Act of 1974—Law and Explanation, Commerce Clearing House, Inc., New York, 1974.

The Private Pension Controversy, Bankers Trust Company, New York, 1973.

"The Push for Pension Reform" (a special *Business Week* report), *Business Week*, Mar. 17, 1973. p. 46.

Chapter 6

1. B. L. Metzger, *Profit Sharing in Perspective* (2nd ed.), Profit Sharing Research Foundation, Evanston, Ill. 1966, p. 13. One of the foundation's key publications.

2. B. L. Metzger and Jerome A. Collette, *Does Profit Sharing Pay?* Profit Sharing Research Foundation, Evanston, Ill., 1971, p. 66. And not surprisingly, the authors say yes!

3. "The Story of the Savings and Profit Sharing Fund of Sears Employees," Sears, Roebuck & Co., Chicago, Ill. May 1974 (news release), p. 6 Quite a story!

4. Proxy statement, The Proctor & Gamble Company, Sept. 5, 1972, p. 4.

5. John C. Perham, "Executive Piggybanks," *Dun's*, May 1973, p. 61.

6. *Bankers Trust 1972 Study of Employee Savings and Thrift Plans*, Bankers Trust Company, New York, 1972, p. 18. The best source of data and examples on savings and thrift plans.

7. B. L. Metzger, *Investment Practices, Performance and Management of Profit Sharing Trust Funds*, Profit Sharing Research Foundation, Evanston, Ill., 1969, p. 358. A comprehensive compendium of plan details and design issues.

8. B. L. Metzger, "Investment Management of Pension and Profit Sharing Trust Funds," *Pension & Welfare News*, Aug. 4, 1969, p. 50.

9. *Research Institute Recommendations*, Research Institute of America, New York, Feb. 18, 1972, p. 2.

Other Sources

Cheeks, James E., *How to Compensate Executives*, Dow Jones-Irwin, Inc., Homewood, Ill., 1974. See Chapter 12, "Pension and Profit Sharing Plans Designed for Executives," p. 164.

Cooper, John W., "P/S Investment Options, or 'To Each His Own,'" *Pension & Welfare News*, May 1971, p. 16.

Dunn, J.D., and Frank M. Rachel, *Wage and Salary Administration*, McGraw-Hill Book Company, New York, 1971. In particular, see Chapter 15.

Fox, Harland, and Mitchell Meyer, *Employee Savings Plans In the United States* (Personnel Policy Study No. 184), National Industrial Conference Board, New York, 1962.

Gordon, George, *Profit Sharing in Business and Estate Planning*, Farnsworth Publishing Company, Inc., Rockville Centre, N.Y., 1970.

Holzman, Robert S., *Guide to Pension and Profit Sharing Plans*, Farnsworth Publishing Company, Inc., Rockville Centre, N.Y., 1969.

Phillips, Harold, *Employee Benefits Planning*, Insurance Field Company, Inc., Louisville, Ky., 1968.

Chapter 7

1. Alfred P. Sloan, Jr., *My Years with General Motors*, Doubleday & Company, Inc., Garden City, N.Y., 1964, p. 408. Must reading for anyone interested in business.
2. *McKinsey Top Executive Compensation Survey*, McKinsey & Company, Inc., New York, 1968–1974 surveys. This survey, now in its nineteenth year, is based on a detailed analysis of the proxy statements of over 550 leading companies, drawn primarily from the *Fortune* 500 industrials and *Fortune's* comparable lists of the leading banks, insurance companies, and utilities.
3. Ronald J. Dornoff and Ronald L. Tatham, "An Incentive Plan for Baseball Players," *Business Horizons*, October 1971, p. 61.
4. Proxy statement, International Textbooks Company, 1971.
5. John P. Kensey, "Dividing the Incentive Pie in Divisionalized Companies," *Financial Executive*, September 1970, p. 52. Proposes one interesting method of relating bonus payout to the performance results of a division.
6. *Forbes*, Feb. 15, 1972, p. 62.
7. Crawford H. Greenewalt, *The Uncommon Man*, McGraw-Hill Book Company, New York, 1959, p. 99. Provocative.
8. Robert Townsend, *Up the Organization*, Fawcett World Library, New York, 1971, p. 62. Townsend's comments on incentives are stimulating.
9. *Newsweek*, Oct. 11, 1971, p. 82.

Other Sources

Baker, John C., *Executive Salaries and Bonus Plans*, McGraw-Hill Book Company, New York, 1938. The early history of bonus plans is fascinating.

Patton, Arch, "Why Incentive Plans Fail," *Harvard Business Review*, May/June 1972, p. 58. Incentive plans often do fail and this article identifies several common mistakes.

Perham, John C., "Payoff in 'Performance' Bonuses," *Dun's*, May 1974, p. 51.

Pitts, Robert A., "Incentive Compensation and Organizational Design," *Personnel Journal*, May 1974, p. 338.

Roberts, Reed M., Jr., "Tie Bonuses to Corporate Profits," *Financial Executive*, June 1973, p. 12.

Salter, Malcolm S., "Tailor Incentive Compensation to Strategy," *Harvard Business Review*, March/April 1973, p. 94.

Schuster, Jay R., and Jon D. Sutcliffe, "Cash Incentive vs. Stock Options," *Financial Executive*, October 1973, p. 92. Still a timely issue.

Shwayder, Keith R., Julian L. Carr, and Frank J. Schmieder, "Financial Considerations of an Executive Incentive Compensation Program," *Financial Executive*, September 1971, p. 18. A good discussion of the many financial considerations in plan formulas and the administration of bonuses.

Chapter 8

1. John C. Baker, *Executive Salaries and Bonus Plans*, McGraw-Hill Book Company, New York, 1938.

2. Joseph R. Daughen and Peter Binzen, *The Wreck of the Penn Central*, Little, Brown & Company, New York, 1971.
3. Proxy statement, Supermarkets General Corporation, April 23, 1971, p. 10.
4. Bruce R. Ellig, "Qualified Stock Options: Alive and Well," *Compensation Review*, Spring 1971, p. 17.
5. Proxy statement, The Chubb Corporation, Mar. 19, 1971, p. 14.
6. Proxy statement, Columbia Broadcasting System, Inc., Mar. 9, 1971, p. 15.
7. George H. Foote, "Performance Shares Revitalize Executive Stock Plans," *Harvard Business Review*, November/December 1973, p. 121. The best treatment of this innovative capital accumulation vehicle.
8. James H. Lorie and Lawrence Fisher, *Rates of Return on Investment in Common Stocks*, This book summarizes the groundbreaking early research done at the University of Chicago on returns from common stocks.
9. Harland Fox, *Qualified Stock Options for Executives*, The Conference Board, New York, 1970, p. 22. Good source of data.

Other Sources

Accounting Principles Board of the American Institute of Certified Public Accountants, "APB Opinion No. 25: Accounting for Stock Issued to Employees," *The Journal of Accountancy*, January 1973, p. 68. This ruling continues to cause problems for corporations. It is well summarized in this article.

Brooks, John, *The Go-Go Years*, Weybright & Talley, New York, 1973. Provides a fascinating perspective on the 1960s.

Kraus, David, and David J. McLaughlin, *Current Trends in Executive Stock Plans*, McKinsey & Company, Inc., New York, 1970. The trend uncovered in this survey continues.

Loomis, Carol J., "How the Terrible Two-Tier Market Came to Wall Street," *Fortune*, July 1973, p. 82.

Lorie, James H., and Mary H. Hamilton, *The Stock Market: Theories and Evidence*, Dow Jones-Irwin, Inc., Homewood, Ill., 1973. Updates earlier research.

"New Guidelines on Inside Information," *Financial Analysts Journal*, January/February 1974, p. 20.

Patton, Arch, *Men, Money and Motivation*, McGraw-Hill Book Company, New York, 1961. See in particular Chapter 10.

Sexton, John J., and James M. Boyle, "How Proposed Section 83 Regs Create Traps in Restricted Stock and Stock Option Areas," *The Journal of Taxation*, September 1973, p. 184.

Chapter 9

1. Proxy statement, Eastern Air Lines, Inc., May, 1964.
2. David J. McLaughlin, *The Emerging Company*, McKinsey & Company, Inc., Los Angeles, 1972, p. 129.
3. *The Wall Street Journal*, June 14, 1973, p. 24.
4. For other examples and a general discussion, see John C. Perham, "How to Make a Million—Quit," *Dun's*, September 1973, p. 51.
5. The formula used to calculate annual pension is N (years) $\times$ 0.01 $\times$ soc. sec. maximum $+ N$ (years) $\times$ 0.02 $\times$ annual income $-$ soc. sec. maximum, where the social security maximum is assumed to be $13,200, average annual income is $150,000 for the nondeferred case and $100,000 for the deferred case ($50,000 is deferred), and the number of years is 10.

6. George H. Foote, "When Deferred Compensation Doesn't Pay," *Harvard Business Review*, May/June 1964, p. 106.

Other Sources

Cheeks, James E., *How to Compensate Executives*, Dow Jones-Irwin, Inc., Homewood, Ill., 1974. See Chapter 5, "Why High-Salaried Executives May Favor Deferred Compensation," p. 52.

Executive Compensation Service, *Plans and Programs for Providing Deferred Incentive Compensation*, American Management Association, New York, 1969.

Perham, John C., "Deferred Compensation: More Promise than Payoff," *Dun's*, June 1973, p. 49.

Stayton, John P., and John L. Lesher, "Recent Developments in Deferred Compensation," *Business Horizons*, April 1969, p. 73.

Wood, Ernest O., and John F. Cerny, *Tax Aspects of Deferred Compensation* (2nd ed.), Prentice-Hall, Inc., Englewood Cliffs, N.J., 1969.

Chapter 10

1. Initial offering prospectus, Nov. 4, 1971, Playboy Clubs International, Inc., pp. 3, 23.
2. For a discussion see "Tax Laws Encourage Companies to Reward Officials with 'Perks,'" *The Wall Street Journal*, July 15, 1971.
3. *Research Institute Recommendations*, Research Institute of America, New York, Aug. 20, 1971, Section 2, p. 4.
4. Burton W. Teague, *Financial Planning for Executives* (Conference Board Report No. 608), The Conference Board, Inc., New York, 1973.
5. *Merchants & Manufacturers Association Executive Compensation Survey*, Merchants & Manufacturers Association, Los Angeles, 1969, 1973, p. 10.
6. *The Wall Street Journal*, Dec. 13, 1971, p. 14.
7. For a recent survey of perk trends see "Executive Perquisites," *Financial Executive*, July 1974, p. 44.
8. Janet Smith, "Status Symbols are Changing, Too," *Dun's*, May 1970, p. 52.

Other Sources

Cheeks, James E., *How To Compensate Executives*, Dow Jones-Irwin, Inc., Homewood, Ill., 1974.

Chapter 11

1. "For Ray Kroc, Life Began at 50. Or Was it 60?" *Forbes*, Jan. 15, 1973, p. 24. For further discussion see "The Burger That Conquered the Country," *Time*, Sept. 17, 1973, p. 84, and "Will Big Mac Meet Its Match in the Land of the Rising Sun?" *Forbes*, May 15, 1973, p. 118.
2. R. Fitch, "H. Ross Perot: America's First Welfare Billionaire," *Ramparts*, November 1971, p. 42. For further discussion see "Ross Perot's Prescription for Wall Street," *Business Week*, May 26, 1973, p. 64, Arthur M. Louis, "Ross Perot Moves on Wall Street," *Fortune*, July 1971, p. 90, and "How Perot Operates duPont, Glore Forgan," *Business Week*, Oct. 2, 1971, p. 72.

3. "The Money Men," *Forbes*, Mar. 1, 1969, pp. 66–67.
4. "Where There's Life," *Forbes*, Sept. 1, 1974, p. 42.
5. Material collected includes initial offering prospectus, secondary prospectus, proxy statements, annual reports, and speeches to security analysts.
6. Allan T. Demaree, "Ewing Kauffman Sold Himself Rich in Kansas City," *Fortune*, October 1972, p. 98.
7. Initial offering prospectus, July 2, 1969, p. 3.
8. For a more comprehensive discussion see "The Wheeler Who Deals in STP," *Business Week*, May 31, 1969, p. 56, and Mitchell Gorden, "Fluid Drive," *Barron's*, Oct. 26, 1970, pp. 5, 12.
9. "No Get-Rich-Quick Scheme," *Barron's*, Feb. 12, 1973, pp. 3, 15, 17, and "Undervalued Situations," *ibid.*, pp. 9, 24–25. For further discussion see Stephen D. Sholes, "The Search for Venture Capital—Preparatory Steps," *Financial Executive*, August 1974, p. 46.
10. Donald K. Clifford, Jr., *Managing the Threshold Company*, McKinsey & Company, Inc., New York, 1973.
11. Prepublication press release issued by Consumers Union summarizing an article on STP oil treatment, appearing in the July 1971 issue of *Consumer Reports*. For complete findings see "STP: Does Your Car Really Need It?" *Consumer Reports*, July 1971, p. 422.
12. For further analysis of this phenomenon see Craig A. Simmons, *Immediate, Short, and Longer Run Performance of New Issues*, University of Pennsylvania, The Wharton School, Philadelphia, Pa., 1974.
13. For an explanation of letter stock and the Security and Exchange Commission's Rule 144 see "With Letter Stock, the SEC Postman Always Rings Twice," *Magazine of Wall Street*, Aug. 2, 1971, pp. 18–19, 39, and Lynn Williams, "How to Sell Letter Stock," *Dun's*, November 1970, p. 51.
14. Arch Patton, *Stock Options and National Growth–The Lessons of Route 128*, McKinsey & Company, Inc., New York, 1970.
15. Presentation by Ewing M. Kauffman, president, and M. M. Dalbey, executive vice president, before the Denver Society of Security Analysts, Jan. 21, 1969, *The Wall Street Transcript*, Feb. 17, 1969.
16. Thomas R. Navin, "Passing On the Mantle," *Business Horizon*, October 1971, p. 83.
17. Proxy statement, Mar. 16, 1973, p. 9.
18. Speech before security analysts, 1971.

Other Sources

Barmash, Isadore, *Welcome to Our Conglomerate—You're Fired!* Delacorte Press, New York, 1971.
Brooks, John, *The Go-Go Years*, Weybright & Talley, New York, 1973.
Dessauer, John H., *My Years with Xerox*, Doubleday & Company, Inc., Garden City, N.Y., 1971. We think of it now as a giant company but only a few years ago it was a struggling new venture.
Hutchinson, G. Scott, *Why, When and How to Go Public*, Presidents Publishing House, New York, 1970.
Miller, Herman P., *Rich Man, Poor Man*, Thomas Y. Crowell Company, Inc., New York, 1971. Contains a great deal of interesting data.

Raw, Charles, et al., *Do You Sincerely Want To Be Rich? The Full Story of Bernard Cornfeld and the I.O.S.*, Viking Press, New York, 1971.

Springer, John L., *If They're So Smart, How Come You're Not Rich*, Henry Regnery Company, Chicago, 1971. This is a well-documented story of the investment advisory business.

Tobias, Andrew, *The Funny Money Game*, Playboy Press, Chicago, 1971.

Chapter 12

1. Dorothy Fields, "Moorea's Barefoot Businessmen," *Los Angeles Times West*, Jan. 15, 1967. Jerry Hulse, "Three Rascals in Paradise," *Los Angeles Times*, July 23, 1967.
2. *The Conference Board Record*, April 1971, p. 30.
3. *Minneapolis Tribune*, May 3, 1974.
4. "Women: Tyros and Tokens," *Time*, July 15, 1974, p. 33.
5. Wyndham Robertson, "The Ten Highest-Ranking Women in Big Business," *Fortune*, April 1973, p. 81.
6. Daniel Bell, *The Coming of Post-Industrial Society*, Basic Books, Inc., New York, 1973.
7. Eric Goldman, "What We Have Here Is a Prosperity Psychosis," *New York Times*, Jan. 1, 1974.
8. *Business Week*, Feb. 2, 1974, personal business section.
9. Ross Newhan, "Vida Blue 'Prisoner' of Finley, Lawyer Charges," *Los Angeles Times*, Feb. 26, 1972, Part III, p. 1.
10. Bernard A. Gelb, ed., and Rosanne W. Reilly, chief chartist, "The Two-Way Squeeze, 1974," *Road Maps of Industry*, The Conference Board, New York, No. 1735, Apr. 1, 1974.
11. James D. Smith, Stephen D. Franklin, and Douglas A. Wion, *The Distribution of Financial Assets* (a working paper), The Urban Institute, Washington, D.C., Sept. 22, 1973.
12. *Business Week*, Feb. 2, 1974, personal business supplement, p. 71.
13. Max Ehrmann, *Desiderata*, 1927 (reprint ed., Brooke House, Los Angeles, 1972).

Other Sources

Gordon, George Byron, *You, Your Heirs, and Your Estate*, Farnsworth Publishing Company, Rockville Centre, N.Y., 1962 (revised 1973). Provides useful advice and background on estate taxes and estate planning.

Kahn, Herman, and Anthony J. Wiener, *The Year 2000*, The Macmillan Company, New York, 1968 (copyright 1967 by The Hudson Institute, Inc.).

Karrass, Chester L., *Give & Take*, Thomas Y. Crowell Company, New York, 1974.

———, *The Negotiating Game*, The World Publishing Company, New York, 1970. A good how-to book on negotiating.

Lyons, John T., ed., *Personal Financial Planning for Executives*, American Management Association, New York, 1970. A somewhat uneven compendium.

Meyer, Caroline, "How to Think Through a Job Offer, *Money*, July 1973, p. 60.

Odiorne, George S., "Management by Objectives: Antidote to Future Shock," *Personnel Journal*, April 1974, p. 258.

Pietschmann, Richard John, "Salaries in Professional Sports," *Mainliner Magazine,* December 1973, p. 18.

Smith, Carlton, and Richard P. Pratt, *The Time-Life Book of Family Finance,* Time-Life Books, New York, 1969.

Wellemeyer, Marilyn, "The Class the Dollars Fell On," *Fortune,* May 1974, p. 225.

Glossary
and
Index

This glossary provides the reader with a set of simple working definitions of all important compensation and tax terms and capsule descriptions of the principal pay plans. It also includes references to specific sections of the book where these terms and phrases are discussed more fully and thus should prove useful as an index. However, I have not attempted to note every place a particular form of pay is mentioned only incidentally; nor is this intended to be an index of the several hundred company and individual names mentioned.

ACCIDENTAL DEATH AND DISMEMBERMENT INSURANCE (AD&D): A form of double indemnity coverage built into most group life insurance plans. It provides for double the normal death benefit in the event of accidental death and a fraction of the benefit in the event of certain disabling accidents. *See pages 62, 67–68.*

ALL-RISK ACCIDENT INSURANCE: A form of group insurance, usually voluntary and paid for by the employee, which enables the individual to purchase substantial sums of life insurance payable only in the event of accidental death. All-risk differs from the more established AD&D in that coverage is more comprehensive and potential benefits are much greater. *See pages 3, 65, 68, 78.*

BONUS FORMULA: The formal provisions in an incentive bonus plan that determine the total funds available for bonus purposes in a given year. Individual bonus awards are made from this total bonus pool. *See pages 123–127.*

BONUS POOL: The total amount of bonus funds generated by an incentive plan in a given year and available for awards. In most companies, the pool approximates the total bonuses that would be paid if all participants received "normal" awards. *See pages 124, 126, 129.*

CAPITAL GAINS TAX: A special tax rate, currently a maximum of 25 percent on the first $50,000 of gain and 35 percent on the excess, that applies to certain forms of compensation, particularly qualified stock options *(see Chapter 8)* and lump-sum distributions from qualified profit-sharing plans *(pages 103–104, 117–118).* For a discussion of the evolution of the capital gains tax *see pages 38–41;* for a general explanation *see pages 43–44, 47–48;* for the impact of the 1969 law on capital gains *see pages 45–48, 53, and Exhibit 11 (page 143).*

CAREER-AVERAGE PENSION: A form of pension in which the benefit earned each year is calculated in terms of that year's income; this contrasts with pensions based on some form of final average pay, say the last five years before the employee retires. *See page 88.*

CHILD'S PENSION: A provision in a qualified pension plan that provides for the payment of part of the accrued pension to the dependent children of a deceased participant. *See pages 95–96.*

CITY TAXES: The income tax levied by certain U.S. cities. *See pages 55–57 and Table 3–4.*

COMPANY LOANS: A relatively recent compensation form under which the corporation loans an executive money directly, usually at a low interest rate and with liberal repayment terms. The device is most commonly used in connection with stock option financing *(pages 155–156)* and as a perquisite designed to help the executive build his personal net worth *(pages 174–175).*

COMPANY-SPONSORED TAX SHELTER: A relatively rare compensation device under which the company organizes a special limited partnership for its executives, usually to provide them with both a tax shelter and an opportunity to build personal net worth. The device is most often used in privately held companies. *See pages 55, 216.*

COMPA-RATIO: The mathematical relationship between the average actual salaries within a salary grade and the midpoint of that grade. If all salaries were at the mathematical midpoint of their respective ranges the compa-ratio would be 100. In most companies the compa-ratio is about 95, meaning that average actual salaries in a grade total 95 percent of the range midpoint.

COMPREHENSIVE MEDICAL INSURANCE: A form of group medical plan under which a percentage of *all* covered expenses is reimbursed. It differs from more prevalent company plans under which hospital, surgical, and dental expenses are covered under several policies. *See page 77.*

COMPREHENSIVE PERSONAL LIABILITY INSURANCE: A relatively recent executive insurance benefit under which key executives are covered with an umbrella policy that provides them with personal liability protection, up to $1 million or more, against such risks as libel suits and personal injury claims. *See page 79.*

CONTRIBUTORY PENSION PLAN: A pension plan in which the employees must contribute part of the cost, normally a percentage of salary, in order to participate. *See pages 91–93.*

CONTRIBUTORY PLAN: Any form of employee benefit or perquisite that requires the individual to pay all or part of the cost from his after-tax earnings.

COST-OF-LIVING ESCALATOR CLAUSE: A clause in certain union contracts (increasingly extended also to nonunion employees or built into pension plans) which provides for increases in wages or benefits in accordance with changes in the Consumer Price Index or other measures of inflation. In connection with pensions *see page 98.* For a discussion of the impact of inflation on deferred compensation *see page 164* and on pay generally *see pages 213–214 and Table 12–1.*

COVERED EARNINGS: That portion of an individual's current income that is recognized in the calculation of a benefit. Some companies calculate pension, profit-sharing, and insurance benefits on the basis of salary alone, while other companies use both salary and bonus. *See page 89* for a discussion of the effect of covered earnings on the pension.

DEFERRED COMPENSATION: Payment that the corporation is committed to make to an executive at some future date, normally after retirement. The compensation can be a voluntarily deferred bonus, a portion of salary, or an additional amount stipulated in an employment contract. *See Chapter 9.*

DISABILITY PENSION: The portion of an individual's accrued normal pension payable when the employee becomes disabled prior to normal retirement but *after* having met vesting requirements. In contrast, disability insurance, which also pays upon disability, has *no* connection with company pension programs. *See pages 95–96* and, as the pension relates to disability insurance, *page 75.*

EARLY RETIREMENT PROVISION: The clause in a pension plan or supplemental personal policy that governs the conditions under which an employee can retire prior to the normal retirement age. The provision also sets forth the degree to which the accrued pension payments will be adjusted to reflect the earlier retirement. *See pages 94–95.*

EARNED INCOME: As defined by the IRS, income received as payment in connection with one's occupation. Under current law and regulations, most forms of executive compensation, including salaries, bonuses, and gains from nonqualified stock options, are classified as earned income. *See page 43.* For an explanation and review of the interaction of earned income with other tax provisions *see pages 45–47 and Exhibit 3 (pages 50–51).*

EMPLOYEE CONTRIBUTION: The money that individual employees pay to participate in company benefit plans, especially common in the areas of pension plans *(page 91),* savings plans *(pages 112–116),* and insurance plans *(Chapter 4).*

EMPLOYMENT CONTRACT: A formal, written agreement between an organization and an executive spelling out the terms and conditions of employment (and frequently including such compensation specifics as stock options and deferred compensation) as well as the arrangements that will prevail in the event of resignation or separation. *See pages 161–162;* in connection with deferred compensation as an issue in negotiation *see page 220.*

EXECUTIVE DINING ROOM: On-premises company eatery available to certain levels of executives, provided in most organizations as both a perquisite and a convenience. *See pages 179–180.*

EXECUTIVE HOUSING: Company-provided housing, typically offered when an executive is on temporary assignment away from his or her home base or when he or she can be expected to encounter unusual costs or difficulty in finding accommodations. Occasionally executive housing is offered as an indirect form of compensation for high-level executives. *See pages 181–182.*

EXECUTIVE PHYSICAL PROGRAM: The policies and procedures under which executives are reimbursed for periodic physical examinations. Frequently these ground rules change with rank. *See pages 178–179.*

EXERCISE PROVISIONS: The clauses in a stock option award governing the timing, amounts, and costs at which the options can be exercised by the recipient. *See pages 154–155;* for a discussion of the trend to longer exercise periods under nonqualified plans *see page 145,* and, for the range of current practices, *see Exhibit 10 (pages 140–141).*

FINAL AVERAGE PAY: An individual's earnings during the final period of employment or participation in a compensation plan, typically the last three, five, or ten years' average pay. It is used particularly in connection with a calculation of pension benefits. *See page 88.*

FORFEITURES: Funds relinquished by a terminating employee in a qualified profit-sharing or thrift plan. Sometimes these funds are used by the company to reduce future company contributions to the plan; sometimes they are allocated to current participants to increase their shares. *See page 108.*

FORMULA PENSION: The category of pension covering most salaried employees, under which a rate formula is applied to individual earnings to calculate the employee's pension. *See pages 84–85, 88–91.*

FOUNDERS' STOCK: Stock in a new venture issued to the founders and, in some cases, other key executives. Typically, such stock is priced below the amount paid by early investment backers. *See pages 195–196;* see also LETTER STOCK.

FUNDED PENSION PLAN: A pension plan that has a fund specifically set aside for the payment of promised benefits to retirees. The fund consists of company contributions, employee contributions (in some cases), and the income from the investment of the fund. *See Chapter 5.*

FUNDING: The process by which money is set aside for given compensation obligations of the corporation, typically used in connection with incentive bonus plans *(pages 123–127),* pension plans *(page 93),* and profit-sharing plans *(pages 107–110).*

GENERAL SALARY INCREASE: An increase in base salary granted to a large group of employees to adjust for increases in the cost of living, to correct inequities, or to improve the competitiveness of a company's salaries.

GROUP LIFE INSURANCE: an employee benefit that provides participants with life insurance (usually term insurance) at rates below those available for individual policies. Rates usually remain constant regardless of the employee's age or health. For the early history *see pages 61-62;* on possible inequities *see pages 65-66.* For a fuller explanation and discussion of how to evaluate this insurance *see pages 66-73.*

INCENTIVE BONUS: A plan under which cash awards are made, almost always annually, with the amount of the award usually varying in relation to company or unit profitability and individual executive performance. *See Chapter 7.*

INCOME AVERAGING: A provision in the tax code that allows a taxpayer to spread one year's income as though it were also earned over the preceding four years. This provision is most helpful for people who experience a dramatic increase in income in one year. *See pages 49-53.* For its application to specific forms of pay *see Exhibit 3 (pages 50-51).*

INDIVIDUAL RETIREMENT ACCOUNT (IRA): A personal account for retirement savings authorized in the Employee Retirement Income Security Act of 1974. Under this provision employees who do not participate in a qualified retirement plan can deduct up to $1,500 each year (but no more than 15 percent of compensation) for contributions to a personal retirement fund. This amount is tax deductible and earnings on it are *not* taxable until distributed.

INDUSTRY PERQUISITES or "PERKS": Special employee or executive privileges, unique to a given industry, which are provided at substantial discounts, e.g., free or reduced-rate air travel in the airline industry. *See page 171.*

INTEGRATED PENSION PLAN: A pension plan that adjusts the employee's pension benefits downward to reflect the company's contribution to social security. *See pages 85, 90-91.*

INVESTMENT OPTIONS: The investment choices offered the individual participating in a qualified profit-sharing or savings plan. Usually he or she can choose among several mutual funds with different degrees of risk and potential gain. *See pages 110-112.*

JOINT AND SURVIVOR OPTION (J&S): An optional form of payment in most qualified pension plans, under which the participant agrees to take a reduced benefit in order that the surviving spouse be guaranteed a benefit in the event of the pensioner's death. *See page 97.*

KEOGH PLAN (HT-10 Plan): A form of self-financed pension, liberalized in the 1974 pension reform law, under which the self-employed can set aside the lesser of 15 percent of earned income or $7,500 per year for retirement purposes without being taxed currently on that amount. *See page 92.*

LETTER STOCK: Stock issued to founders, early executives, and investors that is not registered with the Securities and Exchange Commission and thus is subject to restrictions on sale or disposition. It is called letter stock because, normally, a letter of intent to invest, not to trade, must be filed with the appropriate regulatory body; it is also known as unregistered stock. *See pages 195–196;* see also FOUNDERS' STOCK.

LONG-TERM DISABILITY INSURANCE (LTD): A form of employee group insurance under which the participant is guaranteed the continuation, until a specified age (normally sixty-five), of a portion of his or her earnings in the event of a long-term disability. *See page 62* for a discussion of its evolution and prevalence; *see pages 73–76* for an explanation and planning considerations.

LUMP-SUM DISTRIBUTION: A payment option whereby the employee receives at one time the entire accrued value of his or her account in a profit-sharing or thrift plan *(pages 117–118)* or the total cash value of a qualified pension plan *(page 98).*

MAJOR MEDICAL INSURANCE: A form of group insurance under which participants are reimbursed for significant medical expenses not covered under hospital or surgical policies; sometimes called catastrophe insurance, since its intent is to protect employees against the financial impact of very serious illnesses. For its evolution *see page 62;* as part of medical coverage *see pages 76–78.*

MERIT SALARY INCREASE: The increase in base pay granted a salaried employee, theoretically intended to recognize increased job competence and good performance, distinguished from rises in the cost of living, for example. As a practical matter, however, this means is also used in most companies to adjust salaries for increases in the cost of living, to keep salaried workers on a par with organized employees, and to maintain a degree of internal equity in salary relationships. For a discussion of the importance of compensation philosophy *see pages 30–32;* on the size of the increase, *page 20;* for the impact of inflation, *pages 213–214.*

NONQUALIFIED STOCK OPTION: A stock option that is not eligible for capital gains tax treatment; also known as unqualified stock option. For tax treatment as earned income *see pages 39, 45–46;* for the historical evolution, *pages 138, 139, 145–147;* for timing advantages, *page 155.*

NORMAL BONUS: See TARGET BONUS.

NORMAL RETIREMENT DATE: The age, typically sixty-five, when an employee can retire under the company's pension or profit-sharing program with no loss of benefits. *See page 94.*

OPTION FINANCING: The arrangement under which an individual with a stock option pays for the shares over a period of time. When available, financing provisions range from personal bank loans negotiated by the individual, but often with the unofficial help of the company, to low-interest loans made available or cosigned by the company. *See pages 155–156.*

PENSION: Benefit plan that provides for the payment of income to individuals who retire. Qualified pension plans are funded and meet all IRS nondiscrimination tests, and the individual is not taxed until payment begins. *See Chapter 5.*

PERFORMANCE SHARE: A long-term stock bonus with vesting and payout terms that depend on certain corporate performance conditions, such as earnings per share growth; a form of long-term incentive and also a capital accumulation vehicle. *See pages 148–149.*

PERQUISITE or "PERK": A special benefit or privilege provided as an additional, indirect form of compensation, e.g. company cars, special entertainment allowances, club memberships. *See Chapter 10.*

PERSONAL FINANCIAL COUNSELING: A service provided by an independent professional firm to an individual executive or a group of executives under a plan organized and/or partially paid for by the company. The counselor analyzes an individual's financial affairs, suggests investment strategies, and gives advice on specific financial decisions. This is a relatively new executive compensation vehicle. *See pages 175–176;* for suggestions on personal financial and pay planning *see Chapter 12.*

PHANTOM STOCK OPTION: A form of executive stock that simulates an option on paper; also known as shadow option. Under a phantom stock plan, a grant of stock units is made and the executive receives the appreciation in market price (and sometimes dividends) over a period of time. *See pages 145–147 and Exhibit 10 (pages 140–141).*

PLAN MAXIMUM: The maximum benefit an executive can receive under a given plan, typically expressed as a dollar amount or percentage of pay. Maximums can appear in virtually any compensation scheme but are most prevalent in pension plans *(pages 89–90)*, profit-sharing plans *(page 109)*, and incentive bonus plans *(page 130).*

PORTABILITY: Any provision that permits an employee leaving a company to make a tax-free transfer of the assets behind a vested pension (if the employer agrees) or the distribution from a profit-sharing or savings plan to an individual retirement account.

POSITION EVALUATION: The process whereby the worth of a position or job to an organization is analyzed and the job is compared with other positions in the enterprise and formally placed within the company's salary grade structure. For a discussion of the impact of job levels and promotions on salaries *see pages 19–25;* as part of the compensation philosophy *see page 31.*

PREFERENCE INCOME: As defined by the IRS, specific types of income that are subject to a penalty tax of 10 percent. For a definition *see page 43;* for an explanation and illustration *see pages 46–47;* for types of pay affected *see Exhibit 3 (pages 50–51);* and for the impact of preference income on gains from qualified stock options *see pages 47–48, 142, and Exhibit 11 (page 143).*

PROFIT-SHARING PLAN: A formal plan under which all employees share in the company's profits, typically in relationship to their pay and service. Under a *cash* profit-sharing plan, the award is distributed each year *(pages 102–103, 129);* under a *deferred* profit-sharing plan, contributions are invested and paid out when the employee dies, leaves the company, or retires *(Chapter 6).*

PROMOTIONAL SALARY INCREASE: An increase in base salary granted when a person moves to a higher job in the organization and compensation hierarchy. In most companies the promotional increase is about double the normal merit increase, but it represents a real salary-bargaining opportunity for the individual. See *pages 21, 23–24* for a discussion of the size and importance of promotional increases.

QUALIFIED PROFIT SHARING: A form of deferred profit sharing that conforms to Section 401(d) of the Internal Revenue Code and thereby qualifies for special tax breaks. For the definition *see pages 103–104;* for a full discussion *see Chapter 6.*

QUALIFIED STOCK OPTION: A stock option plan that qualifies for capital gains tax treatment. Under such a plan a stock must be awarded at market value, exercised over no longer than a five-year period, and then held for three years before it is sold if it is to be taxed at capital gains rates. For the historical evolution *see pages 3–4, 39;* for relevant tax provisions *see page 42.* For further discussion *see Chapter 8 and Exhibit 10 (pages 140–141).*

QUALIFIED STOCK PURCHASE: A formal, IRS-governed plan under which employees can purchase company stock, at 85 percent of market price, on a payroll deduction basis over a fixed period of time. *See pages 48, 106.*

RESTRICTED STOCK OPTION: The form of executive stock option most prevalent from 1950 through 1964. Options were granted at 95 percent of market value, exercisable over ten years, and proceeds from sale of this stock were taxable at capital gains rates. For the role of this form of option in compensation planning *see pages 3–4;* for tax advantages, *page 39;* for comparison with qualified stock option, *pages 139–142;* and for a concise explanation of provisions, *Exhibit 10 (pages 140–141).*

ROLLOVER BONUS: A bonus partially paid out in the year in which it is earned, with the balance paid over the following several years. *See page 134.*

SALARY INCREASE BUDGET: A sum set aside in a company's or unit's budget to provide for salary increases during a calendar year.

SALARY STRUCTURE: The dollar framework within which jobs are ranked according to their compensation value. In most organizations the structure consists of a series of salary grades, with each grade having a range of salary levels. A typical company's salary structure will have twenty or more successively higher grades with salaries in each grade averaging 10 to 15 percent higher than those in the preceding grade. *See pages 127–128* for a discussion of the impact of the salary structure on bonuses.

SAVINGS PLAN: A formal compensation plan designed to provide (1) a supplemental source of retirement income in addition to a pension and (2) a source of savings and capital accumulation for employees; also known as thrift plan. Under the typical plan the individual contributes a percentage of pay, usually from 1 to 6 percent, which is matched by the company and invested in one of several employee-selected investment options. *See pages 105–107* for the early history and prevalence; for a full discussion *see Chapter 6.*

SETTLEMENT OPTIONS: The provisions in a special compensation plan governing the form and timing of the payout benefit, used particularly in connection with pension plans *(pages 96–98),* profit-sharing and thrift plans *(pages 117–118),* and incentive bonus plans *(pages 133–135).*

SHADOW OPTION: See PHANTOM STOCK OPTION.

SOCIAL SECURITY INTEGRATION: The technique whereby a pension or profit-sharing retirement plan is discounted for social security benefits. This is done through a formula, through the exclusion of certain earnings from benefit calculation, or through subtracting social security benefits under the so-called offset approach. *See pages 90–91* for further discussion and *page 99* for its impact on benefit levels.

SPECIAL AWARD PLAN: A formal motivational plan providing for special payments to individuals who make an extraordinary onetime contribution to the company.

SPOUSE PENSION: A pension provision that authorizes payment to the spouse of a portion of the employee's accrued pension in the event the employee dies prior to the normal retirement date; also known as widow's pension. In the United States, insurance is frequently used in lieu of the spouse's pension clause. *See pages 95–96.*

STATE INCOME TAXES: The taxation of income by states. *See pages 55–56* for trends, *Exhibit 4 (pages 58–59)* for a summary of current status, and *pages 56–57, 118* for a discussion of state tax influence on career location and retirement decisions.

STOCK APPRECIATION RIGHTS: A special benefit attached to certain stock option awards. Appreciation rights increase in value directly with increases in the per-share market price. Under most plans the appreciation rights are paid upon exercise to help finance the option or pay the taxes incurred. *See pages 146–147 and Exhibit 10 (pages 140–141).*

STOCK OPTION CANCELLATION: A program under which a company cancels outstanding stock options whose exercise price is substantially higher than the current market price; the company then issues new, lower-priced options to replace the canceled options. *See pages 147–148.*

TANDEM OPTIONS: A combination qualified and nonqualified option used between 1969 and 1973 but rendered ineffective as a compensation device by recent IRS rulings. *See page 146 and Exhibit 10 (pages 140–141).*

TARGET BONUS: In an incentive bonus plan, an amount expressed in dollars or as a percentage of salary that represents the bonus payment a participant would receive in an average year for a fully acceptable individual performance; also known as normal bonus. *See pages 129–130.*

THRIFT PLAN: See SAVINGS PLAN.

TRAVEL ACCIDENT INSURANCE: A group insurance policy under which employees traveling on company business receive additional life insurance protection. *See page 67.*

UNQUALIFIED STOCK OPTION: See NONQUALIFIED STOCK OPTION.

UNREGISTERED STOCK: See LETTER STOCK.

VARIABLE ANNUITY. A pension benefit which fluctuates in value with changes in the worth of the assets—typically common stocks—in which it is invested. The variable pension was designed to provide an adjustment mechanism for inflation on the theory that stock prices would rise over time. In recent years they have not, and many variable pensions are lower than the traditional fixed pension would have been. *See pages 97–98.*

VARIABLE PRICE OPTION: A form of nonqualified stock option under which the exercise price *decreases* as the stock price *increases* in relation to the stock price at the time of the award; also known as yo-yo option. *See page 147.*

VESTING: The achievement of an irrevocable right to a benefit, usually attained by reaching a certain age or tenure. Most prevalent in pension plans *(pages 93–94)* and profit-sharing plans *(pages 116–117)*.

WIDOW'S PENSION: See SPOUSE PENSION.

WITHDRAWAL PROVISIONS: The timing and terms under which, in a savings plan and occasionally a qualified profit-sharing plan, either individual contributions or a portion of the accrued company contributions can be withdrawn by the participant. *See pages 113–114.*

YO-YO OPTION: See VARIABLE PRICE OPTION.